D0213120

THE PROFESSION OF DRAMATIST
IN SHAKESPEARE'S TIME, 1590–1642

PRINCETON UNIVERSITY PRESS · 1971

The Profession of Dramatist in Shakespeare's Time 1590-1642

GERALD EADES BENTLEY

Copyright © 1971 by Gerald Eades Bentley
ALL RIGHTS RESERVED
LCC: 75-154990
ISBN: 0-691-06205-6

Publication of this book has been aided by the Whitney Darrow
Publication Reserve Fund of Princeton University Press

This book is composed in Linotype Caslon
Printed in the United States of America by
Princeton University Press, Princeton, New Jersey

To Ellen

174460

Preface

FOR MORE than two centuries there has been much speculation about the circumstances of the composition of individual plays by the best-known Elizabethan dramatists—
especially Shakespeare. Many of these studies have been
illuminating, but not infrequently they have postulated
circumstances which would have been highly abnormal, if
not impossible, in the usual situation of a professional dramatist in the reigns of Elizabeth, James, and Charles. But
what were the ordinary working conditions during the
years of the greatest flowering of the English drama? This
book is an explication of the normal working environment
circumscribing the activities of those literary artists who
were making their living by writing for the London
theatres.

A good many of the facts I have marshaled in this
explication are to be found, usually in other contexts, in
the fourteen volumes of *The Elizabethan Stage*, *The
Jacobean and Caroline Stage*, Greg's edition of *Hens-*

PREFACE

lowe's Diary, and J. Q. Adams's edition of *The Dramatic
Records of Sir Henry Herbert*. Others come from contemporary lawsuits, contracts, and agreements, the front matter
of seventeenth-century editions of plays, miscellaneous publications of the time, and a few from remarks of dramatic
characters making obvious allusions to customs or attitudes
familiar to their audiences.

Perhaps I ought to explain the chronological limits
which have been set. The terminal date is obvious enough.
On 2 September 1642 the Puritan-dominated Parliament
issued "An Order of the Lords and Commons Concerning
Stage-Playes," directing "that while these sad Causes and
set times of Humiliation doe continue, publike Stage-
Playes shall cease, and bee forborne." For eighteen years
thereafter only the most sporadic and profitless dramatic
performances were staged in England, and no professional
playwright could carry on his old vocation. The earlier
date is less obvious, for some argument could be made for
beginning at 1558 or at 1576. I have selected 1590 because by that date the organization of acting companies
and theatres was well developed, many men were writing
plays, and it was becoming possible for the steadiest of
them to make a living preparing scripts for the regular
London acting companies. Before 1590, moreover, records
are so scanty, and such a large proportion apply to amateur
or semiprofessional theatrical activities, that conclusions
about working conditions must be very shaky. One cannot
even be sure that a profession of play-writing had yet
developed.

The Elizabethan spelling, capitalization, and punctua-
tion of the longer quotations has been reluctantly modernized, but for one- or two-line passages, such as extracts
from title pages or pithy remarks from legal testimony,
I have succumbed to long habit and retained the form of
the original.

viii

Most of the material used here I collected while I was engaged in research for *The Jacobean and Caroline Stage*, often with only the vaguest idea of what use I could ever make of it. Accordingly my indebtedness to the research institutions which have fostered my work extends over a long period. I am grateful for the hospitality and help of the Public Record Office, the Guildhall Library, Somerset House, the British Museum, the Bodleian, Cambridge University Library, the Huntington, the Folger, the Houghton, and the Newberry Libraries. They provide not only precious collections of books and manuscripts but also that atmosphere of devotion to learning which is a comfort and a stimulus to their readers.

This book has been improved by the generous advice of Alfred Harbage and Miriam Brokaw, who saw problems and suggested solutions which had eluded me. Patrick O'Donnell checked hundreds of quotations and references and pointed out a number of faulty inferences. Joanna Hitchcock has been the most meticulous and helpful editor I have ever had. To all of them I am grateful.

G.E.B.
Princeton
May 1971

Contents

THE PROFESSION OF DRAMATIST
IN SHAKESPEARE'S TIME, 1590–1642

CHAPTER I

Introduction

I N T H E G R E A T D A Y S of the "Elizabethan" drama the production of plays for the London populace was largely in
the hands of professionals. Indeed, the rise of professionalism in dramatic affairs in the last quarter of the sixteenth
century is one of the distinguishing marks of the emer-
gence of "the Age of the Drama." Before the accession of
Elizabeth and even halfway through her reign, English
drama was almost wholly amateur.

The episodes of the great medieval English cycles were
staged and acted by men who were earning their living as
glovers, shipwrights, bakers, cordwainers, bowyers, fletch-
ers, mercers, and butchers, not by professional actors and
producers. The plays they performed are nearly all anonymous, but there is no evidence whatever that they were
written by men supporting themselves by dramatic writing,
and there is much evidence to the contrary. Even the
moralities and interludes of the sixteenth century, though
they were often performed by groups of strolling profes-

sional players, were written by men whose time was principally devoted to nondramatic activities, as a glance at the most important writers of plays before the reign of Elizabeth will show. Henry Medwall and John Bale and Nicholas Grimald were clergymen; Nicholas Udall and George Buchanan were schoolmasters and scholars; John Rastell was a lawyer and printer; John Heywood was a musician and entertainer. The dramatic entertainment of the Middle Ages and early sixteenth century in England was produced in buildings or at sites used only occasionally for acting: there were no permanent theatres. Thus the enterprise of writing and presenting plays was largely an amateur one before 1558: part-time playwrights, part-time playhouses, part-time managers and producers, and, until the time of the strollers and the court troupe, part-time actors.

A little of this amateur dramatic activity extended into the later years of Elizabeth and the reigns of James and Charles, for plays continued to be performed by students at schools and at the colleges in Oxford and Cambridge; by lawyers for their entertainments at the Inns of Court; occasionally by apprentices in London; sometimes by guests and the household at great houses such as Draiton and Chartley, where the servants and family of the Earl of Essex produced plays and masques, or at Apthorpe, where the plays and shows of the Earl of Westmorland were performed by his children and servants. But these amateur enterprises were the exceptions. The overwhelming majority of the plays witnessed by the subjects of Elizabeth in her later days and by those of her two successors were performed in buildings planned and built for the presentation of plays, and acted by men and boys whose profession was acting. This much professionalism in the drama of the days of the greatest English achievement has been generally acknowledged for a long time.[1]

1. Professionalism was recognized as early as 1699 in the first account of the English drama of the earlier seventeenth century,

4

Since professionalism in the presentation of plays during the reigns of Elizabeth, James, and Charles has been so commonly observed for nearly three centuries, and since the development of such professionalism has often been accounted one of the significant stages in the development

Historia Histrionica . . . A Dialogue of Plays and Players. The first ten pages of this pamphlet, dealing with personal reminiscences of drama in the reigns of James and Charles, discuss professional actors and professional playing places and the existence of amateur productions is scarcely noticed, though a good deal is said about them in the second half, which is concerned mostly with secondhand information about medieval and sixteenth-century dramatic activities. Edmund Malone, in his *Account of our Ancient Theatres* and *Historical Account of the Rise and Progress of the English Stage*, both published in 1790, concentrates on playing by professional actors in buildings to be used as theatres. The same is true of the standard nineteenth-century histories of the "Elizabethan" dramatic achievement. J. P. Collier's three-volume *History of English Dramatic Poetry to the Time of Shakespeare and Annals of the Stage to the Restoration*, 1831, includes much discussion of amateurs in the long section dealing with English plays from the twelfth century to 1575, but the following 360 pages of his *Annals* are devoted almost wholly to productions of professional actors. Similarly Frederick Gard Fleay's *Chronicle History of the London Stage, 1559–1642*, published in 1890, deviates from the professional theatre only in its discussion of the masques at court; each of his seven discursive chapters has a separate section retailing the actions of each professional company, and another summarizing the history and occupancy of each professional theatre.

In the twentieth century the same realization that professional actors and professional theatres dominated the presentation of plays to Londoners is basic for the writers of the major studies. In his standard four-volume work, *The Elizabethan Stage*, 1923, Sir Edmund Chambers devotes his second volume to actors and theatres. In his section on "The Play-Houses" about 95 percent of the space is given to professional theatres; in the section on performing groups about 75 of the 294 pages are given to boy companies, a few of which were amateur or only semiprofessional; nearly all the names in his dictionary of actors are those of professionals like Edward Alleyn, Christopher Beeston, Richard Burbage, Henry Condell, Nathan Field, John Heminges, William Sly, and Richard Tarlton.

In more specialized studies, the same proportions reflect the same

of mature English drama, it is somewhat surprising that the development of professionalism in the *writing* of plays has not been observed as frequently as the development of professionalism in the *presenting* of them. In fact, none of the standard histories cited in note one develops the distinction between amateur or occasional writers for the stage and fully professional playwrights; indeed, most of them show little awareness that there was a difference.

This unawareness seems, at first glance, to be very curious indeed. Nearly all those dramatic historians who have considered "Elizabethan drama" have noted that, with

judgment of the comparative importance of professionalism. Joseph Quincy Adams published his *Shakespearean Playhouses: A History of English Theatres from the Beginning to the Restoration* in 1917. Adams begins with the fifteenth century, and his initial discussions concern innyards which were occasionally used for the presentation of plays. But he devotes only 17 pages to these part-time playing places, and more than 400 pages to the permanent theatre buildings, like the Globe, the Fortune, the Red Bull, the Swan, the Rose, the Blackfriars, the Phoenix, and Salisbury Court. Even these proportions underrate the professional dominance, for at least one of his innyards, that of the Boar's Head in Whitechapel, had a permanent stage and permanent seats for a paying audience, and in 1604 the Boar's Head was a principal theatre for Queen Anne's men and had been for at least two years (see G. E. Bentley, *The Jacobean and Caroline Stage*, Oxford, 1941–1968, vi, 121–31).

The same dominance of the professionals is apparent in John Tucker Murray's *English Dramatic Companies, 1558–1642*, 2 vols., 1910. The first volume devotes 322 pages to the adult professionals and only 45 to all the boy companies, some of which—like Beeston's Boys—were highly professional. The second volume is given over to acting troupes in the provinces, and these records are often too laconic to be revealing about the identity of the visiting players. The most numerous records concern the provincial tours of the professional companies of London, but a number of the names of other troupes are not mentioned in any other documents, and they may have been almost anything, even amateurs. But in any case, there is no evidence that these purely provincial troupes—professional or amateur—had any perceptible influence on the development of the "Elizabethan" drama.

occasional exceptions—like the halls of great houses or of royal palaces or of the Inns of Court—the buildings for which Shakespeare, Jonson, Webster, and Fletcher prepared their masterpieces were structures designed and built for the performance of plays and seldom used for anything else; i.e., they were *professional* buildings. And they have noted that the men who acted in these performances were, with scattered exceptions, such as the officers of an English ship at sea, or the children of the Earl of Westmorland, or students at Oxford and Cambridge, supporting themselves and their families by acting plays, when not prevented by plague or bankruptcy; i.e., they were *professional* actors. Why has there been so little discussion of the fact that professional playwrights developed in this period as did professional actors and professional playing places? Even the violent theatre-haters of the time, like William Prynne, recognized that there were professional dramatists as well as professional actors. On the long and intemperate title page of his notorious *Histriomastix, The Players' Scourge, or Actors' Tragedy*, published in 1633, he proclaims

> . . . that the Profession of Play-poets, of Stage-Players; together with the penning, acting, and frequenting of Stage-playes are unlawful, infamous, and misbeseeming Christians. . . .

The reason that professionalism among the "Elizabethan" dramatists has been so seldom discussed or even recognized by critics and historians in the nineteenth and twentieth centuries is not far to seek. In spite of the fact that a large part of the drama which William Prynne so hated and feared was written by professional playwrights (i.e., men who, for long periods, were writing plays for profit), the greatest of these writers have usually been thought of in the category of poets, not of dramatists. Their professionalism has received comparatively little attention because their productions have commonly been examined

7

as literary phenomena rather than as working scripts for professional actors in a professional theatre. Most often the plays have been analyzed and evaluated as poetry or as philosophy; sometimes as psychology, or (more recently) as sociology. This common antiprofessional attitude towards the masterpieces of the professional dramatists can be seen in hundreds of examples. The attitude is neatly summarized in a couple of sentences from a review published in February 1970 of a book which had first appeared in 1956: "———reads Shakespeare's plays as though they were difficult poems. Readers like myself, who think that's the right way to do it, place this book among the permanent modern contributions of Shakespeare criticism."

In fields such as nondramatic poetry, philosophy, psychology, or sociology the experience and maturity of the writer studied is certainly of importance, but his professionalism is of little consequence. The poet and the philosopher work alone; the cooperation of most nondramatic writers with their colleagues in presentation—copyists, printers, editors, booksellers—is often of biographical interest, but only occasionally is it a prime consideration in the impact made by his creation upon its intended audience.

In the world of the theatre, on the other hand, the impact of the author's creation is in good part determined by the playwright's cooperation with his colleagues in presentation. The tailoring of the literary product to the qualities of the actors, the design of the theatre, and the current conventions of production is of vital importance in achieving the effects which the author planned. The production of plays, in whatever era, is always a cooperative art. Though the Renaissance poet or writer of romances could compose as many songs as he liked in the parts of as many characters as he chose, the playwright could not. If he was a professional working for a repertory group (as all "Elizabethan" professionals were) he knew that songs could be written into the parts of only those actors who

8

sang well; he knew that the roles of women and children must be limited to the number which could be handled by the boys presently in his company; he knew that if he wanted more adult male characters than the number of sharers and hired men in his troupe (as he generally did) he must plan the structure of his play to allow for doubling;[2] he knew that he must take into consideration the character of the audience for which he was writing: at the Red Bull it was notoriously vulgar, at the Blackfriars it was notoriously sophisticated.

Because of such inescapable realities of the theatre, professionalism in the playwright is of far greater significance than in the nondramatic poet, the novelist, or the essayist. The relations of Spenser or of Francis Bacon with their printers are always of biographical interest and sometimes of textual importance, but they did not normally require any alteration of the author's conception of *The Faerie Queene* or of *Novum Organum* to allow for the number of compositors in the printing house, or the size of the edition proposed, or the format of the volume to be sold.

Since professionalism is important in the theatre, and since it has been so frequently noted in the development of acting organizations and of playhouses, one ought to profit from a study of professionalism among writers for the theatres in the years of the finest florescence of the English drama, 1590–1642. How many truly professional playwrights were there? Who were they? What proportion of the plays of the time did they write? What were the normal conditions of their working situations? What was their usual output? Who paid them, and how much? How often and in what way did they collaborate? How often and by whom were their plays revised? Who cen-

<hr>

2. See David Bevington, *From Mankind to Marlowe*, Cambridge, Mass., 1962, and William A. Ringler, Jr., "The Number of Actors in Shakespeare's Early Plays," in G. E. Bentley, *The Seventeenth-Century Stage*, Chicago, 1968, pp. 110–34.

9

sored their manuscripts, and for what? What was expected of them besides the preparation of the original scripts for their theatres? What did they have to do with the publication of their plays?

The ensuing chapters of this book are designed to organize and present a representative portion of what has survived of the once copious theatrical materials which can help to answer these questions. Such questions cannot, of course, be resolved in complete detail for each dramatist because of the destruction of the vast majority of all theatre records. But enough remain to enable us to trace the general outlines of the normal professional life of a writer of plays in these years.

CHAPTER II

Amateur Dramatists and Professional Dramatists

A THOUGHTFUL CONSIDERATION of all plays and playwrights in England during the period 1590–1642 underscores the fact that the plays of the time were provided by writers who varied widely in motive and in theatrical experience. Most clearly defined are the amateurs who were not writing primarily for profit, who generally showed a certain disdain for the commercial theatres, who usually hurried their plays into print, who, with a few exceptions, wrote only one or two plays, and whose productions were usually prepared for amateur actors.

At the opposite end of the scale were the regular professional playwrights who supported themselves and their families by providing plays for the London theatres, whose production of play scripts was copious and generally regular, and whose attitude toward publication was much more reserved than that of the amateurs. When I call these men professionals, I am implying nothing about their excellence. The terms "professional" and "professionalism" are used here and throughout this book in sense II: 4b of the *Oxford English Dictionary*,

> Undertaken or engaged in for money or as a means of subsistence; engaged in by professionals as distinct from amateurs.

Although the plays of the professionals are generally better plays than those of the amateurs, professionals sometimes wrote bad plays and amateurs occasionally wrote good ones. Such distinctions, while interesting and important in many contexts, are not relevant here.

Between these two extremes of the amateur and the regular professional are twenty or thirty experienced writers who show some but never all the characteristics of one or another of these two classes. They wrote plays for the commercial theatres, and they generally wrote for profit. They wrote a good many more plays than the amateurs, but their associations with the London acting companies were less close and exclusive than those of the regular professionals. Like the amateurs they generally had significant sources of income (often nondramatic writing or patronage) other than the London theatres, but they did not disdain the financial rewards of play-writing as most of the amateurs did, or at least pretended to do.

Thus the most essential differentiating characteristic of the regular professional dramatist was his primary dependence on the commercial theatres for his livelihood. In a time when the social status of the playwright was low, the biographical data concerning the writers of plays is inevitably scanty, and our knowledge of the sources of a dramatist's income is therefore largely inferential; but it is not so very difficult to classify roughly into amateurs or professionals most of the 250 or so men who are known to have written plays in England between about 1590 and 1642. Indeed, the low social status of people regularly concerned with commercial theatres, a status which inhibited the writing of biographies of even such successful and comparatively respected playwrights as the "great triumvirate" (Ben Jonson, William Shakespeare, and John Fletcher),[1] is in some respects a help. Those men who were anxious to be considered gentlemanly amateurs, in spite of the fact that they had written one or more plays which may have been acted in the London theatres, often arranged (unlike the majority of the regular professionals) to secure a fairly prompt publication of their plays. And in dedications, or addresses to the readers, or prefaces, or prologues they shrilly proclaimed their nonprofessional status.

A fairly characteristic example of the attitude of the amateur dramatist toward professionalism is to be seen in the front matter of the 1639 edition of Jasper Mayne's *The City Match*, acted at court and later in the Blackfriars theatre. The address to the reader says:

> The Author of this Poem, knowing how hardly the best things protect themselves from censure, had no ambition to make it this way public, holding works of this light nature to be things which need an apology for being written at all, nor esteeming otherwise of them, whose abilities in this kind are most passable, than of masquers who spangle and glitter for the time, but 'tis thorough tinsel. As it was merely out of obedience that he first wrote it, so when it was made, had it not been commanded from him, it had died upon the place where it took life. . . .

And the same attitude is reiterated in Mayne's court prologue for his play:

Prologue to the King and Queen

•   •   •   •   •   •

1. The designation is a seventeenth-century, not a modern, one. See G. E. Bentley, *Shakespeare and Jonson: Their Seventeenth Century Reputations Compared*, rev. ed., Chicago, 1969, pt. 1, pp. 67–68, and pt. 2, pp. 8–9, 12, 232.

Such works, he thinks, are but condemn'd to live

.   .   .   .   .   .

For he is not o' th' trade, nor would excel
In this kind, where 'tis lightness to do well.

Jasper Mayne's concern to clear his amateur skirts of any soil "o' th' trade" is repeated by other men who were anxious lest anyone might think that they would demean themselves to provide plays regularly for the commercial theatres.

A further means of differentiating between the professionals and the other writers of plays is the notably larger number of scripts known to have been prepared by those men at least partially dependent upon the commercial theatres for their livelihood. Not only are the known canons far larger for the professionals than for the others, but the difference in output between them was certainly even greater than we can now discover: their involvement with plays of presently unknown authorship, with lost plays, and with plays not even known by title was extensive. The number of these anonymous, lost, and wholly disappeared plays is great, and it is salutary to pause for a moment to consider them.

About 350 anonymous plays are known at least by title from the period 1590–1642.[2] And we are forced to conclude from the evidence of Henslowe's diary that a good proportion of the plays performed in the London theatres have vanished without leaving any evidence that they ever existed—not even an anonymous title.

The theatrical accounts of Philip Henslowe for the period 1592–1602 are spotty, but they are many times as full as any other diurnal theatrical records before the Restoration. Henslowe set down his receipts from the performances of named plays for seven scattered periods between

2. Most of them are listed in E. K. Chambers, *The Elizabethan Stage*, Oxford, 1923, IV, 1–55, and in *Jacobean and Caroline Stage*, V, 1281–1456.

14

February 1591/92 and November 1597, a total of 40-odd months of recorded performances in a period of 69 months. On other pages of the same ledger he set down his payments to writers for furnishing his companies with named plays during the latter half of this decade, that is, 1597–1602. The total number of different plays mentioned in these two independent sets of incomplete records of the activities of this single manager is about 280.

Of these 280 named plays, only about 40 are still extant, and at least 170 would now be totally unknown—even by title—had Henslowe's accounts been destroyed as were the vast majority of all other theatre records of the period 1590–1642. Even in the diary years of 1591/92 to 1602, how many plays from Henslowe's numerous rival and less well-documented theatres have disappeared without leaving a trace? Plays from the repertories of the Theatre, the Curtain, the Blackfriars, St. Paul's, the Swan, and the Globe—170 more?[3]

I doubt that the number of vanished plays is as great as, say, 340, or even 170, for each decade of the later period, 1612–1642. In those later years managers needed fewer new plays because they had available a far greater number of acceptable old plays suitable for revival (especially printed plays) than Philip Henslowe ever enjoyed, and because play publishing was more common than it had been

3. Fynes Moryson remarked on the extraordinary multiplicity of plays in London. After the publication of his *Itinerary* in 1617 he prepared further papers on his observation of European countries in his ten years of travel, papers which remained in manuscript until 1903. In the section on England, probably written about 1617–1620, Moryson says: "The City of London alone hath four or five companies of players with their peculiar theatres capable of many thousands, wherein they all play every day in the week except Sunday . . . as there be in my opinion more plays in London than in all the world I have seen" (Charles Hughes, *Shakespeare's Europe. Unpublished Chapters of Fynes Moryson's Itinerary. Being a Survey of the Condition of Europe at the End of the 16th Century.* London, 1903, p. 476).

15

from 1592 to 1602. Probably we now know at least the titles of a majority of the plays in the Jacobean and Caroline repertories of the second Blackfriars, the Phoenix, the Salisbury Court, and the Globe. But from the repertories of the less esteemed theatres—the Fortune, the Red Bull, the Hope, and the Curtain—we know the names of far fewer plays, even though performances were taking place at the Red Bull and the Fortune for 37 and 42 years respectively, and for only 25 years at the Phoenix and 13 at the Salisbury Court.[4]

From such evidence it seems conservative and reasonable to conclude that between 1590 and 1642 there probably were written as many as 500 plays of which we know not even the titles. Many of them are likely to have been prepared by dramatists already known to us from their extant plays,[5] and thus the canon of the professional dramatists is likely to have been even larger than it now appears. But ignoring the number of their plays which are probably

4. Compare the number of titles in the known repertories of the King's Men at the Blackfriars and the Globe, 1616–1642 (*Jacobean and Caroline Stage*, I, 108–34) and those of the Lady Elizabeth's Company, Queen Henrietta's Company, and Beeston's Boys at the Phoenix and the Salisbury Court (ibid., I, 194–97, 250–59, and 337–42) with the much smaller number assignable to companies acting at the four less esteemed theatres (ibid., I, 156–57, 214–17, 282, 300–301, and 322–23).

5. Examples of plays unknown until the twentieth century though they were written by well-known dramatists are George Chapman's *The Old Joiner of Aldgate* (C. J. Sisson, *Lost Plays of Shakespeare's Age*, Cambridge, 1936, pp. 12–79), and Thomas Middleton's *The Viper and Her Brood* (*Modern Language Notes*, XLII [January 1927], 35–38). Even such a publication-conscious dramatist as Ben Jonson told William Drummond in 1619 "that the half of his comedies were not in print." If Jonson and Drummond were both reliable, this statement means that more than three of his plays are wholly unknown to us now, for in 1619 eleven of his acknowledged plays were in print, and we know of only eight of his other plays written before 1619, including collaborations, which had not been published by that year.

still unknown to us, the presently ascertainable output of the professional playwrights is large, notably larger than that of the semi-professionals and the amateurs.

Keeping in mind these general facts about the production and preservation of plays in England during the years 1590–1642, we can turn to the more particular characteristics of the different classes of playwrights in the period. It is not vital that there should be complete agreement on the category to which every single name is assigned, but it seems to me that the groups of professionals and amateurs were pretty much as outlined in the following sections.

The Amateurs

The amateurs who wrote plays for production in England between 1590 and 1642 are fairly easy to distinguish as a class. There were, of course, many more of them than of the dramatists who wrote for pay, but even with their larger numbers they were concerned with far fewer plays. There are approximately 1,200 plays written by known authors in the period, but of this number only about 265 were written by just over 200 amateur dramatists.

As these figures indicate, most of the amateurs wrote a single play, not infrequently for some special occasion. Such were many of the Latin plays composed for some university event and ordinarily acted in one of the college halls. Examples are Walter Hawkesworth's play called *Labyrinthus*, prepared for the Bachelor's Commencement and acted at Trinity College, Cambridge, in February or March 1602/1603; or John Chappell's *Susenbrotus, or Fortunia*, performed at Royston during a visit of King James and Prince Charles in March 1615/16; or Thomas Vincent's *Paria*, acted at Trinity, Cambridge, on the occasion of a visit of King Charles to the University on 3 March 1627/28.

But the occasional play by an amateur was not always in Latin, even at one of the universities. It might have

17

been in English, like Peter Hausted's *The Rival Friends*, performed before the King and Queen at Trinity, Cambridge, in March 1631/32. Even the commercial theatres in London sometimes performed an amateur's only play. Such was John Clavell's single dramatic composition, *The Soddered Citizen* of about 1630. The play was performed by the King's company at their Blackfriars theatre, and the players had probably cajoled the piece out of Clavell, the author of *The Recantation for an ill led Life*, in order to exploit the sensation of the sentencing and later pardoning of this gentleman-turned-highwayman.

Similarly occasional was *The Launching of the Mary, or the Seaman's Honest Wife*, written during a voyage home from India by Walter Mountfort, an employee of the East India Company, to defend the company from certain charges and no doubt also to bolster his own shaky reputation with his employers.

The Hog hath Lost his Pearl was another such amateur single play, prepared by Robert Tailor for performance by a group of London apprentices in the Whitefriars theatre in February 1612/13. Unfortunately the apprentices' performance—allegedly critical of their betters—was suppressed by the sheriffs, and, so far as is known, Robert Tailor's dramatic career came to an end.

Occasional in a rather different environment was the comedy called *Apollo Shroving*, which William Hawkins, a schoolmaster at Hadleigh in Sussex, prepared for performance by his pupils on Shrove Tuesday 1626/27.

Another one-play amateur was Thomas Rawlins, whose tragedy called *The Rebellion* was acted with great success by the King's Revels company—presumably at the Red Bull. Rawlins was an engraver who later became chief engraver at the Royal Mint; like so many amateur writers of plays he was insistent that he was not a professional dramatist. Though he was himself an artist, Rawlins wrote for the 1640 quarto of his play an address which displays the usual gentlemanly attitude toward professional play-wrights. Condescendingly he warns his readers: "Take no note of my name, for a second work of this nature shall hardly bear it. I have no desire to be known by a thread-bare Cloak, having a Calling that will maintain it woolly."

This attitude toward the profession of play-writing is usual among the amateur dramatists. Indeed, one who reads through the front matter of all the plays of the period comes to see it as one of the hallmarks of the amateur.

But though the usual canon of the amateur dramatist in this period was one play, not all amateurs stopped after a single experience. An example of an amateur who wrote as many known plays as some of the writers for profit was Lodowick Carlell, Huntsman to Charles I, and later Keeper of the Royal Park at Richmond, who said in the prologue to one of his plays that hunting and gamekeeping and feeding his deer occupied his time, "Not some, but most fair days throughout the year."

Lodowick Carlell wrote eight plays—if each five-act part of his two-part plays is counted—four or five of which were performed by the King's company at Blackfriars. Yet he was an amateur and not a professional, or even a semi-professional, and he and his publishers were anxious to keep his status clear. The dedication to two courtiers of his *Deserving Favorite*, whose title page says "As it was lately Acted first before the Kings Maiestie, and since publikely at the Black-Friers" shows his attitude toward professional dramatists: "Approved Friends, this Play, which know at first was not design'd to travel so far as the common stage, is now pressed for a greater journey, almost without my knowledge."

An amateur playwright much more aristocratic than Lodowick Carlell was William Cavendish, then Earl and later Duke of Newcastle. Cavendish, who was also a patron of the drama, during his long lifetime rewarded at least half a dozen dramatists, one of whom, James Shirley, is said to have been an assistant in, if not the principal author of, his lordship's two pre-Commonwealth plays, *The Country Captain* and *The Variety*, both performed at Blackfriars in the last three years of the Caroline theatre.

Another noble playwright was Fulke Greville, Lord Brooke, in his early life a friend of Sir Philip Sidney and later a patron of dramatists, notably William Davenant.[6] Between 1594 and 1601 Greville wrote three tragedies, *Antonie and Cleopatra*, *Mustapha*, and *Alaham*. The first he himself destroyed; the other two are extant in both manuscript and print. Clearly, as Greville himself said, none was intended for the stage, and Greville's amateur standing can scarcely be doubted, but his lines seem to have had a great appeal to his contemporaries.[7]

Somewhat like Greville was William Percy, third son of the Earl of Northumberland, who left in autograph manuscript six plays apparently written between 1600 and 1603. Some of them he evidently intended to be acted by Paul's Boys before the end of the reign of Elizabeth, but there is no evidence that they ever were—or should have been.

Even the aristocratic ladies were sometimes tempted to dabble in the drama. Lady Elizabeth Cary, later Viscountess Falkland, wrote a lost play set in Syracuse, and another, published anonymously in 1613, called *The Tragedie of Miriam the Faire Queene of Jewry*.

These fourteen occasional writers are sample types of the more than 200 amateurs, men and women, who are known to have written plays in England between 1590

6. Nothing has ever been made of the statement by David Lloyd that Greville wanted to be known to posterity as the master of Shakespeare and Jonson, the patron of Chancellor Egerton, Bishop Overall's Lord, and Sir Philip Sidney's friend. See E. K. Chambers, *William Shakespeare*, Oxford, 1930, II, 250.

7. See *Studies in Philology*, XL (April 1943), 200–201.

and 1642. Although about half those I have so far mentioned produced pieces which were performed in the London theatres, this is not true of the majority of amateurs; most of them prepared their plays for performance in Oxford or Cambridge colleges, at schools, at the Inns of Court, or at private houses. A number of these amateurs wrote closet drama which was not intended for performance anywhere.

The largest group of plays by amateurs was made up of those performed in Oxford and Cambridge colleges, a group which includes 30 to 40 percent of all the amateur plays known in the period. There are records of college play-acting in almost every year of the period, sometimes five or six or even eight in a single year.

Very occasionally a college play, written to be performed by the undergraduates and fellows of a college, such as Christ Church, Oxford, or Trinity, Cambridge, was later performed by the professional actors of the London companies. Such was the fortune of Jasper Mayne's *The City Match* and Thomas Goffe's *The Careless Shepherdess*. More notorious was William Cartwright's *The Royal Slave*, which was such a great success when performed by the students of Christ Church before the King and Queen at Oxford that it was staged again at Hampton Court by the King's players, but so far as is known they never acted it at Blackfriars or the Globe.

But these professional London revivals of Oxford and Cambridge plays were most unusual; many of the college plays were written in Latin, and as for the others, the London players no doubt agreed with the comment assigned to the veteran comedian, Will Kempe, by the university authors of the second part of *The Return from Parnassus*, produced in St. John's College, Cambridge, in 1601/1602: "Few of the university [men] pen plays well. They smell too much of that writer *Ovid*, and that writer *Metamorphoses*, and talk too much of *Proserpina* and

Jupiter. Why here's our fellow *Shakespeare* puts them all down, aye and *Ben Jonson* too."[8]

The same suspicions of university plays by the London professional theatre is seen 35 years later in the prologue written to still the misgivings of the Salisbury Court audience at the performance of Richard Lovelace's lost comedy, *The Scholars*: [9]

> A Gentleman to give us somewhat new,
> Hath brought up *Oxford* with him to show you;
> Pray be not frightened—Tho the Scæne and Gown's
> The *Universities*, the Wit's the Town's;
> The lines, each honest *Englishman* may speake;
> Yet not mistake his Mother-tongue for *Greeke*,
> For still 'twas part of his vow'd Liturgy,
> From learned Comedies *deliver me*!
> Wishing all those that lov'd 'em here asleep,
> Promising *Scholars*, but no *Scholarship*.

Another large group of amateur plays—about 40—was made up of closet drama, a type with which the writers for the commercial theatres were concerned only rarely. The plays of Fulke Greville and Lady Elizabeth Cary fall into this class, as do *Imperiale*, by Sir Ralph Freeman, Master of Requests, Thomas Neale's autobiographical *The Warde*, and the four *Monarchick Tragedies* written by Sir William Alexander, Earl of Stirling and tutor to Prince Henry. Late in the period satiric political tracts in the form of closet drama, like *Canterbury his Change of Diet*, begin to appear, and they become fairly common after the closing of the theatres.

Of the dramatic scripts written for private performance, many were entertainments, shows, satires, or little masques rather than plays, but complete plays were sometimes written by amateurs for only slightly known private

8. J. B. Leishman, ed., *The Three Parnassus Plays*, London, 1949, lines 1766–70.
9. See *Jacobean and Caroline Stage*, IV, 722–24.

occasions. Such was William Cartwright's *The Lady Errant* and Francis Quarles's *The Virgin Widow* and, most interesting of all, the series written by Mildmay Fane, Earl of Westmorland, for performance at his house at Apthorpe—*Candy Restored, The Change,* and *Time's Trick upon the Cards.*

Probably a good many more plays than we know now were written by amateurs like Mildmay Fane for productions in great houses like Apthorpe. The autobiography of Arthur Wilson, called *Observations of God's Providence in the Tract of my Life,* implies that such household theatricals were common. Wilson, a retainer of the Earl of Essex, says:

> The winters we spent in England [i.e. not campaigning in the Palatinate]. Either at Drayton, my Lord's grandmother's; Chartley, his own house; or some of his brother, the Earle of Hartford's houses. Our private sports abroad, hunting; at home, chess or catastrophe. Our public sports (and sometimes with great charge and expense) were masks or plays. Wherein I was a contriver both of words and matter. For as long as the good old Countess of Leicester lived (the grandmother to these noble families,) her hospitable entertainment was garnisht with such, then harmless, recreations.[10]

Wilson's own plays, extant in manuscript but not published until the nineteenth century, *The Corporal, The Inconstant Lady, or Better Late than Never,* and *The Swisser,* were presumably originally written for these great house performances, though all of them were later acted at Blackfriars.

In a time of great dramatic activity, more plays than we now know were probably written by totally untalented amateurs. No doubt the great majority of them have mercifully disappeared, but a few are extant in manuscript, or

10. Philip Bliss, ed., *The Inconstant Lady,* London, 1814, p. 119.

known by chance references. One such is the anonymous play of the reign of Charles I called *The Cyprian Conqueror, or the Faithless Relict*, extant only in a manuscript in the Sloane collection.[11] The plotting, stage directions, characterization, and lines are so immature that it is difficult to imagine that anyone anywhere in England would ever have listened to it; but the prologue and epilogue give evidence that the naïve author certainly hoped that they would.

More sensational, at least in its results, was the lost, unnamed play which brought the author, Jasper Garnett, and others before the Star Chamber in 1621. Garnett's play, acted at Kendal Castle in Westmorland, "was intended to present the case of the tenants of the barony" against the encroachments of the landlords. According to the Star Chamber records:

> One of the scenes showed an ingeniously constructed *hell* placed a little to the side and below the stage wherein ravens were supposedly feeding on poor sheep. Henry Ward and Thomas Ducket, two of the tenants, in their character of clown or fool inquired of a boy who stood looking into this hell what he saw there. The boy replied that he "did see Landlords and puritanes and Sheriffs bailiffs and other sorts of people," whereupon the one clown said to the other: "Ravens quotha, no, thou art far by the square, its false landlords makes all that croakings there, and those sheep we poor men, whose right these by their skill, would take away, and make us tenants at will, and when our ancient liberties are gone they'll puke and pool, & peel us to the bare bone."[12]

These amateur dramatists, though numerous and diverse, and indicative of the strong appeal of the drama in these years, were never people who looked to the commer-

11. See *Jacobean and Caroline Stage*, v, 1316–17.
12. Mildred Campbell, *The English Yeoman under Elizabeth and the Early Stuarts*, New Haven, 1942, p. 152.

cial theatres for a living. Though a very small percentage of the amateur plays did get to the London theatres, they were very seldom intended for them. When they did come to town they generally came to the Blackfriars because of royal enthusiasm for them in some other place, as did *The Royal Slave*, *The City Match*, and Carlell's plays.

Those amateur dramatists who expressed themselves on the subject normally looked down upon the commercial theatres and the professional dramatists. They tended to speak of plays, including their own, as trifles or baubles.

Playwrights for Profit

Though the count of about 265 dramatic pieces composed by about 200 amateur playwrights may seem large, it is a small part of the 1,200 plays written by assignable authors (i.e., eliminating anonymous compositions) during the years 1590–1642. Clearly amateurs were only minor participants in the great "Elizabethan" dramatic outburst; it was dominated by the writers who were selling their services to the Elizabethan, Jacobean, and Caroline professional acting companies.

These 900-odd plays which provided most of the entertainment in the London theatres over a period of 52 years offer several notable contrasts to the group of about 265 amateur dramatic compositions and their 200 authors. Most striking of course is the larger number of professional than amateur plays. Equally notable is the much smaller number of playwrights who were concerned with them. Except for a few authors of single plays, the more than 900 scripts for the commercial theatres were provided by some 50-odd writers. A few of them composed or collaborated in only two or three plays, often apparently in special circumstances, such as an emergency in which an actor or manager was persuaded to help out. Thus William Bird, alias Borne, a very active member of the Lord Admiral's–Prince Henry's–Palsgrave's companies and a friend and agent of Henslowe and Alleyn, helped out with *Judas* and with the revision of *Doctor Faustus*; and Charles Massey, a long-time member of the same groups, appears to have contributed to *The Siege of Dunkirk* and *Malcolm, King of Scots*. In 1623 and 1624 Richard Gunnell, the prominent actor and manager, supplied three plays to the struggling company at the Fortune, which he appears to have been managing.[13]

The great bulk of the theatrical fare in these years, something over 850 plays, was provided by 44 playwrights who clearly were not amateurs, though the number of plays they wrote and the time-span over which they worked for the theatres varied widely. Greene, Lyly, Marlowe, Peele, and Nashe wrote a good portion of their plays before 1590 and were dead or had deserted the commercial theatres before the end of the century. Thomas Jordan and John Tatham wrote a few plays for the Caroline companies, but the bulk of their work was done after the closing of the theatres. There are some 22 writers who wrote or collaborated in a dozen or more plays[14] for the commercial theatres in the period 1590–1642, who were clearly being paid for their literary efforts, and who in a general sense may be considered more or less professional, at least for a certain period of years. The list is comprised of the following men:

13. See R. A. Foakes and R. T. Rickert ed., *Henslowe's Diary*, Cambridge, 1961, pp. 185 and 206, and *Jacobean and Caroline Stage*, IV, 749 and 516–19.

14. There will not be universal acceptance of the exact number of plays written by each of these dramatists because scholars disagree on the exclusion or inclusion of a few plays—usually collaborations—in the canon of dramatists like Beaumont, Fletcher, Marston, Massinger, Middleton, and Rowley. On the whole I have been conservative, and I think few would vary from my count by more than two or three plays even in the canon of so uncertain a dramatist as Francis Beaumont. The elimination of masques, entertainments, and pageants reduces the numbers for men like Jonson, Middleton, and Anthony Munday.

Thomas Heywood	Richard Brome
John Fletcher	William Haughton
Thomas Dekker	George Chapman
Philip Massinger	Michael Drayton
Henry Chettle	Robert Wilson
Thomas Middleton	William Hathaway
William Shakespeare	Anthony Munday
James Shirley	John Ford
Ben Jonson	Wentworth Smith
William Rowley	John Webster
John Day	Francis Beaumont

It is useful to note how prolific these men were, especially in comparison with the amateurs, and to consider the concentration of their work for the theatres. Very little biographical information has been unearthed on several of the Henslowe playwrights, like Henry Chettle, John Day, William Hathaway, William Haughton, Wentworth Smith, and Robert Wilson; most of their plays are lost and we are dependent upon the diary for nearly all our information about them. But for at least fourteen of the others there is enough extant information about their company associations, their beginnings, their retirement from active work for the theatres, and the character of their plays to justify some tentative conclusions about their professional careers.

The professional who served the theatre for the longest period, Thomas Heywood, wrote an address to the reader for the 1633 quarto of his play *The English Traveller* some eight years before his death. In his address Heywood said that he had already written or at least "had a maine finger in" 220 plays.[15] John Fletcher wrote or col-

15. This figure provides another basic fact for any consideration of the number of plays written in this time which have vanished without leaving a trace. It is notable that of the 220 plays Heywood says he wrote before 1633, only 56—including collaborations and lost plays known by title—can now be identified, leaving 164 plays which are presently unknown or at least unassignable.

27

laborated in 69, nearly all of them prepared for the King's company. Thomas Dekker wrote at least 64 plays in a total period of 34 years, but for six years of this time he was in jail, and in the later part of his life his play-writing was only sporadic. In the years 1598 to 1602 alone he is known to have written all or parts of 44 different plays for Henslowe. Philip Massinger wrote all or parts of at least 55, the majority of them also for the King's men. Henry Chettle wrote or collaborated on 50 plays in about five years, according to Henslowe's records of his payments to dramatists. Shakespeare wrote 38, nearly all of them for the Lord Chamberlain–King's players. James Shirley also wrote at least 38, first for Queen Henrietta's company, and then, after his return from Ireland, for the King's men. Thomas Middleton wrote 31, excluding about a score of masques and pageants.

These numbers are large for the major dramatists of any time; when we remember that for each of them the number is almost certainly too small, we cannot fail to be impressed by the industry of these professionals. Even Heywood's monstrous 220 is too small a number for him, for he wrote at least two plays and four Lord Mayor's pageants after he had made his statement in 1633.

So far as presently available records show, these eight men were the most prolific playwrights of their day. But there were 14 others who wrote a large number of plays for profit and had many of the characteristics of the regular professionals for at least part of their careers. In some instances I suspect that the smaller number of their recognized plays is due to the fact that a larger portion of their output is lost or is still unrecognized; Anthony Munday is an example. In other cases the smaller number is due to the short period of time for which we have any records about the work of the man; William Haughton is known from Henslowe's diary to have contributed to 25 plays in five years; Richard Hathaway, 18 in five; and Wentworth Smith, 15 in two.

The fourteen additional playwrights who wrote a dozen or more plays for pay and had periods of attachment to London companies were Ben Jonson, who wrote 28 plays in 41 years; John Day, with 25 plays in ten years; William Rowley, 24 plays in 18 years; Richard Brome, 23 in 13 years, or 24 in 18; William Haughton, 23 in five years; Michael Drayton, 23 in five years; George Chapman, about 21 in 15 years; Robert Wilson, 20 in 20 years, but 16 of them for Henslowe in three years; Richard Hathaway, 18 plays in five years; Anthony Munday, 17 in nine years besides his entertainments; John Ford, 17 in 17 years; Wentworth Smith, 15 in two years and apparently one for amateurs about 12 years later; John Webster, 14 in about 24 years; and Francis Beaumont, about 14 in eight years.

These 22 men were the most prolific of more than 250 who are known to have written plays in the years between 1590 and 1642. They were all professionals in the limited sense that they were paid for writing a significant number of plays for acting companies at the commercial theatres. The most obvious characteristic of the group as a whole is that they were prolific; among them they provided perhaps half the 1,200 plays known from the period.[16] Nearly all of them wrote the major part of their literary work for actors, though several, like Ben Jonson, Thomas Middleton, and Anthony Munday prepared a number of scripts for actors at Court or in the City pag-

16. A simple addition of the number of plays in which each man is known to have participated gives an exaggerated total because of the number of collaborations involved. Most of Fletcher and Beaumont's compositions were collaborations, and so are counted at least twice in the list; and it is the same with Chettle, Haughton, Wilson, Hathaway, and Smith.

eants, in addition to the larger number designated for the commercial theatre in London. They were paid, of course, by all three groups.

The Attached or Regular Professionals

Within this group of 22 authors who served the commercial theatres there was a smaller group which I shall call attached or regular professionals. These men had a closer and more continuous association with the London theatres than the others. Their production of plays was more regular and consistent. They were, so far as our information goes, primarily dependent upon the theatres for their livelihood. They did not easily or frequently shift their company associations, but tended to work regularly for one troupe for long periods. I suspect that they had oral or written contracts with their companies. They had more reservations about publishing their own plays than Jonson or Chapman or Middleton had.

Perhaps the clearest way to indicate their differences from the other professionals is to point out the reasons why more than two-thirds of the 22 cannot be classified as regular professionals or attached professionals.

The first to be eliminated, and no doubt the one whose elimination may be most questioned, is Ben Jonson. His achievement as a playwright was great, and other writers of the seventeenth century praise him more frequently and more fulsomely than any other dramatist of their time.[17] He wrote a large number of plays, and he certainly had more to say in print about the standards and functions of dramatic composition than any of his contemporaries. Indeed, I should say that for the first period of his writing career Jonson may have been an attached professional or a regular professional, but these years were few. In the

17. See Bentley, *Shakespeare and Jonson*, I, 63–70; II, 52–53, 54–56, 58–59, 169–70, 206. See also the anonymous *Jonsonus Virbius*, London, 1638, passim.

period 1597–1602 he wrote at least eleven plays, six or seven for Philip Henslowe's companies and five for other companies, and there is evidence that for at least part of this period he was himself an actor. Before about 1600 he is not known to have had any significant means of support besides the theatre.

But this is not the pattern for most of Jonson's career, nor for his most distinguished years. From no later than 1602 he was not primarily dependent upon the commercial theatres for his livelihood. He is known to have had patrons for long periods.[18]

From 1604 to 1634 the production of Jonson's magnificent series of 41 court masques and entertainments must have absorbed a large proportion of that fabulous energy which had once gone into plays for the commercial theatres, for instead of producing about two plays a year as he had in his early days, in the later years, from 1604 to 1634, when he was much better known, plays appeared at the rate of only about one every two years. In 1619 Jonson told Drummond that "of all his Playes he had never Gained 2 hundred pounds." This is less than £10 per year, certainly too little to maintain Jonson in the circles he frequented in Jacobean times. From at least as early as 1602 a share of Jonson's creative energy was devoted to particu-

18. In February 1601/1602, John Manningham wrote in his diary, "Ben Jonson, the poet, now lives upon one Townshend and scornes the world," and for the following five years he seems to have lived with Lord Aubigny. In 1606, 1607, 1608, and 1609 the Earl of Salisbury paid him as much for each of four slight entertainments as other dramatists were getting for full-length plays (see Scott McMillan, "Jonson's Early Entertainments: New Information from Hatfield House," *Renaissance Drama*, n.s. [1968], pp. 153–66). In 1619 Jonson told William Drummond of Hawthornden that "every first day of the new year" the Earl of Pembroke sent him £20 to buy books. In these years between 1602 and 1619 more than twenty of his masques and entertainments—including most of the great ones—were produced under the patronage of the sovereign or of great nobles.

lar patrons who, in the mores of the time, were expected to be financially responsive.

These facts make it clear enough that after 1602 Jonson could not have been dependent on the commercial theatres for the major part of his support. But perhaps even more significant is the evidence to be found in his own repeated statements about himself and his work that in these years Jonson did not think of himself as a professional dramatist in the way that Heywood, Fletcher, Massinger, Shakespeare, Shirley, and Brome did.

Rather like Jonson in a number of ways was George Chapman, though his canon is more uncertain than Jonson's because of several dubiously ascribed plays and the very unreliable dating of a number of them. He wrote approximately 21 plays between about 1595 and about 1613, but there are several years in this period when he appears to have written no plays at all; he was not consistent in giving his allegiance to one company for long periods; and the publications of his nondramatic works, especially his translations from Homer, are scattered throughout this period. Chapman may have been an attached professional playwright for about 14 months in 1598 and 1599 when he wrote all or parts of what appear to be seven plays for the Lord Admiral's men. He appears again to have been writing plays fairly consistently during about the last year or so of Elizabeth's reign and the first and second years of James's. These plays were all prepared for boy companies, but Chapman does not appear to have been working regularly for any one of them: he wrote for the Children of the Chapel, for Paul's Boys, and for the Queen's Revels boys. Sometime in this second period of dramatic productivity or just after it Chapman received the patronage of Prince Henry. A later group of plays, mostly produced by boy companies, are too uncertain in date to give any assurance that Chapman was devoting himself wholly to work for the theatres. Furthermore, he was under the patronage of Prince Henry during part of these years, and these were the years of the principal *Iliad* publications.

Though Chapman wrote a number of excellent comedies and tragedies, there is no reason to think that he was an attached professional playwright except for the short period of a year or two when he was preparing scripts for the Lord Admiral's company. In two later periods he was preparing plays for boy companies with some regularity, but the number of these plays is not great and in neither period does he seem to have been wholly dependent upon the theatres for his living. Thus he seems, like Ben Jonson, to have been an author who wrote many plays for profit but was not an attached or regular professional.

After Chapman and Jonson, John Ford and John Webster are probably the dramatists whose literary achievement might suggest to many readers that they may have been attached to London acting companies. Both of them wrote a good many plays for the commercial theatres; both wrote two or three masterpieces; both, for limited periods, produced with some regularity for the playhouses.

But neither Ford nor Webster had the protracted period of steady writing for the theatres which characterizes the attached or regular professional playwrights like Heywood, Fletcher, Massinger, Shakespeare, Brome, and Shirley. Ford apparently wrote 17 plays, but four of the lost ones are undatable and assigned to Ford on rather scanty evidence. Most of the others fall into two periods, 1621–1624, when he collaborated with Thomas Dekker on five plays, and 1628–1638, when he wrote three plays for Blackfriars and five for the Phoenix. From the extant records it appears that Ford probably wrote no plays before the age of 35 and none between the ages of 38 and 42. This is not the pattern of work of the attached professional dramatist, though it does show frequent dealings with the regular acting companies.

Furthermore, the attitude which Ford displays toward his plays in prefaces and dedications resembles that of the amateurs. In his dedication of the 1629 quarto of *The Lovers' Melancholy* to four lawyer friends of Gray's Inn he says: "The account of some leisure hours is here summed up, and offered to examination . . . I care not to please many." And in his dedication to John Wyrly and his wife of the 1639 quarto of *The Lady's Trial* he tells them: "In presenting this issue of some less serious hours to your tuition, I appeal from the severity of censure to to the mercy of your judgments."

Brilliant as he was in some of the tragedies of his later career, 1628–1638, Ford did not then think of himself as a professional playwright, and the pattern of his production is not that of the attached professional.

John Webster, whose canon is somewhat more uncertain than Ford's, was similarly sporadic in his composition. He was writing plays fairly steadily between 1602 and 1605 when he participated in seven collaborations for various companies. None of his dramatic work is clearly assignable to the years 1606 to 1609, but his best plays, *The Devil's Law Case*, *The White Devil*, and *The Duchess of Malfi*, were prepared—two for Queen Anne's company and one for the King's men—during the period 1609–1614. Then there is a long break to the time of his later plays written between 1624 and his death. To me these facts indicate that Webster may have been an attached professional from 1602 to 1605, but that later he wrote plays only occasionally and had no settled company affiliation.

Francis Beaumont is probably thought of by his most ardent admirers as an amateur and by those most interested in his successful collaborations for the King's company as a professional. There is some evidence for each classification. His career before 1608 was that of an amateur. He was born into a family of landed gentry; in February 1596/97 he was matriculated at Broadgates Hall,

Oxford; on 3 November 1600 he was entered at the Inner Temple, where his father had been a Bencher; in 1602 his metrical tale, *Salmacis and Hermaphroditus*, was published; in or before 1607 the Children of Paul's acted his *Woman Hater*, and in 1607 the Children of the Queen's Revels company performed his *Knight of the Burning Pestle*. This is the life pattern of an amateur dramatist, but between 1608 and 1613 Beaumont wrote in collaboration with John Fletcher and others about twelve plays for the King's men and one, *Cupid's Revenge*, for the Queen's Revels boys. In 1613 he married an heiress and presumably retired to her estates in Kent, where he died in March 1615/16.

This summary suggests that for most of his rather short life Beaumont's career corresponded to that of many amateur dramatists, but from 1608 to 1613 he seems to have fallen into the pattern of the attached professionals, writing about two plays a year with John Fletcher and preparing them all for the King's men—with the exception of *Cupid's Revenge*, which may indeed have preceded the collaborators' attachment to King James's company.[19] Because of this sharply divided career Beaumont does not quite belong to the category of the regular attached professionals.

Thomas Middleton was another of the rather prolific professionals who appears never to have had any long sustained company attachment, but to have sold his plays here and there. Early in the century he did two or three plays for the Admiral's men, then half a dozen for Paul's Boys in a period of three or four years, apparently interspersing them with a play or two for the Queen's Revels company and one for Prince Henry's company. From 1608 or 1609 until his death he wrote alone or in collaboration at least three plays for Prince Charles's men, four for the Lady

19. See James Savage, "The Date of Beaumont and Fletcher's *Cupid's Revenge*," *ELH*, xv (December 1948), 286–94.

Elizabeth's men, six or seven for the King's men, and three or four, including two lost plays, which cannot confidently be assigned. This is not the activity of an attached playwright; even the series for the King's men is broken by plays for the Lady Elizabeth's company and for Prince Charles's company. Furthermore Middleton, for a good part of his career, was not solely dependent upon the commercial theatres. In the last fourteen years of his life he did about a score of city shows and pageants, and for the last seven years he was the salaried City Chronologer. Middleton was a talented and successful writer for the theatres, but he was not an attached playwright.

Drayton and Munday were Henslowe playwrights whose dramatic work, except for three or four plays, has disappeared. In the few years they were working for Henslowe they were prolific, but neither had a long-term attachment to the theatre, and neither appears to have had anything to do with commercial theatres for the last 28 or 30 years of his life.

We have too little information on six other playwrights in this list of the 22 most prolific to call them attached or regular professionals. About Henry Chettle, John Day, William Hathaway, William Haughton, Wentworth Smith, and Robert Wilson we know very little apart from some details of Henslowe's payments and loans to them. The overwhelming majority of all their known plays have disappeared; for none of the six do we have certain birth dates and death dates, and for several we have neither; it is their obscurity and not their nontheatrical interests or eclectic placing of their plays which prevents their consideration as attached professionals. Actually there is one fact which suggests that Henry Chettle, the most prolific of the group, was attached. On Lady Day in 1602 he signed a bond to write for the Admiral's men, but nevertheless he wrote or contributed to several plays for the

Earl of Worcester's company in the following thirteen or fourteen months.

THE ELIMINATION of these 14 experienced playwrights, who certainly wrote for profit and had short or scattered periods of more or less close association with the London commercial theatres but not long-term exclusive attachments, leaves eight of the more prolific dramatists in our list of 22 who profited from furnishing plays for the theatres. These eight men I have called the regular professionals, or the attached professionals. In the order of their known dramatic productivity they are:

Thomas Heywood
John Fletcher
Thomas Dekker
Philip Massinger
William Shakespeare
James Shirley
William Rowley
Richard Brome

It is from their careers and their plays that I shall draw a large part of the evidence in the ensuing discussions of the profession of the dramatist in Shakespeare's time.

CHAPTER III

The Status of Dramatists, Plays, Actors, and Theatres

IN THE PRECEDING CONSIDERATION of the classes of playwright during the years 1590 to 1642 there have appeared occasional statements about the normal degree of esteem which literate men of the time accorded to plays and the men who wrote them. Jasper Mayne's publisher said that the author of *The City Match* had no ambition to publish his play, ". . . holding works of this light nature to be things which need an apology for being written at all, not esteeming otherwise of them, whose abilities in this kind are most passable, than of masquers who spangle and glitter for the time, but 'tis thorough tinsel."

Even Ben Jonson, who is never accused of being unaware of the value of his own compositions, was familiar with the Jacobean status of plays, and he expressed the common attitude clearly when he wrote from prison to the Earl of Salisbury in 1605, when he and Chapman had been committed to jail for the affair of *Eastward Ho*. Jonson said:

> . . . I am here (my most honored Lord) unexamined or unheard, committed to a vile prison, and (with me) a gentleman (whose name may perhaps have come to your Lordship) one Mr. George Chapman, a learned and honest man. The cause (would I could name some worthier) though I wish we had known none worthy our imprisonment, is, a (the word irks me that our Fortunes hath necessitated us to so despised a course) a play, my Lord.[1]

In the same year Samuel Daniel, whose literary reputation at that time was at least as great as Jonson's, wrote to Viscount Cranbourne expressing the same low opinion of acted plays in comparison with other literary work. At the time Daniel was in difficulties over alleged parallels to the trial and execution of the Earl of Essex in his tragedy *Philotas*, which had been acted by the Children of the Queen's Revels. None of his earlier or later plays and masques are known to have been acted in the commercial theatres, and the reasons can be seen in the opening lines of Daniel's letter:

> Right honorable, my good Lord:
> My necessity, I confess, hath driven me to do a thing unworthy of me, and much against my heart, in making the stage the speaker of my lines, which never, heretofore, had any other theatre than the universal dominions of England, which so long as it shall keep the tongue it hath will keep my name and travails from perishing. . . .[2]

These assumptions about commercially acted plays made by Leonard Lichfield in 1639 and by Ben Jonson and

1. C. H. Herford and Percy and Evelyn Simpson, *Ben Jonson*, Oxford, 1925–1953, I, 194–95.
2. Laurence Michel, ed., *The Tragedy of Philotas by Samuel Daniel*, New Haven, 1949, p. 37.

Samuel Daniel in 1605 are characteristic of the period. They are much less contemptuous than those reflected in most writings of the 1570s or in the fulminations of the professed Puritans from 1570 to 1660. Lichfield and Jonson and Daniel speak as reasonable men of their time.

It is one of the most familiar observations of the student of literature that the popular and admired writing of one generation is the soporific or the scandal of another. The reaction of most twentieth-century readers to the many hundreds of Elizabethan and Jacobean published sermons is a fully documented example of the former reaction; an amusing speculative example of the latter is the reaction of the chastity-preaching Elizabethans to the popular novel of sexual promiscuity widely read and frequently praised in the reign of Elizabeth II.

But a knowledge of these changing standards and the application of such knowledge in the assessment of the motives, customs, expectations, and compromises of Elizabethan dramatists, especially of Shakespeare, has been painfully rare in the criticism of the last two hundred years. Too often the assumption of the critic—generally tacit— has been that Elizabethan standards and values were those of his own time, and on these assumptions the critic posits the reputation or the response of Shakespeare or Marlowe or Heywood and of the audiences for which they wrote.

An instructive example of the power of this almost irresistible anachronism is afforded by a comment of F. J. Furnivall, who had been looking through the interesting diary and account books of Sir Humphrey Mildmay, preserved in the Harleian collection at the British Museum. In the records of Sir Humphrey's 57 visits to London theatres during the last decade before the Civil Wars there is a mention of one Shakespearean play which he saw, *Othello*, an allusion which Furnivall duly reported to the editor of the *Shakespeare Allusion Book*.[3] Naturally Fur-

3. John Munro, 1932 ed., Oxford, 1932, I, 397.

nivall was disappointed not to find more Shakespeare allusions in these accounts, which are the fullest extant records of the theatre attendance of any playgoer in the three reigns. He continued his comment on the records: "And on turning back to the Diary, leaf 10, back, I find under April 28 'this after Noone, I spente att a play wth good Company'—and so forgot to say what the play was: probably not one of Shakespeare's or it would have overpowered the recollection of the 'good company.'" Now Furnivall was very widely read in English literature of the sixteenth and seventeenth centuries, and he was a careful scholar. Yet when it came to critical assumptions, his Edwardian values easily overpowered his own scholarly observations. A careful reading of Mildmay's diary would by itself have demonstrated to him that he was foisting Edwardian tastes onto a Caroline spectator. Mildmay's London residence was near the Blackfriars, the most distinguished theatre of his time, and his diary shows that he went there more often than to any other playhouse. At this theatre Shakespeare's plays were then in the active repertory, and there are still extant records of the company's performance of ten of them in the decade of Mildmay's accounts. Sir Humphrey must have seen several in his 57 recorded visits to theatres; yet he names only one, *Othello*, whereas he names four of Fletcher's plays, three of Jonson's, and two of Davenant's.[4] Mildmay's typical Caroline tastes are implicit in his own records, yet, where Shakespeare was concerned, a man so informed and so careful as Furnivall could not resist the assumption that Sir Humphrey must have had Furnivall's own Edwardian tastes and not those of an aristocratic patron of the theatres in the reign of Charles I.

Even so astute and careful a scholar as Sir Walter Greg, who knew a good deal more about the theatre and the drama than Furnivall did, could be led into a foolish state-

4. See *Jacobean and Caroline Stage*, ii, 673–81.

ment by attributing twentieth-century conceptions of the status and importance of poetry to an Elizabethan theatre magnate. After he had spent several years editing and analyzing the extensive and illuminating theatre records of Philip Henslowe, Greg prepared several appendices generalizing from Henslowe's records of play purchases and performances. Concluding his discussion of the scale of payments to authors, Greg wrote: "A decade later [i.e., in 1612 and 1613] prices had greatly risen. A third-rate poet like Daborne, evidently deep in Henslowe's toils, gets £10 to £20 a play. . . ."[5] The facts are accurate, as usual, but the assumptions underlying that phrase "a third-rate poet" are twentieth-century and nontheatrical assumptions, exquisitely inappropriate to a hard-driving theatre man like Henslowe. They seem intended to suggest that if a third-rate poet like Daborne got £10 to £20, first-rate poets in these years, like Shakespeare and Webster, must have received a good deal more. But certainly Henslowe and his rival theatre managers were not competing for the praise of twentieth-century poetry lovers; they were trying to buy plays which would bring pennies into the box at the Fortune and the Globe and the Red Bull. In buying plays Henslowe could scarcely have ignored the performance records at his own theatres where, so far as his accounts show, *The Jew of Malta* and *Doctor Faustus* had indeed been popular, but *The Wise Man of West Chester, Jeronimo, Bellendon,* and *A Knack to Know an Honest Man* had outdrawn any of the plays of Chapman, Greene, or Dekker. Poetic distinction may be a criterion for the selection of plays for twentieth-century anthologies, but not for building repertories in Jacobean theatres.

Such misleading aberrations on the part of scholars as experienced and distinguished as F. J. Furnivall and Sir Walter Greg demonstrate the almost irresistible distorting

5. W. W. Greg, ed., *Henslowe's Diary*, London, 1904–1908, II, 127.

power of one's own cultivated standards in assessing the facts of the professional environment of Shakespeare and his contemporaries. The mistakes of Furnivall and Greg underscore the importance of maintaining a clear understanding of the status which their London contemporaries assumed for professional playwrights in the reigns of Elizabeth, James I, and Charles I.

This status changed somewhat in the course of the period 1590–1642, but it was always closely related to the status of actors, theatres, and plays. Because of greater financial success, increasing royal and aristocratic patronage, and the accumulation of printed texts, all four were thought less insignificant by writers in 1640 than they had been thought fifty years before, but even after this half century of rising respectability, the playwright and his professional environment were less esteemed than most readers of Shakespeare, Jonson, Ford, and Webster are likely to assume.

At the beginning of the period we are considering, the condemnation of public plays and of the people concerned with them was fairly general. Still current were the violent diatribes against all phases of the drama—especially the drama in the public theatres—which had followed the opening of the Theatre. The writings of men like John Rainolds, John Northbrooke, Phillip Stubbes, and Stephen Gosson were not forgotten, but many more cool and responsible people expressed their disapproval of plays and theatres in emphatic and unambiguous terms. The Corporation of the City of London and several of the great City companies which it represented were consistent and vocal opponents of the commercial theatre almost throughout the period. In 1592—as in several later years—they were involved in a plan for the suppression of all the theatres in town.

On 25 February 1591/92 Sir William Roe, the Lord Mayor, wrote an official letter to the Archbishop of Canterbury:

Our most humble duties to Your Grace remembered. Whereas by the daily and disorderly exercise of a number of players and playing houses erected within this City, the youth thereof is greatly corrupted and their manners infected with many evil and ungodly qualities by reason of the wanton and prophane devises represented on the stages by the said players, the apprentices and servants withdrawn from their works, and all sorts in general from the daily resort unto sermons and other Christian exercises to the great hindrance of the trades and traders of this City and profanation of the good and godly religion established amongst us. To which places also do usually resort great numbers of light and lewd-disposed persons as harlots, cutpurses, cozeners, pilferers, and such like and there under the colour of resort to those places to hear the plays devise divers evil and ungodly matches, confederacies and conspiracies, which by means of the opportunity of the place cannot be prevented nor discovered, as otherwise they might be. In consideration whereof we most humbly beseech Your Grace . . . to vouchsafe us your good favor and help for the reforming and banishing of so great evil out of this City, which ourselves of long time though to small purpose have so earnestly desired and endeavored by all means that possibly we could. . . . Whereof Your Grace shall not only benefit, and bind unto you the politic state and government of this City which by no one thing is so greatly annoyed and disquieted as by players and plays and the disorders which follow thereupon, but also take away a great offence from the church of God and hinderance to his gospel. . . .

The reply of the Archbishop of Canterbury to this plea from the City government to help drive the players and their plays from London has not been preserved, but its contents are implied in the reply of the Lord Mayor ten days after his first letter:

My humble duty to your Grace. I read your Grace's letter wherein I understood the contents of the same and imparted the same to my brethren the Aldermen in our common Assembly, who together with myself yield unto your Grace our most humble thanks for your good favor and Godly care over us in vouchsafing us your health for the removing of this great inconvenience which groweth to this City by plays and players. As touching the consideration to be made to Master Tilney [Master of the Revels] and other capitulations that are to pass betwixt us for the better effecting and continuance of this restraint of the said plays in and about this City, we have appointed certain of our brethren the aldermen to confer with him forthwith, purposing to acquaint your Grace with our agreement and whole proceeding herein as occasion shall require. . . .[6]

The proposal which the Archbishop had made in his lost letter was evidently that the corporation of the City of London arrange to pay the Master of the Revels an annuity to gain his cooperation in driving the players and theatres and their plays out of London. This inference of the contents of the Archbishop's letter is easily derived from a minute in the court books of the Merchant Taylors' Company recording their reaction to the proposal two weeks later on 22 March. Though the Merchant Taylors did not agree with the method proposed, this great City company which often had private plays in its own hall was entirely in agreement with the attempt to rid the City of the commercial theatre. The entry in their court books reads:

A precept directed from the Lord Mayor to this company showing to the company the great enormity that this City sustaineth by the practice and profane exercise of players and playing houses in this City and the corruption of youth that groweth thereupon [and] inviting the company by the consideration of this mischief to yield to the payment of one annuity to one Mr. Tilney, Master of the Revels of the Queen's house, in whose

6. *Malone Society Collections*, Oxford, 1907, i, pt. i, 68–70.

hands the redress of this inconvenience doth rest and that those plays might be abandoned out of this City. Upon consideration of which precept, albeit the company thinks it a very good service to be performed, yet weighing the damage of the precedent and invocation of annuities upon the companies of London [and weighing] what further occasions it may be drawn into, together with their great charge otherwise which this troublesome time hath brought and is likely to bring, they think this no fit course to remedy this mischief but wish some other ways were taken in hand to expel out of our City so general a contagion of manners and other inconveniences wherein if any endeavors or travail of this company might further the matter they would be ready to use their service therein. . . ."[7]

These were the opinions of metropolitan officials and business leaders of London concerning plays and theatres. But gentry in the country, who usually considered their station well above that of the men of commerce in London, did not have a very much higher opinion of the theatres and their activities. Lady Bacon, the mother of Sir Anthony and Sir Francis, would have been in essential agreement with the Lord Mayor, the Archbishop of Canterbury, and the court of the Merchant Taylors' Company. The writer in Thomas Birch's collection reports that

About the latter end of April, or in the beginning of May, 1594, Mr. Bacon removed from Recburne in Hertfordshire, which was too remote from the capital for the carrying on his numerous correspondences; and he settled himself in London, in a house in Bishopsgate street; tho' the situation of it was highly disliked by his mother, not only on account of its neighborhood to the Bull-inn, where plays and interludes were continually acted, and would she imagined, corrupt his servants, but likewise out of zeal for his religious improvement. . . ."[8]

7. *Malone Society Collections*, iii, 166–67.
8. Thomas Birch, *Memoirs of the Court of Queen Elizabeth* . . . , London, 1754, i, 173.

Lady Bacon's attitude toward plays was colored by her moral, or perhaps we should say economic, apprehensions. But she was by no means unusual in her fears; it was not only the provincial mothers of youthful sons in London who assumed that plays and theatres were instruments of seduction and the disruption of households.

The general idea of plays and theatres which lay behind Lady Bacon's fears is expressed by John Stow in his *Survey of London* published in 1598. Speaking of the development of plays, Stowe says that they began with amateurs,

> But in process of time it became an Occupation; and many there were that followed it for a Livelihood. And which was worse it became the Occasion of much Sin and Evil. Playhouses thronged. And great Disorders and Inconvenience were found to ensue to the City thereby. It occasioned Frays and evil Practices of Incontinency. Great Inns were used for this Purpose, which had secret Chambers and Places, as well as open Stages and Galleries. Here maids, especially Orphans and good Citizens' Children under Age, were inveigled and allured to privy and unmeet Contracts.[9]

A couple of years later another solid Englishman used language in a petition which revealed the common estimate of plays and players. In the year 1600 the son of Henry Clifton, Esquire, of Toftrees in Norfolk was impressed by Nathaniel Giles, Master of the Children of the Chapel Royal—ostensibly to sing in the royal choir. Henry Clifton complained to the Star Chamber that the boy was not really taken to sing, for he had no talent as a singer, but that he had been taken

> unto the said playhouse in the Blackfriars aforesaid and there to sort him with mercenary players and . . . there to detain and compel to exercise the base trade of a mercenary interlude player to his utter loss of time ruin and disparagement. . . . [The boy was] committed to the

9. 1720 ed., London, 1598, book I, p. 247.

said playhouse amongst a company of lewd and dissolute mercenary players . . . [to be trained] in acting of
parts in base plays and interludes. [The boy's father
was assured] that his said son should be employed in
that vile and base manner of a mercenary player in that
place. . . .[10]

These are opinions of theatres, actors, and theatre audiences, but the playwrights were, of course, simply the employees of the actors and theatre managers and provided
for them the means of producing these "great disorders
and inconveniences . . . frays and evil practices of incon-
tinency." Though one could not expect Elizabethans with
the prejudices of the Lord Mayor, the Archbishop, the
Merchant Taylors, Lady Bacon, John Stowe, and Henry
Clifton to have had a very high opinion of playwrights,
others who were far more interested in the drama did not
think very highly of the regular dramatists either.

The man who probably contributed larger sums to the
income of poets than any other individual in his time—
Philip Henslowe—showed no undue respect for his playwrights. Most revealing of his true estimate of dramatists
is his account, in a letter to his son-in-law, the great actor
Edward Alleyn, of the death of one of the actors of the
Lord Admiral's company, Gabriel Spencer, in a duel with
Ben Jonson. The letter was written on 26 September 1598,
at a time when Jonson had already written two or three
plays, at least one of which Henslowe had paid for.

Now to let you understand news, I will tell you some,
but it is for me hard and heavy. Since you were with
me I have lost one of my company, which hurteth me
greatly, that is Gabriel, for he is slain in Hogsden Fields
by the hand of Benjamin Jonson, bricklayer. Therefore
I would fain have a little of your council if I could. . . .[11]

10. F. G. Fleay, *A Chronicle History of the London Stage, 1559–
1642*, London, 1898, pp. 127–32.
11. W. W. Greg, ed., *Henslowe Papers*, London, 1907, pp. 47–
48.

48

No doubt Henslowe was exasperated when he wrote, but often people's true opinions come out at such a time. Jonson had indeed been apprenticed to a bricklayer, but he was 26 years old when Henslowe wrote, and he had been a soldier, an actor, and a playwright since his bricklaying days.

Philip Henslowe naturally thought of playwrights as hirelings of actors and managers, as the hundreds of transactions with them recorded in his accounts attest. But other Elizabethans with no connections with the London professional theatre thought similarly. What university students thought is sometimes recorded in college plays. In 1602 or 1603 the undergraduates at St. John's College, Cambridge, performed a play they had written called *The Return from Parnassus*, part 2. The chief characters in the play are Cambridge students who—like many of their successors—are troubled as to how they will make a living after they leave the university. They consider writing plays, and in act IV, scene 4, they even call in Richard Burbage and Will Kempe, Shakespeare's fellows in the Lord Chamberlain's company, to consult about employment. The more susceptible students are somewhat romantic admirers of the poetry of Shakespeare, and one, in his audition before the two actors, recites the opening of *Richard III*. Yet the students have no respect for the theatrical enterprise and less for the position of the playwright, exploited by the actors. In the following scene the two students have become wandering musicians, and *Studioso* justifies their choice of the one profession over the other:

Better it is amongst fiddlers to be chief,
Than at a player's trencher beg relief.
But is't not strange these mimic apes should prize
Unhappy scholars at a hireling rate?
Vile world, that lifts them up to high degree,
And treads us downe in groveling misery.
England affords these glorious vagabonds,

49

That carried erst their fardels on their backs,
Coursers to ride on through the gazing streets,
Sooping[12] it in their glaring satin suits,
And pages to attend their masterships:
With mouthing words that better wits have framed
They purchase lands, and now Esquires are named.[13]

A much more cultivated man, and one who had more respect for poetry than Philip Henslowe or even the Cambridge undergraduates, expressed by implication his acceptance of the inferior status of plays a few years later. When John Donne wrote his *Catalogus Librorum Aulicorum* he was about thirty years old with a good deal of London experience. Sir Richard Baker, under the heading *Of Men of Note in His* [James I] *Time* says: "And here I desire the reader leave to remember two of my own old acquaintance. The one was Mr. *John Donne*, who leaving *Oxford*, lived at the Inns of Court, not dissolute, but very neat; a great visitor of ladies, a great frequenter of plays, a great writer of conceited verses. . . ."[14] Yet "great frequenter of plays" though he was when he lived at Lincoln's Inn in the 1590s, Donne shows that he did not consider plays in the category of significant literature. His *Catalogus Librorum Aulicorum* was first written, Evelyn Simpson thinks, about 1604 or 1605 and revised in 1611, in the decade of the greatest achievements of Shakespeare, Jonson, Chapman, Marston, Heywood, and Middleton, and well after the deaths of Christopher Marlowe and Robert Greene. The *Catalogus* is a satiric piece in the manner of Rabelais which presents a mock catalogue of 34 works by 30 different authors. Among the contemporary, or near-contemporary, writers whom Donne names and satirizes

12. Sooping = sweeping.
13. J. B. Leishman, ed., *The Three Parnassus Plays*, London, 1949, p. 350 (modernized).
14. *A Chronicle of the Kings of England*, London, 1643, section IV, p. 156, Vvvv2^v.

are Sir John Harrington, Sir Francis Bacon, Sir John Davies, John Florio, Thomas Campion, Nicholas Hill, John Foxe, Sir Hugh Platt, Hugh Broughton, and Matthew Sutcliffe. But he lists no dramatists and no play titles. Mrs. Simpson points out that,

> The name of no dramatist appears in [this] list which was drawn up in the decade which produced the greatest English drama of all time. . . . But in truth the *Catalogue* is one more proof that in Shakespeare's lifetime the drama was not thought of as literature. Plays were to be acted, not read. They were the property of the company of actors rather than of the playwright.[15]

In any event, John Donne evidently did not think that the writers of the plays he had seen in his many visits to the theatres sufficiently well known in literary circles to be worthy of mention in 1604 when *Hamlet* and *Othello* were being performed at the Globe, or even when he made his revisions in 1611 as *The Winter's Tale*, *The Alchemist*, *The Tempest*, and *Catiline* were in the active repertory at Blackfriars.

A much more sweeping and explicit denigration of plays is Sir Thomas Bodley's. About 1598 Sir Thomas began making plans for what has become one of the chief libraries of the world. He bought books in great quantities and shipped them to Oxford; he wrote constantly to his librarian; he persuaded the King to visit his foundation in 1605; he got for his library grants of lands for its endowment; he gave his own lands. Most significant of all for the formation of a great library, in December of 1609 he concluded an agreement with the Stationers' Company of London that they should send to his library in perpetuity a perfect copy of every book printed by a member of the Stationers' Company. Since the members of this guild printed

15. Evelyn M. Simpson, ed., *The Courtier's Library or Catalogus Librorum Aulicorum. . .*, by John Donne, London, 1930, pp. 23–24.

nearly every book published in England, a greater bibliographical benevolence can scarcely be imagined.

Obviously the wholesale preservation of English literature at Oxford was one of the far-sighted aims of the
founder of the Bodleian Library. Much of his correspondence with Thomas James, the keeper of his library, is still
extant, and some of it throws light on the status of plays
and playwrights in the middle of the reign of James I. On
the first of January 1611/12 Sir Thomas wrote:

> Sir, I would you had forborne to catalogue our London
> books, until I had been privy to your purpose. There
> are many idle books, and riff-raffs among them, which
> shall never come to the library, and I fear me that little,
> which you have done already, will raise a scandal upon
> it, when it shall be given out by such as would disgrace
> it, that I have made up a number with almanacs, plays,
> and proclamations: of which I will have none, but such
> as are singular.

In his next letter, written three days later on 4 January
1611/12, Sir Thomas takes up the matter with his librarian again:

> . . . I can see no good reason to alter my opinion for
> excluding such books as almanacs, plays, and an infinite
> number, that are daily printed, of very unworthy mat
> ters and handling, such as, me thinks, both the keeper
> and underkeeper should disdain to seek out, to deliver
> unto any man. Haply some plays may be worth the keep
> ing: *but hardly one in forty.* For it is not alike in English
> plays, and others of other nations; for they are most
> esteemed for learning the languages, and many of them
> compiled by men of great fame for wisdom and learn
> ing, *which is seldom or never seen among us.* Were it so
> again, that some little profit might be reaped (which
> God knows is very little) out of some of our playbooks,
> the benefit thereof will nothing near countervail the
> harm that the scandal will bring unto the library, when

it shall be given out, that we stuff it full of baggage
books. . . . This is my opinion, wherein if I err, I think
I shall err with infinite others: and the more I think
upon it, the more it doth distaste me, that such kind of
books, should be vouchsafed a room, in so noble a
library. . . .[16]

Though the Bodleian Library today has the largest or the
second largest collection of Elizabethan and Jacobean plays
in the world, the playbooks came through the efforts of
eighteenth- nineteenth- and twentieth-century librarians
and collectors and not by the design of its founder. Sir
Thomas was a true Jacobean, and to him, as to so many of
his contemporaries, these precious play quartos of Shakespeare, Jonson, Tourneur, and Webster were "riff-raffs" or
"baggage books."

Even a dramatist who had written a number of plays
himself, though he cannot be considered a regular professional, tended to distinguish between professional dramatists and men who had written plays but were not dependent upon the theatres for a living. The well-known list of
dramatists in the epistle which John Webster wrote for the
1612 edition of his *White Devil* has been frequently discussed, partly because it is a Shakespeare allusion, partly
because it is one of the very few documents of the time
noting the accomplishments of writers of plays, and partly
because of the odd order in which Webster lists the writers.
He expresses his appreciation

of other men's worthy labours; especially of that full
and heightened style of Master *Chapman*, the labor'd
and understanding works of Master *Johnson*, the no less
worthy composures of the both worthily excellent Master *Beaumont*, and Master *Fletcher*, and lastly (without wrong last to be named) the right happy and copi-

16. G. W. Wheeler, ed., *Letters of Sir Thomas Bodley to Thomas
James, Keeper of the Bodleian Library*, Oxford, 1926, pp. 219–22.
Italics mine.

ous industry of M. *Shakespeare*, M. *Dekker*, and M. *Heywood*.

Discussions of Webster's order have usually turned on modern literary values, but Webster's order is a Jacobean hierarchical order. The last three dramatists, of "right happy and copious industry" were regular professional playwrights, and in the year 1612 had been so for fifteen to twenty years. In the normal Jacobean ordering they were placed in a group at the end without individual characterization. Though George Chapman may have been a regular professional for several years around the turn of the century in 1610, 1611, and 1612 he was not writing plays and was better known as the translator of Homer than as a playwright. Jonson had probably been a regular professional from 1597 to 1602, but for the last decade before Webster wrote he was not regularly attached to an acting company. In this decade he had written three times as many court masques and royal entertainments as he had plays, and his reputation as a nondramatic poet was growing. "Master *Beaumont*" and "Master *Fletcher*" were gentlemen who had only recently fallen into the status of professionals.

On the other hand, Shakespeare, Dekker, and Heywood grouped together at the end of the list were all attached professionals. Each had written 30 or more plays at this time; each had been regularly attached to an acting company; each was dependent on the theatre for his living; and two of the three were or had been actors. If one thinks of the social milieu of Jacobean London and not of modern literary values, Webster's ordering of the dramatists he appreciates is what one would expect.

The status of the dramatist was closely related, as we have seen, to the status of players and theatres, both of which improved under the notably increasing patronage of King James I and the members of his court. But there were other factors in this slowly rising status, as noted by the historian Sir Richard Baker, who lived much in London from 1587 to 1645. On 13 September 1619 Edward Alleyn's deed of foundation of his College of God's Gift at Dulwich was read before a gathering of notables in London. Baker pointed to one result in his *Chronicle of the Kings of England*. Under the heading "Works of Piety Done by this King [James I] or By Others in His Time" he says:

> About this time also *Edward Alleyn* of *Dulwich* in *Surrey*, founded a fair hospital at *Dulwich*. . . . This man may be an example, who having gotten his wealth by stage playing converted it to this pious use, not without a kind of reputation to the Society of Players.[17]

Of course players and theatres and the writers who worked for them did not immediately become highly respected, but popular references to actors as rogues and vagabonds did not come quite so easily to people who knew something of the famous actor Edward Alleyn's College of God's Gift at Dulwich.

Bracketing Edward Alleyn's foundation of Dulwich College were two other events which in the next few years also tended to rehabilitate somewhat the reputation of plays and playwrights. These two events were the appearance of the Jonson folio in 1616 and the Shakespeare folio in 1623. *The Workes of Beniamin Jonson* is a landmark. No collection of plays by an English author had ever appeared before, and it was years before Jonson ceased to be derided for his presumption in using the term "Workes" for anything so trivial as plays. With the seven comedies and two tragedies in the folio were published the masques and entertainments prepared for the King, epigrams, and occasional poems, a number of them addressed to persons of great social distinction. Probably no other publication

---

17. *Chronicles of the Kings of England*, London, 1684, p. 423, Mmm4.

before the Restoration did so much to raise the contemporary estimate of the generally belittled form of plays.

The Shakespeare folio of 1623, though so much the more important volume to us now, was only the second such collection, and it did not include such items of social prestige as the masques and entertainments prepared for King James nor the epigrams and poems with noble sponsors. But the two volumes were alike in making a mute claim to dignity which had an irrational effect not visible to modern readers. Before 1616 nearly all plays which got printed had appeared on the bookstalls as unbound cheap quartos looking like almanacs, joke books, coney-catching pamphlets, and other ephemera. The degrading association is neatly expressed by two characters in Shakerley Marmion's play *Holland's Leaguer*, first acted at the Salisbury Court theatre in December 1631.

> *Fidelio.* Then know that I have boasted of your beauty;
>   Nay more, exposed thy virtues to the trial.
> *Faustina.* You have not prostituted them on stalls, To
>   have the vulgar fingers sweat upon them, As they do
>   use your plays and pamphlets?
>
>   [act 2, scene 2]

On the other hand the large folio format was generally reserved for sermons, geographies, the classics, royal books like *The Works of King James*, and other such literature thought to be of permanent significance. The fact that two collections of plays were to be seen on the bookstalls in the dignified and ponderous format of *The Works of King James* had its effect, during the later twenties and thirties, in diminishing the literary contempt for plays. This changing situation is clearly pointed up by the bitter comment of the fanatical Puritan, William Prynne, in his *Histrio-mastix, the Players' Scourge, or Actors' Tragedy* in 1633. In his preface Prynne says:

Some playbooks,[1] since I first undertook this subject, are grown from *Quarto* into *Folio*; which yet bear so good a price and sale that I cannot but with grief relate it, they are now[2] new printed in far better paper than most Octavo or Quarto *Bibles*, which hardly find such vent as they.

[1] Ben Jonson's, Shakespeare's, and others.

[2] Shakespeare's plays are printed in the best Crown paper, far better than most Bibles.[18]

But the increased dignity which the appearance of the Jonson and Shakespeare folios brought to plays and play-wrights must be seen only as a rise from an exceedingly low status to a moderately low one. Plays and their writers were still far from the respect shown for other writings published in folio. Their usual status, improved but not exalted, is illustrated in the dialogue of a Caroline writer, a dialogue which makes use of the very publications we have noticed.

The illustrative lines are an exchange between two Inns of Court students in Thomas Nabbes' play, *Tottenham Court*, a play acted at the Salisbury Court theatre in 1633. Since this theatre was within a few hundred yards of the Inner Temple and the Middle Temple it seems likely that the actors could have expected students from the Inns of Court, notorious play-haunters, to be in the audience at most of their performances.

Sam. Let's home to our studies and put cases.
James. Hang cases and bookes that are spoyl'd with them! Give me *Johnson* and *Shakespeare*; there's learning for a gentleman. I tell thee *Sam*, were it not for the dancing-schoole and Play-houses, I would not stay at the Innes of Court for the hopes of a chiefe Justice-ship.   [act 3, scene 1]

The satiric intent of James's preference for Jonson and Shakespeare, the only two dramatists whose plays had ap-

18. Preface, **6ᵛ.

peared in collected editions before 1633, may not be immediately apparent to readers unfamiliar with Caroline estimates of dramatists, but the intent of his coupling theatres and the dancing-school is unmistakable.

Plays and their authors were not particularly cherished even by those who had reason to have great interest in the drama and the production of plays. We have heard so much in our time of the value of first editions and of unique manuscripts that we tend to transfer some of our values. One of the Caroline holders of unique play manuscripts left a record of her estimate of them. Susan Baskervile was concerned with plays and players and theatres most of her life. She was the wife of a well-known actor and company manager, Thomas Greene, from whom she inherited theatrical properties, and she was the mother of another actor, William Browne. She was involved in a series of suits concerning theatrical affairs and on 25 May 1635 she signed an affadavit concerning her inheritance from her son. She said that she "hath had and received no part of the goods and chattels that William Browne, deceased, died possessed of, save only one cloth cloak, one old horseman's coat, two pair of laced cuffs, and a house clock, a silver tobacco box, and four play books, things of small value."[19] These "four play books" were probably prompt books for plays acted at the Red Bull theatre or the Salisbury Court. They may well have been autograph, but to Susan Greene, alias Baskervile, they were "things of small value."

The status of the professional playwright in the late 1630s is clearly indicated in the praeludium for a revival of Thomas Goffe's *Careless Shepherdess* about 1638 at the Salisbury Court theatre after Goffe's death. This induction, quite different in tone from the play which follows, was

19. Public Record Office, Req. Misc. Books, Affadavit Book, Hilary to Trinity 10 and 11 V Charles I, vol. 138.

evidently written by some theatrically knowledgeable writer connected with the theatre.[20] It is a little scene in which several spectators question the doorkeeper about the play which is to follow, and then discuss theatrical matters among themselves.

> *Thri[ft]*. Sir, was't a Poet, or a Gentleman
> That writ this play? The Court, and Inns of Court,
> Of late bring forth more wit, than all the Tavernes,
> Which makes me pity Playwrights; they were poor
> Before, even to a Proverb; Now their trade
> Must needs go down, when so many set up
> I do not think but I shall shortly see
> One Poet sue to keep the door, another
> To be prompter, a third to snuff candles.
> Pray Sir, has any Gentleman of late
> Beg'd the Monopoly of Comedies?

Thrift implies the inferior social status of playwrights by his use of words like "trade" and his suggestion that they may even descend to the status of the company's lower hired men, such as doorkeepers, prompters, and candle-snuffers. Thrift's ranking is mostly an economic one, but an anonymous writer of an epigram about the same time makes his distinction wholly on the basis of more respectable and less respectable writing.

The subject of the epigram is the prolific professional dramatist, Thomas Heywood. In the decade of the thirties, Heywood, still prolific in his sixties, had written—in addition to at least three or four plays and seven Lord Mayor's shows—a number of prose pamphlets and more extended nondramatic works, like *England's Elizabeth*, *The Hierarchie of the Blessed Angels*, *Pleasant Dialogues and Dramas*, and *The Exemplary Lives . . . of Nine the Most Worthy Women of the World*. To the writer of the epi-

---

20. See *Jacobean and Caroline Stage*, IV, 501–505, and V, 973–74.

gram, published in *Wits Recreations*, 1640, these works, especially *The Hierarchie*, seemed a much more respectable and appropriate activity than play-writing.

> *5. To Mr. Thomas Heywood*
> Thou hast writ much and art admir'd by those,
> Who love the easie ambling of thy prose;
> But yet thy pleasingst flight, was somewhat high,
> When thou did'st touch the angels Hyerarchie:
> Fly that way still it will become thy age,
> And better please then groveling on the stage.

This epigram has often mistakenly been interpreted as advice to Heywood to cease acting. It is true that Heywood had long been an actor, but the last clear record that he was still a player had appeared twenty-one years before in 1619; he is in none of the numerous records of actors in the twenties or thirties. Moreover the anonymous writer of the epigram is clearly speaking of literary activities, and the appropriate contrast to *The Hierarchie* is plays, not acting.

Finally there is a comment of John Dryden at the end of the seventeenth century which brings into sharp relief the comparative insignificance of writers of plays in the minds of audiences and managers. On 4 March 1698/99 in a letter to Mrs. Steward, Dryden wrote:

> This day was played a revived comedy of Mr. Congreve's called *The Double Dealer*, which was never very taking. In the playbill was printed,—'Written by Mr. Congreve; with several expressions omitted.' What kind of expressions those were you may easily guess, if you have seen the Monday's Gazette, wherein is the King's order for the reformation of the stage; but the printing an author's name in a play-bill is a new manner of proceeding, at least in England.[21]

21. Charles E. Ward, *The Letters of John Dryden With Letters Addressed to Him*, Durham, N.C., 1942, letter 59, pp. 112–13.

The ephemeral nature of playbills makes it impossible to check the accuracy of Dryden's statement, for none is extant for the first half of the century, but the theatre is always highly conservative, and Dryden's experience with it had been long and active; at least one can be sure that his own name had not appeared in the bills for the performances of the more than thirty plays he had prepared for London theatres. If it was thought irrelevant to print the laureate's name on the bills for the performance of his plays during the Restoration period, it is unlikely that the names of the playwrights had been so dignified in the theatrical advertising of the reigns of the first James and Charles.

CHAPTER IV

The Dramatist
and the Acting Company

IN THIS PERIOD of the highest development of the English drama, the basic fact in the situation of the professional dramatists is that they were the employees of the acting companies. The relationship could take various forms, but it was always the acting company which the dramatist had to please first; it was the acting company which paid him eventually; and it was the acting company, which, under normal circumstances, controlled what we should call the copyright of his play.

There were certain exceptions to this normal situation. The boy companies, for instance, in whose direction the boy actors had no voice, were controlled by a group of managers of whom one or more might be playwrights, like John Lyly in the 1580s or Samuel Daniel in 1604 or Robert Daborne in 1610. There were cases of royal interference, when an amateur play which had pleased the King

62

was handed over by His Majesty to his London company with orders to perform it—without payment to the author of course. Examples of such interference are William Cartwright's Oxford play, *The Royal Slave*, which so pleased the court at Oxford that Charles ordered his own company to perform it at Hampton Court. Another is Jasper Mayne's *The City Match*, intended for Oxford performance but actually performed at the King's request by the King's men in London.[1] Another exception was created by the playwright of strong and belligerent personality, who, though he had to please the actors before he achieved production in the first place, managed to exercise more control than most dramatists did in the publication of his play. Ben Jonson is the most notable and familiar example—so familiar, in fact, that his highly exceptional conduct and reputation are all too often taken to be normal.

Often, perhaps usually, there were middle men who facilitated the dealings between a company of actors and their writers. The intermediary best known to us now—because his records are the only ones which have been preserved—is Philip Henslowe. His function as play-purchasing agent for the company has often been misinterpreted by modern critics, who are incensed by his commercial attitude toward art and confused by accounting practices which inadequately distinguished his actions as financial agent for Worcester's men or the Lord Admiral's men from his related but independent transactions as pawnbroker, theatre owner, and personal loan agent. In his usual transactions with playwrights preparing manuscripts for the companies, Henslowe merely paid the dramatists, acting on orders from responsible members of the acting troupe and charging the payment against the company. Only rarely did he buy a play without authorization from a company he was financing. There is some evidence that Thomas Woodford acted in a similar capacity at different

1. See *Jacobean and Caroline Stage*, III, 134–40, and IV, 847–50.

times for companies performing at Paul's, Whitefriars, and the Red Bull. There is rather more evidence that Christopher Beeston, a player and leader of Queen Anne's company, was acting in a similar capacity for them from about 1609 to 1617, and still more likelihood that he was doing the same for Queen Henrietta's company and for the King and Queen's Young Company or Beeston's Boys from 1625 to 1638. Apparently Richard Gunnell was fulfilling this function at the Fortune in the 1620s and at the Salisbury Court in the early 1630s. Richard Heton was probably doing the same at the Salisbury Court theatre in 1639 and 1640. Nothing is known of William Davenant's activities as manager of the King and Queen's Young Company in the brief period 1639–1640, but considering his practices as manager twenty years later during the Restoration it might be guessed that he too had dealt with playwrights for the company in his short period of management before the wars. Unlike the heirs of Philip Henslowe, alas, the families of Woodford, Beeston, Gunnell, Heton, and Davenant allowed the ledgers of these entrepreneurs to be destroyed. We have only scattered allusions, law suits, and occasional memoranda to suggest that they fulfilled Henslowe's function for other companies.

But whether there was some financial agent or manager to act as intermediary or not, it was normally the acting company which decided to buy the play or to commission the dramatist to write it. A direct statement showing this sequence is found in a letter from the actor-dramatist Samuel Rowley, a patented member of the Lord Admiral's company, to Philip Henslowe, the financial agent for the company, authorizing an initial payment to John Day, William Haughton, and Wentworth Smith for a play which, we learn from other records, was called *The Conquest of the West Indies*.

Mr. Henslowe, I have heard five sheets of a play of the Conquest of the Indies and I do not doubt but it will be a very good play. Therefore I pray you deliver them forty shillings in earnest of it and take the papers into your own hands and on Easter eve they promise to make an end of all the rest.

Samuel Rowley

The request was carried out by Henslowe, and in his ledger he made the entry: "Lent unto John Day and William Haughton the 4 of April 1601 in earnest of play called The Conquest of the West Indies at the appointment of Samuel Rowley the sum of . . . 40s."[2]

This sequence of the transactions between the acting companies and the dramatists is fully demonstrable only in the records of Philip Henslowe. Of the fifteen or twenty companies operating in London at one time or another in the period 1590–1642, extensive records of this sort have been preserved for only the Lord Admiral's men and the Earl of Worcester's men acting at Henslowe's theatres 1597–1604. In spite of repeated statements to the contrary, however, there is no evidence that the King's company, or Queen Henrietta's company, or the Palsgrave's company, or the Lady Elizabeth's company, or any of the others handled their play purchases very differently unless the dramatist was himself a patented member of the troupe. It seems easy for many critics to forget that all the London acting companies were commercial organizations trying, however unsuccessfully, to make a living for actors, playhouse owners, playwrights, musicians, and theatre attendants. The general organization of the adult companies was much the same whether the actors were the Lady Elizabeth's men or the King's men, whether the dramatists were Richard Hathaway or Robert Daborne or William Shakespeare or James Shirley, whether the theatre was the Rose or the Hope or the Globe or the Phoenix.

Henslowe's system can be seen from the full form, often

2. R. A. Foakes and R. T. Rickert ed., *Henslowe's Diary*, Cambridge, 1961, pp. 294 and 167.

65

abbreviated, of his records of a transaction about payment to a dramatist for a play to be acted by one of the companies he financed.

> Lent [i.e. paid out in cash to be charged against the company] unto _____ [an actor, a patented member of the company] to pay to _____ [the author, or authors of the play] in earnest of _____ [the play, usually unfinished at the time of the first payment] . . . 10s.

These are the essentials of the transaction between the playwright and the producers of his play as usually set down in the only surviving full theatrical records of the period. The actual entry in Henslowe's ledger may be stated in a variety of ways, but the vital information is usually there, however the form of the record may vary.

> Lent unto Thomas Downton the 20 of February 1598 [/99] to lend unto Anthony Munday upon his second part of The Downfall of Earl Huntington Surnamed Robin Hood, I say lent the sum of . . . 20s.
>
> Lent unto Harry Chettle the 9 of September 1598 in earnest of a book called Brute Appointment of John Singer the sum of . . . 20s.
>
> Received by me William Haughton for the use of Thomas Dekker on the 30th of January the sum of . . . 20s. In part of payment for the book of Truth's Supplication to Candle Light.[3]

Sometimes Henslowe's records have misled modern readers as to the essential nature of his play-buying transactions because some of the men we think of as dramatists were also actors and patented members of companies. As such they could act as company representatives, without any reference at all to their literary capacities, as Shakespeare did when he received payment, along with William Kempe and Richard Burbage, for two performances be-

3. Ibid., pp. 87, 98, 64.

fore the Queen by the Lord Chamberlain's men in December 1594. In Henslowe's records actor-dramatists like Thomas Heywood or Charles Massey or Samuel Rowley sometimes act as representatives of the company in authorizing Henslowe's purchase of another man's play for their fellows, as indicated in Henslowe's payment in May 1603: "Lent at the appointment of Thomas Heywood and John Duke unto Harry Chettle and John Day in earnest of a play wherein Shore's wife is written the sum of . . . 40s."[4] Here the coupling of the names of the two patented members of the Earl of Worcester's company, Heywood and Duke, makes it clear that Heywood was acting as a member of the company authorizing payment to the playwrights Henry Chettle and John Day, and not as a dramatist himself. Sometimes Henslowe does not name the agent but simply records that his payment for the manuscript was authorized by the real purchasers of the play for whom he acted:

> Paid at the appointment of the company the 12 of February 1602 [/03] unto Thomas Heywood in part of payment for his play called A Woman Killed with Kindness . . . £3.
>
> Lent unto the company the 12 of October 1598 to pay unto Mr. Chapman in full payment for his play called the Fountain of New Fashions . . . 20s.[5]

In all these various and sometimes confusing forms of entry the essential fact is always the same—the dramatists were the employees of the company, and Henslowe was not buying the play for himself, but simply acting as agent for the Lord Admiral's company or the Earl of Worcester's men.

All the evidence we have suggests that this system was not peculiar to Henslowe or to the last decade of Queen

4. Ibid., p. 226.
5. Ibid., pp. 224, 99.

Elizabeth's reign. The Star Chamber case concerning the writing and acting of George Chapman's lost play *The Old Joiner of Aldgate* by Paul's Boys in February 1602/1603 indicates that Thomas Woodford (later one of the lessors of the Whitefriars theatre) was acting in a capacity not unlike Henslowe's for that theatre. Woodford, who was one of the defendants in the libel suit about the play, admitted in his deposition that:

> ... he did buy a stage play of George Chapmen ... and paid for the same twenty marks [£13 6s 8d] which play was called *The Old Joiner of Aldgate* and was played at some several times the last Hilary term by the Children of Pauls by this defendant's means and appointment, but before the playing thereof the same was licensed to be played by the Master of the Revels. ...[6]

George Chapman, another of the defendants in the Star Chamber case, deposed that:

> before Christmas last past ... Woodford coming to me and being then acquainted that I was about a play called *The Old Joiner of Aldgate*, I then told ... Woodford that he should have the same play of me when it was finished. And so I then sold the same to Woodford but did not finish it until after Christmas last and then I delivered the same out of my hands.[7]

In this case, as in the similar one 21 or 22 years later concerning *Keep the Widow Waking*, all the defendants and many of the witnesses were concerned to avoid charges of conspiracy and defamation, and much of the testimony— including earlier parts of Chapman's—is evasive. Probably Chapman was admitting as little involvement as he could, and he may even have suppressed facts; surely his relation-

6. C. J. Sisson, *Lost Plays of Shakespeare's Age*, Cambridge, 1936, p. 70.
7. Ibid., p. 66.

ship with Woodford was not quite so casual as he implies, since he wrote several plays for the rival boy company and at least one other one for Paul's Boys. Indeed the pointedly contemporary if not libelous play of *The Old Joiner of Aldgate* might almost be taken as an attempt to meet the complaint about the company made by a character in *Jack Drum's Entertainment* a couple of years before.

> *Fortune.* I saw the Children of Paul's last night,
>   And troth they pleased me pretty, pretty well:
>   The apes in time will do it handsomely.
> *Planet.* I'faith, I like the audience that frequenteth there
>   With much applause: A man shall not be choked
>   With the stench of garlic; nor be pasted
>   To the barmy jacket of a beer-brewer.
> *Brabant Jr.* 'Tis a good, gentle audience, and I hope the boys
>   Will come one day into the Court of Requests.
> *Brabant Sr.* Aye, and they had good plays. But they produce
>   Such musty fopperies of antiquity,
>   And do not suit the humourous age's backs
>   With clothes in fashion.   [act 5, scene 1]

However much George Chapman may have omitted or evaded in his testimony, what he does admit clearly shows Woodford advancing the money to pay him for a play which all the testimony in the case shows to have been shortly acted by the boys.

Essentially the same system was operating ten or twelve years later in the affairs of the Lady Elizabeth's company, as shown in correspondence, contracts, and complaints left by Edward Alleyn and now preserved among the muniments of Alleyn's College of God's Gift at Dulwich.

Most explicit is the statement in the articles drawn up between Nathan Field, the leader of Lady Elizabeth's company, on the one part and Philip Henslowe and Jacob Meade, owners of the Bear Garden and later of the Hope theatre on the other. One of the articles of the agreement reads:

> And further the said Philip Henslowe and Jacob Meade do for them their executors and administrators covenant and grant to and with the said Nathan Field by these presents in manner and form following, that is to say that the said Philip Henslowe and Jacob Meade or one of them shall and will from time to time during the said term disburse and lay out such sum or sums of money as shall be thought fitting by four or five of the sharers of the said company to be chosen by the said Philip and Jacob, or one of them, to be paid for any play which they shall buy or condition or agree for. So always as the said company do and shall truly repay unto the said Philip and Jacob, their executors or assigns all such sum and sums of money as they shall disburse for any play upon the second or third day whereon the same play shall be played by the said company without fraud or longer delay. . . .[8]

The vellum of this document has decayed, and the lower part, which would have carried the date and the signatures of the principals and the witnesses, has been torn away, but it is likely that it was completed and signed about the end of June 1613. The document nonetheless shows what the pattern was and how the principals in the handling of the affairs of the Lady Elizabeth's company assumed that dramatists and their manuscripts would be handled.

The operation of this process as agreed between the leader of Lady Elizabeth's company and Henslowe is shown in some of their correspondence preserved in the same muniment room. About the end of June 1613, Field wrote for the company to Henslowe:

Mr. Henslowe:
    Mr. Daborne and I have spent a great deal of time in conference about this plot which will make as bene-

8. W. W. Greg, ed., *Henslowe Papers*, London, 1907, p. 24.

ficial as play as has come these seven years. It is out of his love he detains it for us. Only £10 is desired in hand, for which we will be bound to bring you in the play finished upon the first day of August. We would not lose it, we have so assured a hope of it, and, on my knowledge, Mr. Daborne may have his request of another company. Pray let us have speedy answer, and effectual. You know the last money you dispersed was justly paid in, and we are now in a way to pay you all. So, unless you yourself for want of small supply will put us out of it again, pray let us know when we shall speak with you. Till when and ever, I rest

Your loving and obedient son
Nat: Field[9]

In spite of some confusion about the antecedents of his pronouns whereby "we" sometimes refers to Daborne and Field, as dramatist and company leader, but more often to the sharers of the Lady Elizabeth's company, Field makes it clear enough that as representative of his troupe he is urging their financial agent to make a large down-payment for them to Robert Daborne, who is at work on a most promising play.

However successful Robert Daborne may have been as a playwright, he was none too reliable a character, as his correspondence shows, and it would appear that he was capable of playing Henslowe off against the players. This game is suggested in a letter of his dated 14 October 1613, but it nonetheless shows the agreement of Henslowe, Meade, and Field at work. It also shows some of the troubles which the financial agent for a Jacobean acting company had to go through. Daborne writes:

Mr. Henslowe, I builded upon your promise to my wife, neither did I acquaint the company with any money I had of you because they should seek to you as I know they will and give you any terms you can desire. If they

9. Ibid., p. 84.

do not, I will bring you your money for the papers, and many thanks. Neither will I fail to bring in the whole play next week. Wherefore I pray sir of all friendship disburse one forty shillings, and this note shall suffice to acknowledge myself indebted to you with my quarter's rent £8 for which you shall either have the whole company's bonds to pay you the first day of my play being played, or the King's men shall pay it you and take my papers. Sir, my credit is as dear to me now as ever, and I will be as careful of it as heretofore, or may I never prosper nor mine. So desiring this may satisfy you till you appoint a time when I shall bring you the company's bond, I rest, expecting your no more deferring me.

14 October   Ever at your command,
1613   Rob: Daborne[10]

Daborne's threat that the King's company, playing at the Globe and Blackfriars, were eager to take his play may or may not be true, but he thought it might influence Henslowe, and such competition for manuscripts was not unusual.

This playing off of Henslowe against the company was a very reckless procedure. It was sure to make difficulties at this time when the Lady Elizabeth's company was not very successful and was having internal troubles of its own, as various other documents show. One such document consists of a series of articles of grievance against Henslowe drawn up by the Lady Elizabeth's players in 1615. The company was heavily in Henslowe's debt, and most of the articles charge that Henslowe confused the debts of individual actors in the company with the indebtedness of the company as a whole, or that he withheld from the company articles that were rightfully theirs. It should be remembered, however, that these are the complaints of actors in financial straits, and that no copy of Henslowe's defense has survived. Anyone who has read the bills of the plain-

10. Ibid., p. 76.

tiffs and the answers of the defendants in Elizabethan and Jacobean lawsuits is familiar with the vastly different assertions about the same series of events always made by the two antagonistic parties. At any rate, one of the charges, however exaggerated or unfounded, concerned Henslowe's buying, as their agent, of plays for the repertory of the company. "Also we have paid him for play books £200 or thereabouts, and yet he denies to give us the copies of any one of them."[11] The players here assumed as normal Henslowe's purchase of plays for them; the disagreement concerned possession of the manuscripts. Henslowe would probably have claimed that he kept the manuscripts as security for the company's general debt to him, but the Lady Elizabeth's men wanted to keep them in their own archives, since they said they had repaid the sums he advanced for plays and the manuscripts were legally theirs.

The records of Philip Henslowe preserved by his son-in-law in the muniment room at Dulwich College are so uniquely numerous and varied that one tends to forget that other managers or enterpreneurs surely had nearly as many, but lacked a son-in-law who was at once in the same profession, devoted to it, rich, and the founder of a permanent institution. Casual destruction has been the fate of most Elizabethan and Jacobean records of all kinds, including those theatrical archives of James Burbage, Philip Rosseter, Aaron Holland, John Heminges, Thomas Woodford, Richard Gunnell, Christopher and William Beeston, and Richard Heton. All these men must have kept records which would have paralleled Henslowe's at many points, but all have disappeared and we can glimpse their similar activities only when they are revealed indirectly in the archives of some governmental or ecclesiastical body—in Treasury payments, the Lord Chamberlain's accounts, or the wills preserved at Somerset House, or in

11. Ibid., p. 89.

the documents of lawsuits in Chancery, the Court of Requests, the King's Bench, and the Star Chamber.

One such revealing legal action is set out in a bill of information in the Star Chamber against John Audley and several dramatists and other theatre people to recover damages for the alleged victimization of Anne Elsden. One action complained against was the writing and acting at the Red Bull of a defamatory play in 1624. Thomas Dekker was called as a witness and testified

> ... that John Webster ... William Rowley, John Ford, and this defendant were privy consenting and acquainted with the making and contriving of the said play called Keep the Widow Waking and did make and contrive the same upon the instructions given them by one Ralph Savage. And this defendant sayeth that he this defendant did often see the said play or part thereof acted, but how often he cannot depose. . . .[12]

Dekker's testimony suggests that in 1624 Ralph Savage, who Professor Sisson thought was the successor of Aaron Holland, builder and owner of the Red Bull, was acting as financial backer and intermediary with dramatists in a capacity not unlike that of Philip Henslowe for the actors at the Rose, Fortune, and Hope.

This relationship of dramatist and acting company as employee and employer appears to have been standard. It was still in effect in the 1630s at the Red Bull, the most vulgar of the public theatres,[13] and at the Salisbury Court, one of the exclusive private theatres. It was taken as normal in the suit of *Heton* versus *Brome*, brought in 1640 in the Court of Requests but citing events and conditions going back as far as 1633. In his answer to the bill of complaint, the dramatist Richard Brome, a protégé of Ben

12. *Library*, 4th series, VIII (September 1927), 258.
13. See *Jacobean and Caroline Stage*, VI, 238–247.

Jonson, says that eighteen months before July 1635 the company at Salisbury Court

> did entice and enveigle this defendant to depart and leave the company of the Red Bull players being the Prince's highness servants [i.e., Prince Charles (II) company which had been formed in 1631] and where this defendant was then very well entertained and truly paid without murmuring or wrangling and to come and write and compose and make plays for the said complainants and their said company. . . .[14]

Brome does not give the particular conditions under which he was writing plays for the Red Bull company in the early 1630s, but he does say that he was "very well entertained and truly paid" and evidently considered himself a servant of the troupe at the Red Bull then—Prince Charles's [II] company.

The suit from which this statement comes primarily involved Richard Brome's relations with another company as a dramatist under contract to them. The full details of this contract can be more appropriately discussed later, but it is relevant to note here that on 20 July 1635 Brome contracted with the troupe acting at the Salisbury Court theatre and with the owners of that theatre

> Anthony Berry, William Cartwright, the elder, Christopher Goad, George Stutville . . . Curtis Greville, John Young, Edward May, Timothy Reade, William Wilbraham and William Cartwright the younger the then owners and actors of the said house [Salisbury Court theatre] . . . that he the said Brome should for the term of three years then next ensuing with his best art and

14. Answer of Richard Brome, 6 March 1639/40, to the bill of Richard Heton and the Salisbury Court Players, 12 February 1639/40 in the Court of Requests, as transcribed by Ann Haaker in "The Plague, the Theatre and the Poet," *Renaissance Drama*, n.s. (1968), pp. 296–306.

industry write every year three plays and deliver them to the company of players. . . .[15]

A normal part of the dramatist's preparation of his play for the acting troupe was the reading of his manuscript to them for their approval. Since, as is well known, all the companies of the time were repertory companies, the dramatist knew in advance a good deal about the kind of production his play might get, and a skillful writer of experience could go far in adapting the requirements of at least the major roles to the leading members listening to his reading. In this situation a great advantage lay with the actor-dramatists like Samuel and William Rowley, William Shakespeare, Thomas Heywood, and Nathan Field, whose daily familiarity with the styles and talents of their fellows made it easier for them to exploit special gifts and to anticipate difficulties.

There are various allusions to this usual step of the reading to the company. In March of 1598/99 Henslowe paid Drayton, Dekker, and Chettle £6 5s in two installments for a play called *The Famous Wars of Henry I and the Prince of Wales*. It is indicative of a common attitude of the players and their agents toward the plays the dramatists were preparing for them that when Henslowe made his first payment in behalf of the company for this piece he did not know the title, but he *did* know about a leading role which the playwrights were writing into it. He called the piece "A book wherein is a part of a Welshman written which they have promised to deliver by the twentieth day next following." After his entry recording the payment in full, he notes: "Lent at that time to the company for to spend at the reading of that book at the Sun in New Fish Street . . . 5s."[16] About a year and a half later Robert Shaw reported another play-reading to Henslowe, in this case,

15. Ibid., p. 297.
16. Foakes and Rickert, p. 88.

apparently, of a manuscript which had been completed without any installment payments:

Mr. Henslowe:

We have heard their book and like it. Their price is eight pounds, which I pray pay now to Mr. Wilson, according to our promise. I would have come myself, but that I am troubled with a sciatica,

Yours,

Robert Shaa.[17]

In May and June of 1602 Henslowe financed for the Lord Admiral's men the writing and production of a play probably entitled *Jephtha Judge of Israel* but which Henslowe persistently calls "Jeffa." It was written by Anthony Munday and Thomas Dekker who were paid £5 for their work on 5 May 1602. Evidently the company expected a good deal of the new play, for in the next two months expenditures of £13 17s are recorded for costumes and properties for "Jeffa." The play had its reading before the company, for in the ledger is recorded an expenditure of two shillings "Laid out for the company when they read the play of Jeffa for wine at the tavern. Delivered unto Thomas Downton."[18]

Ten years later the correspondence between the dramatist Robert Daborne and Henslowe shows that Daborne took for granted the reading of his manuscript to the company as the final step in his composition. On 16 May 1613 Daborne wrote asking for further advances and reassuring Henslowe that his manuscript was almost finished, though he was not yet quite ready to read it to the assembled members of the Lady Elizabeth's players. ". . . I doubt not on Tuesday night if you will appoint I will meet you and Mr. Alleyn and read some, for I am unwilling to read to the general company till all be finished, which upon my

17. Ibid., p. 288.
18. Ibid., p. 201.

77

credit shall be to play it this next term with the first."[19]
But Daborne's promises were never reliable and nearly a
month later he had not yet finished the play but was still
taking for granted his reading before the company.

> . . . Before God they shall not stay one hour for me,
> for I can this week deliver in the last word and will that
> night they play their new play read this, whereof I have
> sent you a sheet and more fair written so that you may
> easily know there is not much behind and I intend no
> other thing, God is my judge, till this be finished . . .
> wherefore I pray send me the other twenty shillings I
> desired and then when I read next week I will. . . .[20]

At the end of the year Daborne was working on two
other plays for the Lady Elizabeth's company, one the
revision of an old play, and the other a new one called
The Owl. At the end of a letter dated 31 December 1613
asking for more money in advance, this time ten shillings,
Daborne adds a postscript: "On Monday I will come to
you and appoint for the reading the old book and bringing
in the new."[21] At the foot of the letter Henslowe has
added a note, "Paid upon this bill toward *The Owl* 10s."

Though the dramatist's reading of his completed manuscript to the assembled company seems to have been customary, as these items show, preliminary readings to the
actors of portions of an unfinished manuscript were not
unknown. In his ledger Henslowe made the entry: "Lent
unto Benjamin Jonson the 3 of December 1597 upon a
book which he showed the plot unto the company which
he promised to deliver unto the company at Christmas
next the sum of . . . 20s."[22]

Sixteen years later Robert Daborne was prepared for a
similar reading of an uncompleted manuscript which, as
usual, was behind schedule.

19. Greg, *Henslowe Papers*, p. 70.
20. Ibid., pp. 72–73.
21. Ibid., p. 81.   22. Foakes and Rickert, p. 85.

Some papers I have sent you, though not so fair written as I could wish; I will now wholly intend to finish my promise which though it come not within the compass of this term shall come upon the neck of this new play they are now studying. My request is the £10 might be made up whereof I have had £9. If you please to appoint any hour to read to Mr. Alleyn, I will not fail, nor after this day lose any time till it be concluded.[23]

Henslowe was again accommodating, and a signed receipt for £1, dated 8 May 1613 is written at the foot of the letter.

Rejections

Even in a time of such constant demand for plays as the days of Elizabeth, James, and Charles, a number must have been rejected by the acting companies. Of course the great majority of the plays of whose preparation we have any knowledge were performed; nevertheless a few records of rejections by the players have been preserved.

One would guess that even in a time when the social status of the playwright was low, a fair number of amateur plays would have been boldly or surreptitiously offered to the London acting companies and rejected by them. For though many extant plays of the period were written by dilettantes and often given amateur performance, it is surprising how few of them reached the boards of the metropolitan theatres—at least before the reign of Charles I. Of more than 500 plays known to have been given professional performance in London between 1590 and 1625, less than half a dozen (aside from a group of four or five acted by the King's Revels Boys in 1607–1608) are known to have been written by amateurs. For the most part the presumed rejections of amateur offerings are unrecorded, but one is mentioned in print.

In 1635 the printer Richard Royston brought out John

23. Greg, *Henslowe Papers*, p. 69.

Jones's play *Adrasta, or the Woman's Spleen and Love's Conquest.* John Jones wrote a dedication to his friends in which he said:

> Having long since (honored Gentlemen, and friends) finished this play and fitted it for the stage, I intended to have had there the Promethean fire of action infused into it: being thereto encouraged by the general good liking and content which many of you had vouchsafed to receive in the hearings of it. . . . This I say was encouragement enough for me to prefer this little glowworm . . . to the stage, and to bring it to that noble nursery of action. . . . But the players, upon a slight and half view of it, refused to do it that right. . . .

The modern reader of this play, even "upon a slight and half view of it," is likely to think that the judgment of the players was quite sound.

Of course plays by professionals or semiprofessionals were also rejected on occasion, and a few records of such rejections have been preserved. After Henslowe had paid installments amounting to £1 19s to Richard Hathaway and William Rankin for a play eventually to be called *The Conquest of Spain by John of Gaunt,* he received a letter in April 1601 from Samuel Rowley, a leading member of the Lord Admiral's company, saying: "Mr. Henslowe, I pray you to let Mr. Hathaway have his papers again of the play of John of Gaunt and for the repayment of the money back again he is content to give you a bill of his hand to be paid at some certain time as in your discretion you shall think good."[24] Of course there is no indication of what the company thought was wrong with the play, but their rejection occasioned no serious break with Hathaway, for he wrote at least three more plays for the Admiral's men in the next year and a half.

Nearly forty years later a semiprofessional, Thomas

24. Greg, *Henslowe Papers,* p. 56.

80

Nabbes, left a record that one of the plays he offered an acting company had been refused. Nabbes was fairly experienced, and at the time of his rejection at least four of his plays had had professional London productions at the Phoenix or the Salisbury Court theatres. But his piece called *The Unfortunate Mother* was rejected by the actors, to his considerable annoyance. On the title page it is designated "A Tragedie. Never acted," and in the dedication to Richard Brathwait the author says:

> I have (though boldly being a stranger) elected you to countenance a piece that (undeservedly I hope) hath been denied the credit which it might have gained from the stage; though I can accuse myself of no error in it, more than a nice curiosity (which notwithstanding I must boast to be without precedent) in the method: where I have denied myself much liberty, that may be allowed a Poet from old example, and new established custom.

The method by which he denied himself "much liberty" was probably his careful maintenance of a unity of place within each act, but evidently his scrupulosity did not appeal to the actors.

A more experienced and successful playwright than Jones or Nabbes has also indicated that he had plays rejected by a London acting company. In the suit of *Heton* versus *Brome*, Richard Brome states in his answer to the bill of complaint that in the autumn of 1638 he had signed a new contract to write plays and do other dramatic chores for Queen Henrietta's players at the Salisbury Court theatre.

> And this defendant upon the last agreement in the bill mentioned for twenty shillings a week . . . composed another new play for the said complainants, and before Easter term 1639 this defendant brought them another new play written all but part of the last

scene. But this defendant found that divers of the company did so slight the last-mentioned plays and used such scornful and reproachful speeches concerning this defendant divers of them did advise the rest of them to stop all weekly payments towards this defendant, so as this defendant understood that they took occasion daily to weary the defendant from and out of their employment. . . .[25]

At the time he prepared this answer to Heton's bill Brome was being sued for breach of contract by the players and proprietors of the Salisbury Court theatre for whom he had written a number of plays; it was therefore to his advantage in the suit to emphasize the "scornful and reproachful speeches" of the actors. Nevertheless it can scarcely be doubted that the plays mentioned were refused by the players, though not necessarily with so much scorn as it was to Brome's advantage to assert.

Plays Bought without Reference to the Authors

Though the usual way for an acting company to secure a manuscript for production was to deal with the dramatist who wrote it, there were others. A good many records have been preserved showing that companies sometimes secured the manuscripts of plays and then acted them without any dealings with the author at all, and in most instances evidently without his knowledge. This custom, which so offends the modern concept of literary property, was not illegal, and there are few if any records of protests by the playwrights. The dramatist sold his manuscript to the acting company for which it had been prepared; after that it was no more his than the cloak that he might have sold to the actors at the same time.

In the spring of 1598 Henslowe bought for the company a collection of old plays offered to him by Martin

25. Answer of Richard Brome, as transcribed by Haaker in "The Plague, the Theatre, and the Poet," p. 304.

Slater, a leading actor and later a company manager. Slater had, until recently, been a member of the Lord Admiral's company which had in the past three years produced all these plays; how he got the manuscripts is not known, but the fact that he was later a company manager and a member of the Ironmongers' Company suggests that he probably had some capital, and there are other records of actors who acquired play manuscripts as personal property. Henslowe records that he: "Lent unto the company the 16 of May to buy 5 books of Martin Slater called the 2 parts of Hercules, and Phocas, and Pythagoras, and Alexander and Lodowick, which last book he hath not yet delivered, the sum of . . . £7."[26] Evidently this payment did not completely cover *Alexander and Lodowick*, which Slater for some reason did not deliver with the others, but two months later he brought it in and was paid separately: "Paid unto Martin Slater the 18 of July for a book called Alexander and Lodowick, the sum of . . . 20s."[27]

In September 1601 Henslowe bought for the Lord Admiral's company, from Edward Alleyn, the manuscript of *The Wise Man of West Chester*, almost certainly the same play as *John a Kent and John a Cumber*, the manuscript of which is still extant. He recorded in his ledger: "Paid at the appointment of [the name of some member of the Lord Admiral's company is omitted] the 19 of September 1601 for the play of the Wise Man of West Chester unto my son E. Alleyn the sum of . . . 40s."[28] Since this play had previously been one of the most popular in the repertory of the company, this manuscript bought from Alleyn was probably a revision which had come into his possession. In any case, Anthony Munday, the author, was not a party to the transaction.

Four months later the company again authorized Henslowe to buy plays from Alleyn, again plays which had

26. Foakes and Rickert, pp. 89 and 93.
27. Ibid., pp. 89 and 93.   28. Ibid., p. 181.

been in the repertory five to eight years before. "Paid at the appointment of the company the 18 of January 1601 [/1602] unto E. Alleyn for three books which were played called The French Doctor, The Massacre of France, and The Nut, the sum of . . . £6."[29]

It is notable that Henslowe was buying these second-hand plays at the rate of £2 per manuscript. The rate was the same for Alleyn and for Slater, if one considers the two parts of *Hercules* as one play and notes that Henslowe withheld half the price for *Alexander and Lodowick* until he had the manuscript in hand. The rate was also the same in August following when Henslowe paid Alleyn £4 for two more old manuscripts, one of *Philip of Spain* and another of *Longshanks*, and again the same in October when he paid Alleyn £2 for "his Booke of tambercam."[30] It appears that in the last five or six years of the reign of Elizabeth the going rate for secondhand plays was approximately one-third that for new plays—at least with the Henslowe companies.

This traffic in old play manuscripts was still current thirty years later when the Master of the Revels noted in his office book: "Received of Beeston [Christopher Beeston, manager of Queen Henrietta's company at the Phoenix or Cockpit in Drury Lane] for an old play called *Hymen's Holiday*, newly revived at their house, being a play given unto him for my use, this 15 August, £3. Received of him for some alterations in it £1."[31] The play, which is lost, had been written by William Rowley for his company, the Duke of York's men, sometime before February 1611/12 when it was performed at court. Since at the time of Herbert's entry Rowley had been dead for seven or eight years, it is not likely that the play was given to Beeston

29. Ibid., p. 187.
30. Ibid., pp. 204 and 205.
31. J. Q. Adams, ed., *The Dramatic Records of Sir Henry Herbert*, New Haven, 1917, p. 35.

by the author but by someone who had come by the manuscript. Probably it had been long unacted, since Beeston
considered it necessary to pay for having it revised.

Though in particular cases we seldom know how the
vendor of a play manuscript by some other man came by
his commodity, we do have repeated examples of one
method.

Among Henslowe's papers is a deed of sale made by the
actor Richard Jones to Edward Alleyn and dated 3 January 1588/89.

> Be it known to all men by these presents that I Richard
> Jones of London yeoman for and in consideration of the
> sum of £37 . . . to me by Edward Alleyn of London
> gentleman well and truly paid have bargained and sold
> and . . . have delivered to the same Edward Alleyn all
> and singular such share, part, and portion of playing ap-
> parel, play books, instruments and other commodities
> whatsoever belonging to the same as I the said Richard
> Jones now have or of right ought to have jointly with
> the same Edward Alleyn, John Allen, Citizen and Inn-
> holder of London and Robert Browne yeoman to have,
> hold, and enjoy all and singular my said share of play-
> ing apparel, play books, instruments and other commodi-
> ties whatsoever. . . .[32]

By this deed Richard Jones is making over to Alleyn those
properties, including play books, which he held jointly
with Edward Alleyn, John Allen, and Robert Browne as
the sharing members of some acting company, perhaps the
Earl of Worcester's men. We have here one of the possible sources from which Alleyn secured some of the costumes and play manuscripts which were later bought by
Henslowe on behalf of one or another of the companies
he financed.

But Alleyn and Slater were not peculiar. Twenty to
thirty years later there is still evidence of this same phe-

32. Foakes and Rickert, pp. 273–74.

nomenon of play manuscripts from the repertory of a hard-pressed or breaking company getting into the hands of a solvent or unscrupulous actor. About 1618 or 1619 five of the patented members of Queen Anne's London company, Richard Perkins, John Cumber, William Robbins, James Holt, and Thomas Heywood, brought suit in the Court of Chancery against their former fellow in the company, Robert Lee. They say that Lee had left the troupe two years before and had agreed, for a consideration, to give up playing and to restore to the company "all such clothes, books of plays, and other goods belonging thereunto as he had then or were trusted in his hands or custody. . . ." They say he had returned nothing but had set up another acting company by enticing away seven of their young men and "also detaineth from your orators divers books, apparel, and other goods of theirs to the value of £100. . . ."[33] Lee's answer has not been found, but his defense would probably have been that his former fellows had defaulted on their bonds. In any case Lee had in his possession the manuscripts of plays which had been written for Queen Anne's men. Perhaps he used them in performances by his new company, but there was nothing to prevent him selling them to some other acting company or to a manager like Beeston or an entrepreneur like Edward Alleyn.

Another player and sharer in an acting company is known to have been in possession of play manuscripts. William Browne, a fellow of Prince Charles [II] company acting at the Red Bull made his will on 23 October 1634 and was buried at St. James's, Clerkenwell, on 6 November following. In his will he left to his mother Susan Greene, alias Baskervile, whom he made his executrix,

> All such sum and sums of money, debts, duties, claims challenges, and demands whatsoever as either is ought, or shall be due, owing, or belonging unto me forth, out

33. Public Record Office, Chancery Proceedings, James I, P 16/14.

86

of, and from the Red Bull playhouse . . . whereof I am a member and a fellow sharer, or of or by any of the shares or other persons players there or owners thereof and of in or to any house or houses to the said play-house adjoining. . . .[34]

Later, suit was brought in the Court of Requests against Susan Greene, alias Baskervile, concerning financial relations with the company at the Red Bull. As part of the proceedings she made an affidavit on 29 May 1635 saying that she "hath had and received no part of the goods and chattels that William Browne deceased died possessed of save only one cloth cloak, one old horseman's coat, two pair of laced cuffs, and a house clock, a silver tobacco box, and four play books, things of small value."[35] There is no known record of what Susan Baskervile did with the play manuscripts her son had retained from the archives of Prince Charles's [II] company, but she had long experience of the London theatre world since the time of her first actor-husband, Thomas Greene, and it is not unlikely that she found some manager who would pay her for her manuscripts.

These various records of the ownership and sale of play manuscripts without reference to the author not only suggest one of the ways in which London acting companies came to act plays known to have been written for some other company, but they further emphasize the playwright's lack of control over his own compositions. Far from being a sacred holograph, a dramatist's manuscript was often treated simply as another theatrical commodity, like a cloth cloak or laced cuffs, "things of small value."

34. *Jacobean and Caroline Stage*, II, 391–92 and 636–37.
35. Public Record Office, Req. Misc. Books, Affidavit, Hilary to Trinity, 10 and 11 Charles I, vol. 138.

CHAPTER V

Dramatists' Pay

Though playwrights were the servants of the acting companies and theatres, and though actors, theatres, and dramatists stood rather low in social esteem in these times, a little consideration of contemporary remunerations shows that professional playwrights were not ill paid.

The financial rewards of the dramatist in the reigns of Elizabeth, James, and Charles have too often been lamented in the romantic context of golden words poured out for posterity by the starving drudge in the frigid garret, or, for example, in a scandalized comparison of the £6 Thomas Heywood received for the composition of *A Woman Killed with Kindness* with the £6 13s paid for a single costume to be used in the performance of his tragedy.[1] As a matter of fact, the scattered evidence of

1. This discrepancy between the sum paid for a play and the sum paid for a fine costume is simply sound economy on the part of the Earl of Worcester's men. Every new play was a gamble; it might fail dismally and the sum paid its author would constitute a total

payment records, compensation correspondence, contracts, and the comments of contemporaries suggests that professional playwrights like Chettle, Dekker, Heywood, Middleton, Shakespeare, Shirley, and Brome took in more cash from their professional activities than was usual for writers or for those in some related professions. We can look at a few comparative figures of payments in the time.

Precise information about any payments to nondramatic writers in the three reigns is scanty; anything like a record of consecutive payments or annual incomes of nondramatic writers is almost unheard of. Of course they commonly cry poor, but so do most men in most times; the literary man is simply better equipped to carry his cry to posterity.

In the sixteenth and seventeenth centuries the ancient system of patronage was still in vogue, though writers who mention it generally call it inadequate—often insulting. But printing and publishing became a profitable trade during the reign of Elizabeth, and writers were supplementing or often substituting the publishers' payments in cash or in kind for patronage from the noble or wealthy. Thus many writers drew their incomes from two sources.

There is only one known detailed account of such income from a writer of the time. Richard Robinson, who published from 1576 to 1600, left an account of his literary receipts, called *Eupolemia,* which forms part of a manuscript now preserved in the British Museum.[2] In these accounts Robinson set down his receipts for a number of his publications from *A Record of Ancient Histories,* 1577, to *A Fourth Proceeding in the Harmony of King David's*

---

loss for the company. A fine costume, on the other hand, could be used for years and for many different plays, whether the production for which it had been originally purchased was a long-running success or a complete failure.

2. *Royal 18 A* LXVI, fols. 5–13. A transcript was published in 1924 by George McGill Vogt in *Studies in Philology,* XXI (October 1924), 629–48.

Harp, 1596. Apparently he tried for a gift from a patron in connection with each publication, but he was only intermittently successful. When he presented *Part of the Harmony of King David's Harp* to the Earl of Warwick, he received nothing; when he dedicated *The Laudable Society, Order and Unity of Prince Arthur and his Knights of the Round Table* to Thomas Smith, president of the London Archery Society, he was rewarded with a present of five shillings; Alexander Nowell, Dean of St. Paul's, the dedicatee of *The Dial of Daily Contemplation for Sinners*, gave him ten shillings; he fared better when he dedicated a book of prayers to Sir Philip Sidney, who gave him £2, to which his father, Sir Henry, added 10 shillings more. He did best with the Earl of Rutland and Sir Christopher Hatton, both of whom gave him £3, the former as a reward for the dedication of a translation of Melancthon, and the latter for a dedication in 1583.

Robinson often supplemented these gifts from dedicatees by selling copies of his book which the publisher had given to him as payment. By such peddling he sold 25 copies of the volume he had dedicated to the Dean of St. Paul's and added 25 shillings to the ten which the dean had given him. In the same way he sold 25 copies of a translation he had dedicated to a judge of the Admiralty and added 25 shillings to the 12 he had received from the judge. When the Earl of Warwick gave him nothing for his dedication, Robinson took 100 copies from the publisher, which he succeeded in selling for £10—but he notes that it took him two years to sell them. These peddling activities were clearly intended to supplement inadequate rewards from dedicatees, for Robinson notes in reference to the book for which Sir Christopher Hatton gave him £3: "I bestowed very few of these books abroad by reason of his liberality which kept me from troubling my friends abroad for one whole year's space afterwards."[3]

3. Vogt transcription, *Studies in Philology*, XXI (October 1924), 636.

Robinson's total receipts from his writing in this period of nearly twenty years have been analyzed by Edward Haviland Miller.[4] In three instances Robinson's accounts are incomplete and Miller has supplemented them with receipts estimated from those recorded for the other books. During the period of these accounts Robinson's gifts from patrons to whom he had made dedications amounted to £23 6s 4d; his receipts from peddling the copies of his books which the publisher had given him came to £29 11s 1d; so that his total recorded remuneration from writing between 1577 and 1596 reached the grand total of £52 17s 5d for an average of less than £3 per year.

We have similar records of payments made to writers for the theatres, but these are the only detailed accounts of payments made in the period to writers for patrons and publishers. How far from the average receipts of nondramatic writers were Robinson's? The very few casual records of rewards and payments suggest that Robinson's literary income was not so very far short of those of some other nondramatic writers.

A few scattered allusions to payments or gifts to poets were collected by David Nichol Smith for his account of "Authors and Patrons" in *Shakespeare's England*, 1916. There are several assertions that the publishers' usual rate for a pamphlet was 40 shillings. In the Cambridge University play of about 1600, *The Return from Parnassus*, part 1, act 1, scene 3 opens with the entrance of *Ingenioso* (probably a caricature of Thomas Nashe) and "Danter the Printer":[5]

> *Ingenioso*. Danter thou art deceived, wit is dearer than thou takest it to be. I tell thee this libel of Cambridge has much salt and pepper in the nose; it will sell

4. *The Professional Writer in Elizabethan England*, Cambridge, Mass., 1959, pp. 160–63.

5. John Danter published in London from 1589 to 1599. He printed a number of pamphlets and more than a dozen plays, including two of Shakespeare's, and is known to have sometimes been involved in surreptitious printing.

> sheerly underhand [i.e. sell well by stealth] whereas
> these books of exhortations and catechisms be mould-
> ing on thy shop board.
> *Danter.* It's true; but good faith, Master Ingenioso, I
> lost by your last book, and you know there is many a
> one that pays me largely for the printing of their in-
> ventions; but for all this you shall have 40 shillings
> and an odd pottle of wine.[6]

The same fee was mentioned by John Stephens in "The
Author's Epistle Popular" which he prefixed to his anonymously published closet drama, *Cynthia's Revenge or
Menander's Ecstasy*, in 1613. Stephens sneers at the front-
matter appeals of popular writers of the time, who

> . . . assure the hood winked buzzards of this age that
> every syllable savors of milk sops, doth require an easy
> stomach, slight concoction, simple and weak judgment
> &c *ad infinitum.* Thus do our piebald naturalists depend
> upon poor wages, gape after the drunken harvest of
> forty shillings, and shame the worthy benefactors of
> Helicon. . . .

Whatever the reader may think of the comparative literary
merits of Stephens's interminable play and the hackwork
of the poetasters whom he castigates, his statement of the
usual fee paid by the publishers is clear enough.

About a decade later George Wither, who had done a
good deal of publishing of various kinds, indicated near
the end of his pamphlet, *The Scholars' Purgatory*, that the
usual fee was still the same as it had been in 1600.

> For what need the stationer be at the charge of printing
> the labors of him that is Master of his Art, and will re-
> quire that respect which his pain deserveth? Seeing he
> can hire for a matter of 40 shillings some needy Igno-
> ramus to scribble upon the same subject, and by a large

6. J. B. Leishman, ed., *The Three Parnassus Plays*, London,
1949, pp. 247–48.

promising title make it as vendible for an impression or two as though it had the quintessence of all art?[7]

And as late as the 1640s the standard payment for pamphlets appears to have remained unchanged. When John Aubry put together his notes on Sir John Birkenhead, editor of the famous Royalist newsbook *Mercurius Aulicus* and later a fellow of the Royal Society, he noted Birkenhead's activities after the fall of Oxford and his expulsion from his fellowship at All Souls. Aubry says that Birkenhead "got many a forty shillings (I believe) by pamphlets, such as that of *Colonel Pride,* and *The Last Will and Testament of Philip Earl of Pembroke,* &c."[8]

Publishers sometimes appear to have done better by their writers than they did by Robinson and the pamphleteers, but the circumstances are so ambiguous that one cannot tell how much work by the writer the payments represent. A case in point is the payment to John Stow in 1602.

John Stow was a best-selling English popular historian. His *Summary of English Chronicles* first appeared in 1565 and had gone through ten new editions with revisions before 1602; *A Survey of London* had been first printed in 1598. Both copyrights appear to have passed from the original publishing firms into the hands of the Stationers' Company itself. In 1602, and perhaps for some time before, Stow was making additions and revisions to both histories, which were to be reissued with additions, the former in 1604 and the latter in 1603. In these circumstances the court of the Stationers' Company, at its meeting of 2 August 1602, issued an order: "It is ordered that Mr. Stow shall have £3.0.0 and 40 copies for his pains in the book called *The Survey of London.* And £1.0.0. and 50 copies for his pains in *The Brief Chronicle* [i.e. *A Summary of*

7. *The Scholar's Purgatory,* London, n.d. (1625?), I₁ᵛ, p. 130.
8. Oliver Lawson Dick, ed., *Aubry's Brief Lives,* London, 1949, p. 23.

93

English Chronicles]."⁹ This order seems to authorize payment to Stow for his revisions and additions—which were extensive—in anticipation of good profits. The circumstances are obviously unusual because the high court, representing the entire membership of the guild of printers and publishers and not an individual printer, was involved. Nevertheless the remuneration is very little more than Richard Robinson was receiving, and the popular John Stow, like the less well-known Robinson, was required to peddle his own books.

The account that Richard Robinson left in his *Eupolemia* shows the average rewards from patronage for an ordinary writer in the last two decades of the sixteenth century. Other payments from patrons which are known are very scattered, and one can never tell—as one can with Robinson—to what extent they are representative of the writer's experience. Spenser's reward was a pension which he received only after years of work on *The Faerie Queene*; Prince Henry's individual gifts to writers were numerous, but the greatest one, to Chapman, was *promised*, but apparently never delivered before the death of the Prince; Drayton had from him an annuity of £10 per year, and Sylvester £20; Jonson said in 1619 that the Earl of Pembroke gave him £20 a year to buy books. But these records of patronage seem unusual. Nichol Smith concludes his survey of the patronage situation:

> In the absence of further evidence about the reward for the dedication of minor works, what Peele was given by the Earl of Northumberland for *The Honour of the Garter* may be taken as typical. Peele celebrated in this poem the earl's installation as a knight of the Garter in 1593, and he received for it £3.¹⁰

9. W. W. Greg and Eleanor Boswell, *Records of the Court of the Stationers' Company, 1576-1602*, London, 1930, pp. 90 and lxx–lxxi.

10. *Shakespeare's England*, Oxford, 1916, II, 210–11.

Before comparing these records of payments made to non-dramatic writers with those that professional playwrights received, it is worth recalling that the scale of pay for most intellectual activities during these three reigns also seems very low. University education was certainly no road to riches in the sixteenth and seventeenth centuries.

A calling somewhat comparable to that of the writer—at least in its requirements of literacy and training, though certainly not in respectability—was that of the schoolmaster. The profession was not unassociated with the drama: much of the development of English drama before the period of professionalism was in the hands of schoolmasters and teachers like Nicholas Udall, Thomas Ashton, John Redford, Richard Edwards, and John Ritwise; and even after the complete dominance of professionalism in the seventeenth century, plays were written by schoolmasters like John Mason, Samuel Bernard, Robert White, William Hawkins, and Thomas Singleton. Some of the professional dramatists had—or are said to have had—experience as schoolmasters. William Beeston, the son of Shakespeare's colleague Christopher Beeston, told John Aubrey that Shakespeare "had been in his younger years a schoolmaster in the country."[11] James Shirley was certainly a schoolmaster at St. Albans in the early 1620s before he came to London and became the regular dramatist for Queen Henrietta's company in the reign of Charles I.[12]

Various extant records give the pay of schoolmasters. According to the town charter of 1553 the salary of Shakespeare's schoolmaster at Stratford was fixed at £20 per annum. Sir Edmund Chambers comments on this rate of pay: "This was much more than the £12.5 paid at Warwick or than the amounts usual in grammar schools outside Westminster, Eton, Winchester and Shrewsbury. It

11. E. K. Chambers, *William Shakespeare: A Study of the Facts and Problems*, Oxford, 1930, II, 254.
12. *Jacobean and Caroline Stage*, V, 1065–72.

was better than the emoluments of an Oxford or Cambridge fellowship."[13]

Chambers's observation that the Stratford schoolmaster's salary was abnormally high is confirmed by Robert Burton, who lumps schoolmasters with the comparable curates and lecturers. In *The Anatomy of Melancholy*, part 1, section 2, member 3, subsection 15, where he speaks of the hard fate of the university man, Burton says:

> . . . he is as far to seek [preferment] as he was (after twenty years standing) at the first day of his coming to the *University*. For what course shall he take, being now capable and ready? The most parable and easy, and about which most are employed, is to teach a School, turn Lecturer or Curat, and for that he shall have falconers wages, ten [pounds] *per annum* and his diet, or some small stipend, so long as he can please his Patron or the Parish; if they like him not, as usually they do above a year or two, serving-man-like, he must go look a new Master. . . .

This is the way Burton estimated the graduate's wage in his first edition of 1621. It is significant that though he revised, clarified, and slightly expanded this passage in the editions of 1624, 1628, 1633, 1638, and 1651, he never saw need to alter the sum of £10 as the usual expected wage for a university graduate in a schoolmastership, a curacy, or a lectureship.

Somewhat higher was the rate of pay received by James Shirley after he had received his B.A. from Cambridge and before he became the regular professional for the actors of Queen Henrietta's company. Of course Shirley's teaching days came half a century and more after the years for which we know the schoolmasters' salaries at Stratford-

---

13. *William Shakespeare*, 1, 10. It is true, however, that about the same time as £20 was set up as the stipend for Stratford, Sir Andrew Judd is said to have bequeathed land to Tunbridge to pay a salary of £20 to the schoolmaster and £8 to his usher (John Stow, *Survey of London*, London, 1603, p. 114).

upon-Avon and Warwick, and these were years of rising prices. Yet his salary in the years 1621–1623 was not significantly greater than the Stratford master's had been in 1553. The several payments recorded to him in the account books of the borough of St. Albans are somewhat irregular, but after going through them all Albert Baugh concluded that the normal rate of pay for the schoolmaster was £6 3s 4d per quarter for four quarters, and for his usher £2.[14] The schoolmaster's salary was supposed to be supplemented by a payment of 2d per quarter from the parents of each pupil, but there is no record of how many pupils there were or how regularly this fee was paid. Thus in the early 1620s Shirley took in £24 13s 4d plus probably not more than £2 or £3 in twopenny fees.

Against this background of customary rewards for their services made to nondramatic writers and to schoolmasters and curates we can see more clearly what the true economic situation of the dramatist was. Fortunately there are a good many records of the financial rewards of the playwright.

The most extensive and detailed evidence about payments to theatre writers comes, of course, from the records —diary and correspondence—of Philip Henslowe. From late 1597 to early in 1603 he entered hundreds of payments made to dramatists in behalf of the companies he financed. It is interesting to note that the prices do not vary much, and since we have the amounts paid for well over

14. Albert C. Baugh, "Some New Facts about Shirley," *Modern Language Review*, xvii (July 1922), 228–35.

Shirley's salary as schoolmaster was better than the one Edward Alleyn, the actor-manager-philanthropist, was paying four or five years earlier at the College of God's Gift at Dulwich. On 24 March 1617/18, Alleyn noted in his diary that he had paid to "Mr Young my chapline and Schoolmr" £5 as his quarterly wages. But Mr. Young's usher was better paid than Shirley's; Alleyn records his quarterly wages as £3 6s 8d (J. P. Collier, *Memoirs of Edward Alleyn, Founder of Dulwich College*, London, 1841, p. 147).

one hundred plays, we can be fairly sure of the going rates.

Sir Walter Greg summarized these rates in the commentary volume of his superb edition of the diary:

> From the end of 1597 onwards, we have, on the contrary, very full evidence which shows that the sums paid to authors were gradually rising. This was only part of the general rise in prices. . . . The earliest play for which we have complete records [22 December 1597–5 January 1597/98] is *Mother Redcap* for which Drayton and Munday received £6 in full. This appears to have been the usual sum, though it is probable that in some cases not more than £5 was given, as for each part of *Robin Hood* [Munday, Part I; Munday and Chettle Part II, 15 February–8 March 1597/98]. The first part of *Black Ba[teman of the North*, by Chettle, Dekker, Drayton and Wilson, 2-22 May, 1598] was bought for £7, but for Part II [Chettle, Porter and Wilson paid 26 June–14 July] the authors only got the usual sum of £6. This continued the standard for a long time with occasional variations of £5 on the one hand and £7 on the other. . . . The prices paid by Worcester's men are exactly the same and it may be said that throughout the standard price remains £6, but that while in the earlier period £5 is not uncommon, toward the end payments of £7 and even £8 become comparatively frequent. . . .[15]

In addition to these payments for their contributions to new plays, the professional dramatists of the diary earned additions to their incomes by revising old plays, writing prologues and epilogues, preparing special material for court performances, and occasionally by writing a play so successful that the writers were awarded a special bonus by the company. All these activities together produced an income for a professional dramatist in the years 1597–1603 which surpassed the cash receipts of many other literary

15. W. W. Greg, ed., *Henslowe's Diary*, London, 1904–1908, II, 126–27.

men and notably exceeded the recorded remunerations of some other trained professional men like schoolmasters and curates.

It may be helpful in putting the professional dramatist in a somewhat more accurate economic perspective to make a rough tally of the cash payments known to have been made to a few of them. Of course these figures must be incomplete; even in the diary Henslowe sometimes makes payments for plays or parts of plays and does not name the recipient, who may well have been one of the dramatists whose receipts I have totaled. And there were usually other payments. Normally playwrights had a benefit, a percentage of the receipts at the second or third performance of their new play, and since such payments were made directly by the company, Henslowe had no reason to enter them, as they were not part of his accounts. Sometimes playwrights were given gratuities, as when Edward Alleyn recorded in his own diary on 19 November 1621 "Given to Charles Massey at his play . . . 5 shillings."[16]

It is also true that Henslowe's regular professionals are known to have written occasional plays for other troupes while working mostly for his companies. Thus Dekker wrote *Satiromastix* for the Children of Paul's and the Lord Chamberlain's men, but this seems to have been quite rare. We can be reasonably sure that the totals I have assembled for a few of the professional dramatists from Henslowe's accounts fall short of the total incomes of these men for the periods specified.[17]

16. William Young, *The History of Dulwich College*, London, 1889, II, 224. How common such gifts at first performances were is not known. Henslowe records another such to Munday, Drayton, Wilson, and Hathaway at the opening of *Sir John Oldcastle* in November 1597, and one of 10s to John Day after the playing of the *Second Part of Tom Strode*, and another to Thomas Dekker "over and above his price for his book, *A Medicine for a Curst Wife.*"

17. These figures are conservative. In general I have credited a playwright with a payment only when Henslowe names him. There

The most faithful playwright and the largest earner to
be revealed by Henslowe's accounts is Henry Chettle. In
the diary he is recorded as having a hand in 52 plays, mostly collaborations and several probably unfinished, in the
five years between his first payment entered 25 February
1597/98 and his last recorded one on 9 May 1603. Total
payments of £123 17s 8d are entered to him—an average
of about £25 a year. But his output was sporadic, due at
least in part to irregularities in the theatrical seasons. In
the ten and one-half months from 25 February 1597/98
to 28 November 1598 he was paid £36 12s 4d for his contributions to 17 plays, only three of which were unaided
compositions. No payments to him are recorded in December 1598 or January 1598/99, but in the ten months between 16 February 1598/99 and 17 December 1599 he
was paid £24 5s for his part in nine plays. He was paid

---

are some payments for which no dramatist is named but he is known
from other sources; such payments I have omitted. Sometimes Henslowe's listing of authors suggests omissions. The first payment for
Christmas Comes But Once a Year was £3 to Heywood and Webster;
the second was £2 to Chettle and Dekker; the third was £2 to Chettle only "in fulle paymente." I have my doubts about the accuracy
of these indications of distribution, but I have credited them as Henslowe does. Once he credits a payment to "An: Munday & the rest."
There is a further source of error in the division of a lump sum
among the dramatists named. Though the majority of the plays
bought are collaborations, Henslowe generally records simply a total
of £4 to four men or £3 to three men. In such cases I have credited
the money evenly among the collaborators. I suspect that is often
wrong, for two or three times Henslowe does break down his lump
payment, as when he noted that he had divided £4 5s into 30s, 30s,
and 25s to Wilson, Chettle, and Munday for *Chance Medley*; or
when he divided 50s for *The Second Part of Godwin*: Drayton, 30s;
Wilson, 10s; and Chettle, 10s.
Henslowe left too much room for choice in his bookkeeping, and
some other amateur accountant might get totals different from mine,
but I doubt that we would vary much. I am confident that these
playwrights received somewhat more from the Lord Admiral's men
and from Worcester's men than I have credited them with.

nothing between 17 December 1599 and 16 February 1599/1600, but in the following four months up to 19 June 1600 he received £14 15s for his part in six plays. In 1601 he was paid £16 15s for contributions to four plays in nine months; in 1602, £27 10s 4d for contributions to eleven plays in twelve months; in 1603, £4 for contributions to three plays in four months.

In these last years Chettle may have had some supplementary unrecorded dramatic income from the Lord Admiral's men, for on 25 March 1602 Henslowe recorded that at the appointment of representatives of the company he paid out £3 "at the seallenge of h Chettells band to writte for them."[18] The stipulations of the bond are not given, but it is notable that Chettle agreed to write for the company, not for Henslowe. In the only such dramatist's contract to write for a company which is known in detail (Richard Brome's in 1635–1639) the poet is guaranteed weekly wages.

Thomas Dekker wrote almost as many plays for the companies financed by Henslowe, and he was paid almost as much, but his annual totals fluctuated even more. He had a hand in 45 plays prepared for these companies and was paid a total of £110 9s 2d in six years. But in two of the six years he contributed only single plays—a collaboration with Chettle in late April and early May of 1601 and *The Honest Whore* with Middleton in March 1603/1604. Clearly in these two years he was concerned mostly with nondramatic work or plays for other companies. In the four years during which he received regular payments from Henslowe he contributed 43 plays for a total of £103 9s 2d, or an average of about £25 per annum. In 1598 he worked on 16 plays between 8 January and 30 December and was paid £37 1s 8d. In 1599 he worked on eleven plays in nine months and received £28 7s 6d. In 1600 he worked on seven plays in eleven months for £14 11s; and in 1602

18. Foakes and Rickert, p. 199.

Henslowe paid him £27 19s for contributions to nine plays in ten and one-half months.

These two playwrights, Henry Chettle and Thomas Dekker, were, so far as Henslowe's surviving records show, the most reliable providers of plays for the Lord Admiral's and the Earl of Worcester's men in the last five years of Elizabeth's reign. But there were eight others in the diary who are each shown to have contributed ten or more plays for the Henslowe companies in these years, though none was so prolific or so regular as Chettle and Dekker.

William Haughton was concerned with 24 plays in a period of five years from 5 November 1597 to 8 September 1602 for which he was paid £56 15s. But in three of these years he was paid for only a single play; he was contributing steadily to the companies only in the last half of 1599, in 1600, and in 1601. In the four months from 20 August to 17 December 1599 he worked on five plays; in the eleven months from 13 February 1599/1600 to 1 January 1600/1601 he worked on seven; and in the eight and one-half months from 29 January 1600/1601 to 8 November 1601 he worked on nine. In these years he was paid £10 12s 6d, £15 5s, and £21 2s 6d. Thus in a period of 23½ consecutive months Henslowe paid Haughton in behalf of the companies £47, or about £24 per year.

Michael Drayton participated in a similar number of plays for a similar sum, 23 plays for £50 16s 3d in a period of four and one-half years, between 22 December 1597 and 29 May 1602. But only one was written in 1597, one in 1601, one in 1602, and two in 1600. Drayton's steady work for the Henslowe companies was done between 13 March 1597/98 and 20 January 1598/99, though he did contribute to two more plays in the last two months of 1599. In that period of ten months of steady work he contributed to 16 plays for which he was paid £32 6s 8d. He also received income from boy companies, but the fullest records we have for any period of his life show that when he was producing plays steadily for the Henslowe companies in 1598 he was paid £32 6s 8d in ten months.

The other playwrights who were paid for numerous contributions to the repertories of the Lord Admiral's and the Earl of Worcester's companies, John Day, Richard Hathaway, Anthony Munday, William Smith, Robert Wilson, and Thomas Heywood, wrote less and earned less. The number of plays they contributed varies from 11 to 22.

Considering the very large number of plays Thomas Heywood "had a hand or at least a main finger in" during his long life, it is at first glance surprising that Henslowe paid him for only eleven in the period 6 December 1598 to 6 March 1602/1603. I would infer that in 1598 when he was paid for one play, in 1599 one, and in 1600 none, he was devoting most of his time to acting, for on 25 March 1598 he contracted to act at Henslowe's theatres exclusively for a period of two years or to forfeit £40. In the last four months of 1602 he contributed to seven plays and was paid £20 2s. Probably by 1602 he was a sharer in the Earl of Worcester's company and was expected to devote more time to writing; certainly he had become a sharer before the time of the company's draft patent of 1603–1604.[19]

The earnings of one of the other dramatists for the companies financed by Henslowe are worth noting. George Chapman was not a long-term Henslowe playwright, but he did write for the companies from 16 May 1598 to 17 July 1599. In these fourteen months he was paid £28 10s for contributing to seven plays. These were very good earnings at the end of the sixteenth century.

Unhappily there are no comparable records of the payments to their regular playwrights by competing companies like the Lord Chamberlain's men, but in a period of such intense theatrical competition as these years it is not likely that the Lord Chamberlain's company paid Shakespeare less than Henslowe was authorized to pay Chettle,

19. Chambers, *Elizabethan Stage*, II, 229–30.

Dekker, or Chapman. Indeed, there is a little evidence that during these years of Henslowe's dealings with Chettle, Dekker, Haughton, Heywood, and the others the managers of the *boy* companies were paying *more* for individual plays than he was, though it is unlikely that the boys were purchasing so many new plays. In the suit brought on by the performance of Chapman's *The Old Joiner of Aldgate* by Paul's boys, plaintiffs and defendants agreed that in February 1602/1603 Chapman was paid twenty marks (£13 6s 8d) for his play, about double Henslowe's rate at the time. Some dramatists had directorial functions in the boy companies and shared in the profits. At one time or another in the years 1594–1610 the managing syndicate of the Revels companies or the Chapel companies included the dramatists John Marston, Michael Drayton, Lording Barry, John Mason, and Robert Daborne. When the boys were doing well, the managerial functions were a source of profit for these playwrights, but the various lawsuits and suppressions in which the boys were involved suggest that Chettle and Dekker probably did better for themselves by writing steadily for the Lord Admiral's, and the Earl of Worcester's companies.

These earnings of professional dramatists writing for the Henslowe companies form an interesting contrast to the earnings of Richard Robinson, a nondramatic writer in the immediately preceding years. Over a period of nineteen years Robinson records his total earnings from literature as £52 17s 5d. In five and one-half years the acting companies paid Henry Chettle a total of £123 17s 6d; over a period of six years they paid Thomas Dekker £110 9s 2d; in a single year they paid George Chapman £28 10s. The average yearly earnings of Richard Robinson from publishers and patrons combined was a little less than £2 17s. From the acting companies Chettle averaged about £25; Dekker averaged £19.

Robinson's best years are almost impossible to isolate,

since he lists his books under the year of publication, and in the same entry lumps in receipts for later editions in subsequent years; moreover he usually does not say how long it took him to sell the copies paid him by his publisher, though in one instance he notes that it took two years. I can find no indication that in his best year his receipts can have exceeded £7 or £8, whereas Henslowe's records show that the actors paid Chettle £36 12s 4d in one period of ten and one-half months, Dekker £37 1s 8d in one year, and Chapman £28 10s in one year.

No other records of the earnings of dramatists remotely comparable in fullness to Henslowe's diary exist in the period. Scattered correspondence and comments make it clear enough that the price of plays was increasing, apparently faster than the general price rise in the reign of James. In 1613 and 1614 Robert Daborne was involved with Henslowe in a correspondence which has been preserved in the archives of Dulwich College.[20] On 17 April 1613 Daborne signed a memorandum agreeing with Henslowe to deliver to him "before ye end of this Easter Term" a tragedy called *Machiavel and the Devil* for which he was to receive £20, of which he had already had £6. On 25 June 1613 Daborne wrote offering another play, *The Arraignment*, and asserting that if Henslowe did not take the play "Before God I can have £25 for it as some of the company knows." In August Daborne wrote in some financial straits about a collaboration, *The Bellman*: ". . . we will have but £12 and the overplus of the second day . . . and from £20 a play am come to £12, therefore in my extremity forsake me not." On 28 March 1613/14 Daborne wrote about *The She Saint* and seemed to settle on £12 as his expected initial payment, though he seemed to imply additional later payments. "I desire you should disburse but £12 a play till they be played."

These letters written by Robert Daborne indicate that—

20. Greg, *Henslowe Papers*, arts. 70, 71, 72, 84, 97.

at least as far as this playwright and Philip Henslowe were concerned—the going rate for plays in 1613–1614 was double to triple Henslowe's rate in 1598–1601. It may be only a coincidence that a college dramatist, Thomas Tomkis, was rewarded at a similar rate for his play, *Albumazar*, in the following year. In the bursar's account books for Trinity College, Cambridge, for 1615 is the entry, "Item, given Mr. Tomkis for his pains in penning and ordering the English Comedy at our Master's appointment, £20."[21]

The most explicit surviving figures about a dramatist's rate of pay are those revealed in the suit of *Heton* versus *Brome* about Richard Brome's contract as regular dramatist for the Salisbury Court theatre in the years 1635 to 1639. The various provisions of the two contracts may be discussed more conveniently later, but here the money Brome was to receive as regular company playwright is relevant. According to his contract of 20 July 1635, to run for three years, Brome was to receive 15 shillings a week plus a benefit performance for each new play he wrote for the company. If Brome was to be paid for 52 weeks, his earnings were expected to be £39 plus benefits.

Of course the dramatist's return from these benefit performances could be expected to vary a good deal with the weather, the competing attractions, the political situation, and the appeal of the particular play, but Brome himself makes an estimate of what it would be. He says that because the plague restrained playing just after the presentation of his second play he was not paid his benefit, "And this defendant's said clear day's profit of the said second new play was never allowed unto him to the damage of five pounds and upwards." Brome also says that one of the plays he wrote for the Salisbury Court theatre "styled and called *The Sparagus Garden* was worth to them by general conjecture and estimation and as by their own

21. *Notes and Queries*, 3rd ser., XII (August 1867), 155.

books and writings being produced this defendant verily believeth may appear the sum of one thousand pounds and upwards."[22] No doubt his estimate of £1,000 profit on *The Sparagus Garden* is exaggerated, as was common in suits, but it does suggest that his expectation of £5 or more from his benefits is not unreasonable. Thus Brome's yearly income on the contract of 20 July 1635 might well have been expected to be £54 for 52 weeks.

Evidently the company did not think the terms of this contract excessive, for in August 1638 a new agreement was made, according to which Brome was to be given a 33 percent increase and paid 20 shillings a week, the contract to run for seven years.[23]

These terms indicate what the company thought a playwright might be paid, 1635–1639. The fact that the suit *Heton* versus *Brome* shows that because of the bad plague of 1636–1637 and for other reasons the contract stipulations seem to have been violated by both parties does not alter the estimation of what reasonable pay for the Salisbury Court playwright was thought to be.

It is probable that these contractual payments to Richard Brome amounted to a good deal less than certain other professional dramatists were receiving from their companies in these years, for the Salisbury Court theatre was one of the less distinguished and less profitable in the 1630s. The two most distinguished London theatres in the reign of Charles I were clearly the Blackfriars and the Cockpit

22. Ann Haaker, "The Plague, the Theatre, and the Poet," *Renaissance Drama*, n.s. (1968), pp. 302 and 301.

23. Ibid., 298, 299, 304. These terms of 20*s* a week are confirmed by another source, generally called Heton's Papers. These are notes for an agreement which the manager of the Salisbury Court theatre, Richard Heton, drew up for the company, setting out their respective charges. According to one item the company is to pay "half the poet's wages, which is 10 shillings a week" (*Jacobean and Caroline Stage*, II, 686).

or Phoenix in Drury Lane.[24] Their regular dramatists in
1635 were Philip Massinger and James Shirley, and it is
probable that these two were paid more by the King's men
and Queen Henrietta's men than the Salisbury Court company could afford to give Brome.

There is a certain amount of specific evidence—beyond
their popular reputations—that the Blackfriars at least was
a good deal more profitable than the Salisbury Court. It
will be recalled that Brome expected his benefit to bring
him "five pounds and upwards" on a *new* play after the
expenses of the house had been deducted. Now from 1628
to 1633 Sir Henry Herbert had a similar benefit arrangement with the Blackfriars, namely the take minus the expenses of the house. The difference was that his benefit was
on the *second* day of a *revived* play, notoriously less popular than a *new* play. For five years Sir Henry recorded his
receipts from this benefit at the Blackfriars. The benefit
paid on the different plays recorded were £17 10s, £9 16s,
£12 4s, £13, and £15.[25] These sums which Sir Henry Herbert was paid are from two to three times as much for the
second performance of a *revived* play as Brome expected to
receive from his benefit performance of a *new* play at the
Salisbury Court theatre. Philip Massinger's arrangements
at Blackfriars are likely to have been similar to Brome's at
the Salisbury Court, i.e., wages and benefits. If so, they are
likely to have yielded a good deal more than Brome's
estimated £54.

THESE ACCUMULATED FIGURES indicate, it seems to
me, that the professional playwrights made more money
than other literary men of their time, and more than they
could have made as schoolmasters or curates—professions
which might have been open to many of them. Not only

24. See *Jacobean and Caroline Stage*, VI, 12–15, 33–35, 47,
59–61.
25. See ibid., I, 23–24.

do the extant accounts of payments show very respectable incomes for the time, but unrecorded payments for special gifts, occasional plays sold to other companies, benefit performances (except for Richard Brome), and occasional non-dramatic writings (such as the pamphlets of Heywood, Dekker, Middleton, and Rowley) certainly added to the income of most professional playwrights.

It is also notable that these extant figures, though they represent fees from four or five different companies, in no case represent the payments made to those dramatists regularly attached to the most stable and the richest acting organization of the time, the Lord Chamberlain–King's men. This company had more and better theatres than any other; it held its actors longer, it seems to have had no difficulty in hiring actors away from other troupes, its receipts from court performances were always greater than those paid to any other performing group, its plays were more often preserved and praised than those of any other, and it hired and held the best dramatists of the time. It seems almost certain therefore that the regular dramatists of this company with the greatest prestige and the greatest wealth of the time would have been paid more than the regular dramatists of lesser companies. If Chettle, Dekker, Haughton, Drayton, Chapman, and Brome were paid well, clearly the King's men's sequence of William Shakespeare, Nathan Field, John Fletcher, Philip Massinger, and James Shirley would have been paid better.

The widespread impression of the ill-paid Elizabethan dramatist derives in part, of course, from romantic predispositions about the artist, predispositions which (for the anti-Stratfordians) make the unmistakable evidence of Shakespeare's substantial estate seem such an unanswerable argument against the identification of the man of Stratford with the poet of *A Midsummer Night's Dream*. And selected evidence from documents of the time—evidence like the rate of composition for the dramatists of the Lord

Admiral's and the Earl of Worcester's companies and their repeated borrowings recorded in Henslowe's diary, like the begging and borrowing letters of Robert Daborne, Nathan Field, and Philip Massinger, like the poverty poems and prefaces of Massinger, Jonson, Randolph, and Greene, like the imprisonment of Dekker and Field and Massinger— such evidence can be made to suggest that the sufferings of these playwrights demonstrate their low payment.

But debts and borrowings and financial straits do not necessarily indicate abnormally low incomes, as any court of bankruptcy could demonstrate. If the poverty complaints of Massinger, Jonson, Randolph, and Greene are to be quoted, they ought to be balanced against the evidence of property bequeathed in the wills of theatre people like Edward Alleyn, Samuel Rowley, Thomas Greene, Philip Henslowe, William Shakespeare, John Heminges, John and Elizabeth Condell, James Shirley, and John Shank.

Dekker, Daborne, Massinger, and Brome may have complained about their poverty, but they were not ill-paid for the plays they wrote.

CHAPTER VI

Dramatists' Contractual Obligations

CLOSE AND CONTINUED ASSOCIATION of certain play-wrights with certain companies has been implied in several contexts in preceding chapters—"Amateur Dramatists and Professional Dramatists," "The Dramatists and the Acting Company," and "Dramatists' Pay." So many scholars have noted such an association of William Shakespeare with the Lord Chamberlain–King's company that the observation has become a commonplace. How conventional was such an association? What did it entail? And was it formalized or simply a free selection by an independent artist of his favorite among several competing companies?

It is likely enough that arrangements between drama-tists and acting companies were not completely uniform among all the fifteen or so companies of the period. And it is further likely that there was some development in the relationships—probably in the direction of greater formalization—during the 52 years under consideration. But the organized presentation of plays tends to become conventionalized in any era; it has many times been shown that the theatre is usually conservative.

One would expect, therefore, that different as the companies were, the adult companies at least would tend to conform to a pattern in their relations with their principal dramatists as they did in admission prices, length of plays, plan of theatre buildings, use of boys, and the size and character of actors' organizations. And one would expect that these playwright–company relationships would sooner or later be formalized in a contract.

The only contract between dramatist and acting company which is known in detail is that entered into by Richard Brome and the actors and proprietors of the Salisbury Court theatre on 20 July 1635 and renewed with minor alterations in August 1638. Since the theatre was so conventional in its arrangements, it is probable that Richard Brome's two contracts in 1635 and 1638 were traditional and similar in their basic provisions to those of "ordinary"[1]

1. The term "ordinary poet," which is used in this period in connection with the theatres is evidently used according to definition 3b under the entry for the adjective "ordinary" in the *OED*: "Of officials, persons employed, etc.: Belonging to the regular staff or to the fully recognized staff of such. . . . Now mostly represented by *in-ordinary*."

The theatrical usage is well illustrated by one of the complaints about the hardships caused by the closing of the theatres. It occurs toward the end of the pamphlet, *The Actors' Remonstrance, or Complaint. . . . As it was presented in the names and behalf of all our London Comedians. . . .* January 24, 1643[/44]. "For some of our ablest ordinary poets, instead of their annual stipends and beneficial second days, being for mere necessity compelled to get a living by writing contemptible penny pamphlets. . . ." (Reprinted by William Carew Hazlitt in *English Drama and Stage*, London, 1869, pp. 259–65.)

playwrights for other major companies, at least in the reigns of James and Charles. It ought to be useful, therefore, to review the explicit provisions of Brome's contracts and then to note evidence of the responses to such presumptive requirements in the activities of other attached professional dramatists.

The details of these two contracts are known from a suit brought against Richard Brome in the Court of Requests by the "owners of the playhouse in Salisbury Court, London" and the members of Queen Henrietta's company, the acting troupe at that theatre.[2] As usual in lawsuits, plaintiffs and defendant disagreed on the charges of the plaintiffs. Fortunately for us however, the disagreement was wholly concerned with the acts of the two parties in carrying out their agreements; there was no disagreement about what the contracts provided. The troubles seem to have arisen largely from the sufferings of both parties under the long closing for the plague from 12 May 1636 to 2 October 1637,[3] and each seems to have had some justification for its violations. But since our concern here is with what a company customarily asked its regular dramatist to do, and with what the dramatist expected to do, the points of agreement of the two parties provide what we

2. The bill and the answer in the suit were discovered by C. W. Wallace at the Public Record Office early in this century. He never published them or revealed their location, but he inserted two or three sentences about the contract in a popular article in *The Century Magazine* in 1910. In response to a letter from Clarence Edward Andrews he revealed a few more facts, which Andrews published in *Richard Brome: A Study of his Life and Works*, New York, 1913.

A few years ago the Henry E. Huntington Library acquired the Wallace Papers with transcripts of the bill and answer. Ann Haaker checked these transcripts in the Public Record Office and published them with an introduction under the title "The Plague, the Theater, and the Poet," *Renaissance Drama*, n.s. 1 (1968), pp. 283–306.

3. See *Jacobean and Caroline Stage*, II, 661–65.

need. It might be interesting if we could tell the extent to which each was irresponsible, or arbitrary, or dishonest, but that is not material here.

Perhaps it will be most helpful to consider the various provisions of the contracts separately and to note under each heading such evidence as comes to hand that other attached professional dramatists working for other companies tended to meet the same requirements.

Exclusiveness

Both Brome's contracts specify that he would do no writing for any other company during the terms of the agreements. The plaintiffs assert that according to the terms of the contract of 1635 "the said Richard Brome should not nor would write any play or any part of a play to any other players or playhouse, but apply all his study and endeavors therein for the benefit of the said company of the said playhouse." And they further assert that this clause was simply restated in the second contract of July 1638, "And that he should not write, invent or compose any play tragedy or comedy or any part thereof for any other playhouse."

Now the violation of these clauses in both contracts was one of the principal issues in the suit. Therefore Brome's admission that he had agreed to such a stipulation and his attempts to excuse himself for violating it strongly imply that such clauses were so common that everyone would have assumed their existence. Brome in his answer to the bill of complaint admits that he "did agree . . . that he would write for no other company but apply his labors totally unto them as aforesaid. . . ." He further recognizes the company's legitimate contractual expectations when he excuses himself for composing fewer than three plays a year by asserting that

> some of the complainants on behalf of the residue of
> them did undertake and assuredly affirm to this defend-

ant . . . that their main purpose in expressing such a number of plays was but only to oblige this defendant to dedicate all his labor and plays totally unto their sole profits.[4]

In excuse for his violation of this exclusive clause Brome explains that as the plague continued his salary was not paid—at least in full—and that in his poverty and desperation he went to William Beeston who lent him £6 on his agreement to write a play for Beeston's company at the Cockpit. But the Salisbury Court players got the play back from Beeston and persuaded Brome to come back to them.

Obviously Brome accepted his obligation to write exclusively for the company at the Salisbury Court—hence his excuses for his deviation. Moreover, there is a suggestion that William Beeston, the old theatre-hand who had possession of Brome's manuscript, recognized the irregularity of Brome's conduct; otherwise it is difficult to understand why he was willing to turn over the manuscript of a profitable play to a rival company. The plaintiffs in their bill of complaint say that Brome "did sell and deliver one of the plays which he made for your subjects in the said time unto Christopher Beeston, gentleman, and William Beeston." And Brome admits that because of his financial straits he did violate the exclusive clause in his contract:

And as to the new play which the complainants suppose this defendant to have sold unto the said Christopher or William Beeston, this defendant confesseth it to be true that the stoppage of his weekly means and unkind carriage aforesaid forced this defendant to contract and bargain for the said new play with the said William Beeston, but yet the said complainants and their company had it and acted it and by common estimation got a thousand pounds and upwards by it.[5]

4. Bill of complaint, Haaker transcript, pp. 297 and 298; Brome's answer, ibid., pp. 301–302.

5. Bill, Haaker transcript, p. 298; answer, ibid., p. 305.

Though no contract has yet been found for any other professional playwright, several of the well-known attached professionals can be shown to have followed this practice of exclusive composition, presumably under the terms of an agreement, like Brome's, with the companies to which they were attached.

In the case of Brome's contemporary, James Shirley, there are enough license records and title-page statements to demonstrate that he wrote exclusively for King Charles's company after he returned from Ireland, regularly furnishing them with an autumn play and a spring play in 1640, 1641, and 1642. No play written for any other company can be found in his canon during this period. In his earlier career in London, 1625–1637, before he left for Ireland, Shirley wrote regularly for Queen Henrietta's men at the Phoenix, producing plays at about the same rate as he later did for the King's men. This pattern of exclusive attachment to the Queen's men was broken once, as Brome's was broken later. For unknown reasons *The Changes, or Love in a Maze*, licensed in January 1631/32, was performed by a rival company at the Salisbury Court theatre, and both the prologue and the epilogue for the play emphasize Shirley's transferred allegiance and the company's hopes for their new and struggling troupe. Could the reason have been the expiration of a seven-year contract and disagreement about its renewal? Whatever the reason, the breach in Shirley's allegiance to Queen Henrietta's men was soon healed, and all his subsequent plays in this period of his life were demonstrably the property of the Phoenix company.

Philip Massinger was the "ordinary poet" for King Charles's company between the incumbencies of John Fletcher and James Shirley, i.e., 1626–1639 inclusive. Before 1626 Massinger frequently wrote for the company, usually in collaboration with Fletcher, but he also wrote several other plays in those years for the Lady Elizabeth's company. After Fletcher's death he apparently wrote exclusively for the King's men—with one probable exception. The evidence is not complete because a number of Massinger's plays, though known by title, are lost and furnish no evidence of date or ownership, and Malone and Chalmers were not so consistent in copying the licenses for his plays from the office book as they were for Fletcher's and Shirley's. But at least half his plays after 1625 were demonstrably written for the King's men, and none of them—with the possible exception of *The Great Duke of Florence*—is known to have been written for any other company. That play, apparently written in 1627, was published in 1636 as acted by Queen Henrietta's men. There is some confusion about it, and the piece may be one of Massinger's earlier productions for the Phoenix, but the weight of the evidence now available seems to indicate a single aberration, like Shirley's composition of *The Changes* for the Salisbury Court.

John Fletcher's attachment to King James's company at the Blackfriars and the Globe appears to have been similarly exclusive. Since most of his plays were licensed before the period of Sir Henry Herbert's office book, and since their popularity was so great that the company withheld most of them from publication until 1647, the evidence for date of production and original ownership is less complete than for Shirley or Brome. It is complete enough, however, to suggest and almost to demonstrate that he was attached exclusively to the King's company from Shakespeare's retirement to Fletcher's death in the plague of 1625. None of his own plays or his collaborations in this period can be shown to have been written for any other company, and the great majority are in the King's repertory of unprinted plays submitted to the Lord Chamberlain in 1641.[6]

Shakespeare's exclusive attachment to the same company

6. See *Jacobean and Caroline Stage*, I, 65–66 and 108–15.

is well known. After the organization and establishment of the Lord Chamberlain's men late in 1594, no Shakespearean play can be shown to have been composed for any other company, and for most of them the evidence of composition for the Lord Chamberlain–King's company is complete. Shakespeare's exclusive attachment was probably a part of his involvement as a patented member and leading sharer in the organization, but exclusive it certainly was.

The regular dramatists for the other leading adult companies in the reigns of James and Charles probably worked with similar exclusiveness, but the dates and ownership of their plays are confused or totally unknown, and the histories of such troupes as Queen Anne's men, the Prince Henry–Palsgrave's company, and the Lady Elizabeth's company are so meager and their continuity so broken that their policies cannot be demonstrated.

There is evidence, however, that the custom of guaranteeing the exclusiveness of a successful playwright's services came into being fairly early. Not only is there the example of Shakespeare's preparing all his plays for the Lord Chamberlain's men, but there are entries in Henslowe's accounts which suggest that the system was developing at the time he was writing.

At the beginning of the new year 1598 (old style) Thomas Heywood signed an agreement with Henslowe. The principle was exclusiveness, and the seven witnesses to the contract were six of the leading members of the Lord Admiral's company and the dramatist who was writing plays for them; but the services specified, though exclusive, were not literary, and the attachment was not to the company but to Henslowe:

> Memorandum that this 25 of March 1598 Thomas Heywood came and hired himself with me as a covenant servant for two years by the receiving of two single pence according to the statute of Winchester and to begin at the day above written and not to play anywhere

public about London, not while these two years be expired but in my house. If he do then he doth forfeit unto me the receiving of these two pence, forty pounds and witness to this

Anthony Munday	William Borne
Gabriel Spencer	Thomas Downton
Robert Shaw	Richard Jones[7]
Richard Allen	

On the face of it this seems to be an ordinary agreement with a hired man of the company. But six leading members of the company and their dramatist are not likely to have been present simply by chance when Heywood signed, and why should they have been called in for a mere hired man? Again, the hired man is attached to Henslowe and not to the company as was usual. This agreement does not constitute a dramatist's contract, but there are enough odd features about the entry to spur speculation.

The entry Henslowe made about a year later on 28 February 1598/99 is still not quite a contract for the exclusive services of a dramatist to a company.

> Lent unto Harry Porter at the request of the company in earnest of his book called *Two Merry Women of Abington* the sum of forty shillings and for the receipt of that money he gave me his faithful promise that I should have all the books which he writes either himself or with any other; which sum was delivered upon the 28 of February.
> I say ... 40 shillings.
> Thomas Downton   Robert Shaw[8]

Here again the agreement was witnessed by two members of the Lord Admiral's company, and not by all the principal sharers, but Henslowe did note that his payment was made "at the request of the company." Moreover, this

7. Foakes and Rickert, p. 241.
8. Ibid., p. 105.

agreement did specify plays, though the dramatist was bound to Henslowe, not the company.

The third entry in Henslowe's accounts represents an agreement which has the essentials of the exclusive clause in Brome's contract thirty-three years later. Only the month date is given, but the position of the entry shows that the year was 1602. "Lent unto Harry Chettle March 25 at the appointment [of] Thomas Downton and my son E. Alleyn at the sealing of H. Chettle's bond to write for them the sum of . . . £3."[9] Downton and Alleyn were both leading members of the Admiral's company, and both frequently authorized Henslowe to make payments in behalf of the company. Here the sealing of a bond is mentioned, not simply the signing of an agreement, and the payment of £3 is not related to payment for a play—as Porter's £2 was connected with *The Two Merry Women of Abington*—but seems to have been related to the contract only. This entry would appear to record something very close to, though not necessarily so detailed as, Richard Brome's contract with the Salisbury Court organization.

All in all, then, the clause in each of Brome's contracts stipulating that he should give all his plays to the Salisbury Court players and write nothing for any other company would seem to represent a traditional arrangement between a settled company and its principal dramatist. Although there is not enough evidence to prove finally that every major troupe had such an understanding with its "ordinary poet," there is enough to make it apparent that such an arrangement had become a convention in the reigns of James and Charles.

Annual Quota of Plays

The two contesting parties agree that the contract of 20 July 1635 required Brome to write for the company three plays a year for three years. Brome says that he gave

9. Ibid., p. 199.

a total of six plays to the company in the three years of the first contract (the plaintiffs say five) though some were very late because of the confusion at the time of the plague when the company was taking in little or no money and the playwright's salary was either stopped or only partly paid. Brome says that at the signing of the first contract he objected to the quota of three plays a year "as being more than he could well perform." And he comments that several members of the company, on behalf of others,

> did undertake and assuredly affirm unto this defendant that howsoever they had desired to have three plays yearly for three years continuance together to be undertaken and promised by this defendant yet upon trust and confidence and by the true and fair intent and plain meaning of all parties, the plaintiffs neither should nor would exact nor expect from this defendant the performance or composition of any more plays than so many only as this defendant could or should be able well and conveniently to do or perform and that their main purpose in expressing such a number of plays was but only to oblige this defendant to dedicate all his labor and plays totally unto their sole profits.[10]

The plaintiffs say that the second contract of August 1638 also stipulated three plays a year, but Brome does not mention the quota, though he does mention the contract and the increased rate of pay to 20 shillings a week.

The parties agree that Brome did write two plays a year (or the plaintiffs say about one and two-thirds) for the company, and Brome seems to indicate that at the beginning he thought this was about his capacity, or at least that three a year was too much.

Those other professional dramatists whose company attachments were steady and whose plays can be dated with some precision seem to have come quite close to this rate of two plays a year. James Shirley, whom Brome succeeded

10. Answer, Haaker transcript, pp. 301–302.

as dramatist at Beeston's Phoenix theatre, had written for Queen Henrietta's company at this rate. Sir Henry Herbert's licenses for most of Shirley's plays were copied from the office book by Malone and Chalmers. Beginning with *Love Tricks with Compliments*, licensed 11 February 1624/25, shortly after he came to London from St. Albans, and ending with *The Duke's Mistress*, licensed 18 January 1635/36, a few months before the plague closing during which Shirley went to Ireland and wrote for the St. Werburgh Street theatre in Dublin, we have the Master of the Revels' licenses for 20 plays. In addition *The Arcadia* and *The Wedding* certainly belonged to the Phoenix company and were evidently written in this period, though Malone and Chalmers did not copy their allowances from the office book. Thus Shirley's output as regular dramatist for Queen Henrietta's company was 22 plays in 11 years— about the same annual production as Brome's.

When Shirley returned to London after his three years of absence in Ireland, he became regular dramatist for King Charles's company in succession to Philip Massinger, who had died in March 1639/40. His work for this company shows a sequence even more regular, a spring and an autumn play each year. Herbert licensed *Rosania* (June 1640), *The Imposter* (November 1640), *The Politic Father* (May 1641), *The Cardinal* (November 1641), and *The Sisters* (April 1642). Apparently the autumn play for 1642 was *The Court Secret*, but it was not licensed by Herbert because, as he wrote in his office book, "Here ended my allowance of plays, for the war began in Aug. 1642." This inference is supported by the statement on the 1652 title page of *The Court Secret*: "Never Acted, But prepared for the Scene at Black-Friers."

Shirley's predecessor as regular dramatist for the King's company was apparently working to a similar schedule, but for him the evidence is less complete. Some time after the death of Fletcher, probably in 1626, Massinger seems to have become the regular playwright for the company, but Malone and Chalmers were evidently not so interested in his plays as in Shirley's and failed to copy the license entry of the Master of the Revels for many of them. A number of Massinger's plays which we know at least by title have no preserved license, and several of them are extremely uncertain in date.

There are seventeen or eighteen plays by Massinger definitely recorded as the property of the King's men, most of them precisely dated by the licenses of the Master of the Revels, and produced between 1626 and 1639 inclusive, beginning with *The Roman Actor*, which Sir Henry licensed for the company on 11 October 1626, and ending with the lost play *The Fair Anchoress*, which was allowed for them on 26 January 1639/40. Two others, *The Forced Lady* and *The Italian Night-Piece*, though lost, are known to have been acted by the King's men in the twenties or thirties. Seven other lost plays known by title and attributed to Massinger in the Stationers' Register would make up the total to 26 or 27, quite close to two plays a year for fourteen years, especially considering that in this period the theatres were closed for seven months in 1630 and in 1636–1637 for nearly seventeen. These figures for the quota and regularity of Massinger's work as contracted dramatist for the King's men fall short of a conclusive demonstration that he produced for the King's company at the same rate as Brome for the Salisbury Court theatre and James Shirley for Queen Henrietta's men and the King's men, but they show that his rate must have been similar to theirs.

Massinger's predecessor as regular dramatist for the King's company was John Fletcher. The evidence for his rate of production for the company is more involved than that for Massinger: first, because most of his plays were produced before Sir Henry Herbert began to keep his office book, much the most complete production record extant for the Jacobean and Caroline theatre; secondly, because his popularity in the theatre persuaded the King's men to withhold most of his works from publication until after the closing of the theatres, thus depriving us of more evidence of production date; thirdly, because so many of his plays were collaborations which obscure the total work of the author more than the generally unaided plays of Massinger, Shirley, and Brome; and finally, because the dates of his exclusive attachment to the King's company are less clear than those for the other three. Certainly he was principal dramatist for the company from Shakespeare's death to his own, but how long before? Shakespeare's compositions for the company were greatly reduced from 1608 or 1609 to 1612 or 1613, and they ceased entirely from 1613 to 1616. It seems to me likely that Fletcher's regular association probably began about 1609 or 1610, for at least ten of his plays in the company's repertory appear, on the rather shaky evidence we have, to date from the period 1609–1615. From the period 1616 to 1625 we have 32 plays, including lost pieces like *The Devil of Dowgate*, *The Jeweller of Amsterdam*, and *A Right Woman*, and excluding plays in the Caroline repertory of the King's company but known to have been composed originally for other troupes—plays such as *The Scornful Lady*, *The Honest Man's Fortune*, and *Monsieur Thomas*.

Thus we know that Fletcher participated in about 42 plays written for the King's company in the years 1609–1625. But at least 21 of them have been shown to be collaborations including work of Beaumont, Field, Shakespeare, Rowley, and especially Massinger. If we assume that Fletcher's lines in these collaborations would have been, on the average, approximately half the play, then his contribution to the repertory of the King's men in the period from 1609 to his death in August 1625 would have been about 32½ plays in a period of 16½ years. This is reasonably close to the norm of two plays a year found in the contracted work of Brome, Shirley, and Massinger.

Fletcher's predecessor as principal dramatist for the Lord Chamberlain–King's company was, of course, William Shakespeare. Though the problem of dating the plays is more complex for Shakespeare because of the scantiness of the external evidence before the death of Queen Elizabeth, many times more scholars have devoted their efforts to Shakespearean dating problems than to Fletcherian ones. As a consequence there is fair general agreement on the approximate dating of most of the 38 plays. Most scholars have recognized a falling-off in the frequency of composition after *Timon of Athens*, about 1608. Probably the most generally accepted chronology is set out by Sir Edmund Chambers. This list shows an average of two plays per year from the season of 1590–1591 to that of 1607–1608, and after that, six plays (including two collaborations) in the next five years. While a number of scholars might quibble with the precise seasons in which many of these first 32 plays fall, the average of two a year is clear enough.[11]

11. See *William Shakespeare*, 1, 270–71. The statement of John Ward is of interest here. Ward was vicar of Shakespeare's parish, Holy Trinity, Stratford-upon-Avon, from 1662 to 1681. He kept extensive notebooks and included several remarks about the poet who had been buried in his church 45 years before Ward came to the parish. He could never have known the playwright and probably never knew any of the members of the company of the King's men, but the stories he collected in Stratford are worth consideration. Ward wrote:

> . . . he frequented the plays all his younger time, but in his elder days lived at Stratford and supplied the stage with two plays a year, and for that had an allowance so large that he spent at the rate of £1,000 a year, as I have heard (ibid., 11, 249–50).

Allowing for the exaggerations of most local gossip and the haziness about time-spans 50 to 75 years in the past, Ward's remarks do no violence to our other information if we assume that "two plays a year" applies to the period *before* and not after retirement.

For the other professional dramatists the evidence is too obscure or too incomplete to allow any conclusions. The great majority of the 220 plays in which Thomas Heywood says that he "had either an entire hand or at least a main finger" are not even known by title, much less by date. Nor can one tell how many of the plays in this huge total were two-, three-, four-, or even five-man collaborations. Rowley and Field, though clearly attached professionals, were important actors and were evidently not expected to devote full time to writing as Brome, Shirley, Massinger, and Fletcher were. Dekker's company affiliations—after his Henslowe career—are too unsettled to suggest any contractual production, and so are Middleton's, except for his early years with boy companies. The chief Henslowe dramatists certainly *participated* in more than an average of two plays a year for the companies whose accounts are preserved in the diary, but the great majority of their plays were collaborations, often three, four, five, or even six writers participating in a single composition. Often it is impossible to tell whether the plays for which Henslowe recorded serial payments were ever completed, though in a number of instances it is clear that they were not. In these circumstances it seems folly to attempt to work out any pattern of composition for Haughton, Munday, Hathaway, Wilson, or Wentworth Smith. For what it is worth, I am inclined to doubt that the Lord Admiral's company or Worcester's men had any set agreed quotas with these men during the years of Henslowe's payment records, 1597–1604.

Salary

According to the contract of 20 July 1635 the salary was to be 15 shillings per week plus a benefit. Both parties quote this figure, and Brome even names the pay day: "In consideration whereof the said complainants or some of them or some of their company did agree to pay fifteen shillings weekly upon every Saturday unto this defendant. . . ."

In the 1638 contract this weekly salary was increased to £1 and the benefit stipulation continued as in the first contract. Both parties to the suit agree on these figures. Apparently the pound-a-week salary was not considered excessive at the time, for in February 1639/40 the plaintiffs claimed that Brome had left them for a higher salary:

> And upon the said [William] Beeston's promise to be his good friend and to give him more salary than your subjects by the agreement aforesaid, he, the said Richard Brome did voluntarily fail to present unto your subjects any more of the said plays for which he was in arrears with your subjects. . . . But the said Brome being tampered withall by the said Beeston as aforesaid hath and doth refuse and deny to compose make or present unto your said subjects the said three plays which by the first article he is in arrears in and behindhand with your subjects as aforesaid, but wholly applies himself unto the said Beeston and the company of players acting at the playhouse of the Phoenix in Drury Lane. . . .[12]

I know of no other direct references to the payment of a weekly salary to a dramatist by a company, though I have little doubt that at certain times other companies operated in the same way as this suit indicates Queen Henrietta's company acted in the 1630s. It is notable that the King's Revels company made the original contract with Brome, which was taken over by Queen Henrietta's men when they replaced the King's Revels at the Salisbury Court, and it must therefore have been their custom to pay a dramatist a weekly salary too. Brome says in his answer in the suit that the original company in the contract, the King's Revels, had enticed him away from Prince Charles [II] company at the Red Bull:

12. Haaker transcript, pp. 302 and 299–300.

> And upon their [i.e., the King's Revels company's] spe-
> cious pretense and promises of reward and bountiful
> retribution and love did entice and inveigle this defend-
> ant to depart and leave the company of the Red Bull
> players being the Prince's highness servants, and where
> this defendant was then very well entertained and truly
> paid without murmuring or wrangling. . . .[13]

From this statement of the dramatist one might assume
that he had been paid a weekly wage by Prince Charles's
company as he was by the others, but he does not explicitly
say so.

Benefit Performances

Both plaintiffs and defendant in the suit agree that under
the first contract Brome was to receive the profits from a
benefit performance of each new play in addition to his
weekly wage. (The plaintiffs say that the same provision
was written into the second contract, but Brome neither
affirms nor denies this.) In their complaint Queen Henrietta's men say it was stipulated in the first contract that:

> . . . the said covenantees should pay unto the said Rich-
> ard Brome the sum of fifteen shillings per week during
> the said term of three years and permit the said Brome
> to have the benefit of one day's profit of playing such
> new play as he should make according to the true intent
> and meaning of the said articles (the ordinary charges
> of the house only deducted). . . .

And they say that the same benefit provision was set out
in the new contract of August 1638:

> that they should pay unto or for the said Richard Brome
> the sum of twenty shillings per week and permit and
> suffer him to have one day's profit of the said several
> new plays (except as before excepted) in manner as in

13. Answer, ibid., p. 301.

the said first recited articles of agreement is mentioned and expressed. . . .[14]

And in his answer Brome verifies this benefit provision with a little more detail. He says that in the first contract the company agreed:

> to pay fifteen shillings weekly upon every Saturday unto this defendant to have the clear benefit of any one day's playing unto himself within the space of ten days after the first playing of any such play at this defendant's election (the common charge deducted as by the said articles). . . .

And Brome confirms that the company allowed him the profits of his benefit upon at least one occasion. He says that he gave them the manuscripts of two new plays within the first three-quarters of the year after the contract was drawn up on 20 July 1635: "And true it is that this defendant for the first of the said two plays had one day's clear profit as they affirmed by their account deducting as aforesaid according to the said articles." However, the second play was delivered just before the plague closing of 12 May 1636 and the "said clear day's profit of the said second new play was never allowed unto him to the damage of five pounds and upwards. . . ."[15]

There is complete agreement between the two parties that Brome was to receive the take minus the regular house charges at one benefit performance of each play he wrote. Benefit performances for dramatists are many times referred to; the only odd feature of the Brome–Salisbury Court agreement is Brome's statement that he was to select the day of his benefit: "The clear benefit of any one day's playing unto himself within the space of ten days after the first playing of any such play at this defendant's election. . . ." Most references to the custom state that the

14. Bill, ibid., pp. 297 and 299.
15. Ibid., p. 302.

benefit was the second or the third day of performance. Ordinarily in the repertory system of the time a new play would not have been performed more than three or possibly four times in the first ten days of its stage life; perhaps this odd clause was intended to give Brome the option of taking receipts on the second, third, or fourth performance. The only advantage I can see of the third or fourth performance over the second is a gamble on better weather.

The fact that most dramatists had benefit performances of their new plays seems to have been common knowledge in seventeenth-century London. It is not clear just when it began, but William Davenant implies very early. Toward the end of the first act of his *The Playhouse to be Let*, there is a conversation between Player and Poet concerning the proposed play. Player says

> There is an old tradition
> That in the times of mighty Tamberlane
> Of conjuring Faustus, and the Beauchamps bold,
> You poets used to have the second day.
> This shall be ours, sir, and tomorrow yours.

Though the play was written to be acted in 1663, Davenant had had plenty of experience of the Caroline theatre: he had written ten or more plays to be acted by the King's company at Blackfriars or the Globe; for almost a year he managed the company at the Phoenix theatre; and in 1638 and 1639 he was developing plans for a huge new theatre of his own. Certainly he knew a good deal about theatre customs before the war, but these lines imply benefits for Marlowe and Heywood[16] in the last ten or fifteen years of Elizabeth's reign. There is no other evidence of benefit performances at such an early date, unless two entries in the accounts of Philip Henslowe are to be so interpreted.

16. *The Bold Beauchamps* is lost, and though there are half a dozen or more references to it as a popular piece, only one, in the 1660s, attributes it to Heywood. See Arthur Melville Clark, *Thomas Heywood, Playwright and Miscellanist*, Oxford, 1931, pp. 13–15.

In April or May 1601 Henslowe noted that he had "paid unto John Day at the appointment of the company 1601 after the playing of the second part of Strowd the sum of ... 10s." And in September 1602 there is another suggestive entry: "Paid unto Thomas Dekker the 27 of September 1602 over and above his price of his book called *A Medicine for a Curst Wife* the sum of ... 10s."[17]

The first payment, that to John Day, is recorded as a payment from the company, but the round sum suggests a reward rather than the more usual share of receipts due on a benefit performance. In the case of *A Medicine for a Curst Wife*, previous payments in the months of July, August, and early September show that Dekker had already received a total of £10 for this play. The 10 shillings paid on 27 September was thus evidently not a part of the regular payment for the play, but the round sum again suggests a reward and not a benefit.

But the custom appears to have been well established, and Thomas Dekker evidently assumed that his audience was familiar with it when in 1611 he wrote the prologue for his play *If This Be Not Good the Devil Is in It,* acted by Queen Anne's men at the Red Bull and published in 1612. After some rather cynical remarks about the reception of plays, the prologue continues,

It is not praise is sought for now, but pence,
Though dropped from greasy-aproned audience.
Clapped may he be with thunder that plucks bays
With such foul hands, and with squint-eyes does
    gaze
On Pallas shield, not caring (so he gains
A crammed third day) what filth drops from his
    brains.

A benefit performance on the second day, not the third, seems to be referred to in a letter of Robert Daborne to

17. Foakes and Rickert, pp. 168 and 216.

Philip Henslowe about payment for the play he was writing: ". . . I pray sir go forward with that reasonable bargain for the Bellman. We will have but twelve pounds and the overplus of the second day. . . ."[18]

Edmund Malone, who had the original manuscript of Sir Henry Herbert's office book for some time but published only such extracts as seemed pertinent for his discussions of the theatre of Shakespeare's time, did make a few generalizations about what he found in these allowance records. He says, ". . . I have learned from Sir Henry Herbert's office-book, that between the years 1625 and 1641 [dramatists'] benefits were on the second day of representation."[19] Malone seems to imply that these benefits were the custom in all companies in Caroline London, but it would be comfortable to have his evidence.

The epilogue to Richard Brome's play *The Novella*, whose title page says that it was "Acted at the Black-friars by his Majesties Servants, Anno 1632," suggests a benefit performance some time after the opening, though it is none too precise:

> Cause 'tis the custom, by the Poet, sirs,
> I'm sent to crave a plaudit; and the spurs
> That prick him on to 't is, his promised pay
> May chance to fail if you dislike the play.

More explicit is the prologue to Jasper Mayne's play *The City Match*, which was acted by the King's company at Blackfriars in 1637 or 1638 after a previous performance at court. The arrogance of the amateur, and his contempt for the professional playwright, are also apparent in this prologue.

> Whether their sold scenes be disliked or hit
> Are cares for them who eat by the stage and wit.

18. Greg, *Henslowe Papers*, p. 75.
19. James Boswell, ed., *The Plays and Poems of William Shakespeare. . . Comprehending . . . an Enlarged History of the Stage, by the late Edmund Malone*, 21 vols., London, 1821, III, 158.

He's [the author is] one whose unbought
    muse did never fear
An empty second day or a thin share;
But can make th' actors, though you come
    not twice,
No losers, since we act now at the King's price,
Who hath made this play public, and the same
Power that makes laws, redeemed this from the
    flames.

At about the same time that *The City Match* was acted at Blackfriars, a lost play by Richard Lovelace was performed at Salisbury Court. The prologue and epilogue were published in the collection of Lovelace's verse, *Lucasta*, in 1649. Both prologue and epilogue express the same amateur fear of commercial contamination as Mayne's verses do. The last four lines of the epilogue refer to the usual author's benefit on the second day:

> Profit he knows none
> Unless that of your approbation,
> Which, if your thoughts at going out will pay,
> He'll not look farther for a second day.

More explicit reference to the exact procedure in the theatre after the dramatist's benefit performance is set out at the end of the epilogue of William Davenant's *The Unfortunate Lovers*, which was licensed for performance on 16 April 1638 and acted before the Queen by the King's men at Blackfriars a week later.[20]

> And though he never had the confidence
> To tax your judgment in his own defence,
> Yet, the next night when we your money share
> He'll shrewdly guess what your opinions are.

This allusion at the first performance of the play to "the next night when we your money share" not only indicates the second performance as the dramatist's benefit night,

20. See *Jacobean and Caroline Stage*, III, 220–22, and VI, 34–35.

but implies that the actual cash of the receipts was shared after the performance.

An authoritative allusion to the common practice occurs in the anonymous pamphlet, *The Actors' Remonstrance*, which purports to represent the actors at Blackfriars, the Phoenix, and the Salisbury Court. The piece was published on 24 January 1643/44, about a year and a half after the closing of the theatres, and laments the hard lot of the theatre people who have been deprived of their livelihood. After mentioning the trials of the housekeepers, the actor-sharers, the hired men, the comedians, the boy actors, the doorkeepers, the musicians, the tire-men, and the tobacco-men, the authors of the pamphlet come to the dramatists: "For some of our ablest ordinary poets, instead of their annual stipends and beneficial second days, being for mere necessity compelled to get a living by writing contemptible penny pamphlets."[21]

Finally Henry Harington alludes to the custom in the verses he wrote for the Beaumont and Fletcher folio of 1647.

> You wits o' th' age
> You that both furnished have, and judged the stage,
> You, who the Poet and the Actors fright,
> Lest that your censure thin the second night.[22]

Additional Chores

Besides plays, Brome wrote other dramatic material for the company at the Salisbury Court theatre. In the plain-

21. Reprinted by William Carew Hazlitt in *The English Drama and Stage*, London, 1869, pp. 259–65.

22. Beaumont and Fletcher folio f₄ᵛ. There are other allusions to the custom of the dramatists' benefit night in the verses signed "Thy Friend C. G." before John Tatham's *Fancies Theatre*, 1640; the prologue to John Denham's *The Sophy*, 1642; the epilogue scene to Thomas Killigrew's *The Parson's Wedding*, 1663, but performed in 1639 or 1640; "Dr. Smith's Ballet," in *Musarum Deliciae, or The Muses' Recreation*, 1656; and the induction scene 1, 2, of the anonymous *Lady Alimony*, 1659.

tiffs' account of the contract they say nothing of these extra chores, and Brome himself does not state specifically that they were required by the contract. But he does enumerate several other contributions necessary to a repertory theatre which he says he furnished. In defending himself against the plaintiffs' accusation that in the plague period he did not contribute as many plays as his contract called for, Brome asserts:

> . . . In lieu of which he hath made divers scenes in old revived plays for them and many prologues and epilogues to such plays of theirs, songs, and one Introduction at their first playing after the ceasing of the plague, all which he verily believeth amounted to as much time and study as two ordinary plays might take up in writing. . . .[23]

Brome's statement that new scenes, prologues, epilogues, songs, and the induction involved as much writing as two new plays ought to be taken with a grain of salt because two new plays was exactly the amount the plaintiffs charged that he had agreed to bring to them before Michaelmas 1638 to make up for his alleged arrears. On the other hand I see no reason to doubt that he did do such necessary repertory chores for them, since there is evidence that other dramatists did such work.

Prologues and Epilogues

There is a good deal of evidence that prologues and epilogues were often written separately from the play to which they were attached and frequently by the dramatist attached to the company, and not by the author. Probably the clearest evidence of this custom is found in *Poems &c By James Shirley*, 1646. The book is a miscellaneous collection of his shorter works brought together by the author after the closing of the theatres. One section of the volume is entitled "Prologues and Epilogues; Written to several plays presented in this Kingdom and elsewhere."

23. Answer, Haaker transcript, p. 305.

"Elsewhere" is Dublin, where Shirley worked as dramatist for the Saint Werburgh Street theatre between the periods of his regular service to Queen Henrietta's company at the Phoenix and to the King's company at Blackfriars and the Globe. In this section of the book Shirley prints six of the prologues and epilogues to his own plays, but he also prints "A Prologue to Mr. Fletcher's play in Ireland," "A Prologue to *The Alchemist* acted there," "A Prologue to a play there called *No Wit to a Woman's*," "A Prologue to a play there called *The Toy*," "To another there," and "To a play there called *The General*."

Obviously these prologues which Shirley indicates that he had written as part of his duties to the Irish theatre were chores of the same sort that Brome says he carried out for the Salisbury Court; Shirley is not even able to remember the name of one of these plays by other men, though he evidently still had the manuscript for his prologue among his papers in 1646.

New prologues and epilogues for revived plays and for court performances were already commonplace in Henslowe's time. There is no convincing evidence that the Henslowe dramatists had contracts with their companies, but the companies did authorize Henslowe to make payments for special prologues and epilogues. In January 1601/1602 the diarist noted that he had "paid unto Thomas Dekker at the appointment of the company for a prologue and an epilogue for the play of Pontius Pilate the 12 of January 1601[/1602] the sum of . . . 10s." There is no other record of a play called *Pontius Pilate* and no good reason to think Dekker had written it himself. Later in the same year the Lord Admiral's company authorized Henslowe, through its usual representative, Thomas Downton, to pay for writing special prologues and epilogues for court performances of Greene's old play, *Friar Bacon and Friar Bungay*, and for another unnamed play.

Lent unto Thomas Downton the 14 of December 1602 to pay unto Mr. Middleton for a prologue and an epilogue for the play of Bacon for the court the sum of . . . 5*s*.

Lent unto Thomas Downton the 29 of December 1602 to pay unto Harry Chettle for a prologue and an epilogue for the court the sum of . . . 5*s*.[24]

Numerous prologues and epilogues mention that they were written for a revival or refer to the author of the play as dead, and must therefore have been written by another, probably as a rule the regular dramatist of the company staging the revival. There are several in the Beaumont and Fletcher canon, most of them probably written by Massinger or Shirley.[25]

Evidently the company dramatist sometimes saved time by using an old prologue or epilogue for a different play. The same prologue is printed with *Thierry and Theodoret* and *The Noble Gentleman*; Dekker's *Wonder of a Kingdom* and Rowley's *All's Lost by Lust* have the same prologue; the prologue printed in the 1613 edition of Beaumont and Fletcher's *Knight of the Burning Pestle* is almost the same as that printed in the 1584 edition of John Lyly's *Sapho and Phao*, a play which had been acted 25 years before, but also at the Blackfriars theatre.

These examples indicate that Brome's chore of writing prologues and epilogues for the plays of other men was not peculiar to the Salisbury Court theatre, and suggest that the task was probably a customary one for the "ordinary poet" of a well-established theatre.

---

24. Foakes and Rickert, pp. 187 and 207.

25. See, e.g., the prologues or epilogues in the 1637 quarto of *The Elder Brother*, and those for *The Loyal Subject*, *The Nice Valour*, *The Lovers' Progress*, *The Custom of the Country*, and *The Noble Gentleman* in the 1647 folio. See also those in the 1633 *Jew of Malta* and the prologue in the 1656 quarto of Goffe's *Careless Shepherdess*, referring to events long after Goffe's death.

New Scenes in Old Plays

Brome says that among his other chores for the Salisbury Court company he had "made divers scenes in old revived plays for them." This method of giving new life to old plays in the repertory was not peculiar to the Salisbury Court, and probably most such scenes were written by the company dramatist, but in most instances there is no external evidence of the authorship of the added scene. Precisely what Brome was talking about is illustrated in a license granted by Sir Henry Herbert to the Salisbury Court company about a year before Brome signed his contract and while he was still working for the Red Bull. Herbert allowed, "An old play with some new scenes, *Doctor Lamb and the Witches* to Salisbury Court the 16th August, 1634 . . . £1." In this instance it is possible to make a good guess at the occasion and circumstances of the additions to the old play.[26]

The same routine additions to old plays were being made at the Fortune theatre a couple of years later. Again the evidence is found in Herbert's office book. "Received of old Cartwright for allowing the [Fortune] company to add scenes to an old play, and to give it out for a new one this 12th of May 1636 . . . £1."

Such additions to old plays were by no means peculiar to the inferior theatres. The same thing was done by the King's men and the results presented at court, as shown by the title page of the third edition of *Mucedorus* in 1610, which says that the play was "amplified with new additions, as it was acted before the King's majesty at Whitehall on Shrove Sunday night. By his highness servants usually playing at the Globe."[27]

26. See below, chap. IX, pp. 253–55.
27. See "*Mucedorus*, Most Popular Elizabethan Play?" *Studies in the English Renaissance Drama*, ed. J. W. Bennett, Oscar Cargill, and Vernon Hall, Jr., New York, 1959, pp. 248–68.

In 1602 when Dekker and Heywood were working regularly for the Earl of Worcester's men and the Lord Admiral's men they performed this chore on plays they had not written originally, as indicated by Henslowe's payments:

> Lent unto John Thare the 7 of September 1602 to give unto Thomas Dekker for his additions in Oldcastle, the sum of . . . 10*s*.

> Paid unto Thomas Heywood the 20 of September [1602] for the new additions of Cutting Dick, sum of . . . 20*s*.

Probably best known of all is the payment made at the company's order to two of the leading members of the Lord Admiral's troupe for their additions to a very famous play: "Lent unto the company the 22 of November 1602 to pay unto William Bird and Samuel Rowley for their additions in Doctor Faustus the sum of . . . £4."[28]

There are many examples of plays on which other playwrights had carried out Brome's chore for his company of making "divers scenes in old revived plays for them"; a number of others are cited below in the chapter on revisions. All Brome's statement adds to our knowledge of revisions is (as might have been guessed) that such addition of new scenes was normally one of the duties of the regular dramatist for the company owning the play.

Added Songs

The addition of songs—sometimes just more songs—to old plays is also a phenomenon confirmed by other sources. The 1638 edition (fifth) of Heywood's *Rape of Lucrece*, originally written thirty or more years before for his company (Queen Anne's men) at the Red Bull, carries a statement on the title page: "The Copy revised, and sundry Songs before omitted, now inserted in their right places."

---

28. Foakes and Rickert, pp. 216 and 206.

139

In this edition five additional songs are printed. Just when these new songs had been written is not apparent, but they are not in earlier editions of the play, which, in 1639, was still in repertory.

Somewhat similar to the statement in *The Rape of Lucrece* is the announcement on the title page of the second issue of *A Fair Quarrel* in 1617: "With new additions of Mr. *Chaugh's* and *Tristram's* Roaring, and the Bawd's song. *Never before printed. As it was acted before the King, by the Prince* his Highness Servants." The new songs are inserted after act 4 in four leaves which were added to this edition. Since William Rowley was both a collaborator in the original composition of the play and a patented member of Prince Charles's company, it seems likely that he wrote the new songs for the company.

Another well-known play to which songs were added is Shakespeare's *Macbeth*. Many scholars have observed that before the play was first printed, in the 1623 folio, material had been interpolated into it, and most agree that the Hecate material, including two songs in the third and fourth acts, were such interpolations. The songs also occur in Middleton's play *The Witch*, almost certainly later in composition than *Macbeth*. But the man who added the songs to *Macbeth* was not necessarily Middleton, since the manuscript of *The Witch* belonged to the King's men and any reviser with access to the Blackfriars archives could have transferred the songs from *The Witch* to *Macbeth*. In any event, the addition of these songs to *Macbeth*, however ill advised it may seem to Shakespeareans, is the sort of chore Brome said he performed for Queen Henrietta's company twenty-five or thirty years later.

Introductions or Inductions

The chore which Brome indicates in his list as "one Introduction at their first playing after the ceasing of the plague" is probably the least familiar one, since most occasional inductions of this type were of such ephemeral interest that they were never printed. But such inductions or introductions are a natural development in a repertory theatre where the friendly relations of audience and actors were a greater source of continued profit than enthusiasm for a particular play or dramatist. This is, of course, also the reason for the popularity of prologues and epilogues in repertory theatres—witness the number which say so little about the play to be performed that they have sometimes been attached to other plays.[29]

The type of induction which Brome and probably all other regular company playwrights wrote might be called the occasional induction; it is not like the more familiar ones that Jonson wrote for a half a dozen of his plays and Shakespeare for *The Taming of the Shrew*. These familiar inductions are essentially a part of the play; they could not be used for another play on a similar occasion. The only Jonson induction which approaches the occasional type is that for *Bartholomew Fair*, which is partly occasional in that it has much on the players and the particular playhouse and may indeed have been written for the opening of the new Hope theatre, but has mostly to do with the fair and Jonson's depiction of it, and could not have been used for any other play.

Precisely like the "Introduction at their first playing after the ceasing of the plague" which Brome says he wrote for the Salisbury Court theatre in 1637 is one which Thomas Randolph wrote when he was probably regular dramatist for the same theatre seven years earlier, after the plague of 1630. This one also failed to achieve print, but it is extant in a British Museum manuscript (Add. MS 37

29. Readers of Elizabethan plays are often confused about prologues and epilogues, partly because they tend to think about plays as pieces for the study, and partly because the most familiar prologues—those for *Romeo and Juliet*, *Henry V*, *Every Man in His Humour*, *The Alchemist*—are those least characteristic of the form.

425 fols. 54-55). The manuscript is headed simply "Prae-ludium," but it is endorsed "T. Randall after the last Plague." It consists of about two hundred lines of dialogue between Histrio and Gentlemen, mostly concerned with the trials of the players during the plague closing; it could have been used before any play.[30]

A similar introduction, induction, or praeludium was probably the lost piece which the King's company pre-sented at court on 5 November 1630. It is known only from the bill the King's men presented for their perform-ances at court in 1630 and 1630/31. The item reads, "The 5 of November, an Induction for the House and The Mad Lover." Apparently this forepiece for Fletcher's popular play was a celebration of the opening of the new Cockpit playhouse designed by Inigo Jones for the court.[31]

Similar occasional pieces concerned with the actors and the theatre, not with the play, were written by John Tatham when he appears to have been attached to the Red Bull players in and about 1640. Tatham called his pieces prologues, and they are not dialogue, but the occasions are as nonliterary as Brome's and Randolph's. One was printed in his *Fancies Theatre*, 1640, and the other in his *Ostella*, 1650, and neither was given any connection with any play. They are entitled *A Prologue spoken upon the removing of the late Fortune players to the Bull* and *A Prologue spoken at the Cock-pit at the coming of the Red Bull play-ers thither*. It is significant that Tatham's titles for these pieces make mention of the occasion and not of the play they preceded. When he printed the prologue for an ordi-nary occasion, he named the play, as Shirley did for the

30. See "Randolph's *Praeludium* and the Salisbury Court Thea-tre," *Joseph Quincy Adams Memorial Studies*, ed. James G. Mc-McManaway, Giles E. Dawson, and Edwin E. Willoughby, Washing-ton, D.C., 1948, pp. 775–83.

31. See *Jacobean and Caroline Stage*, I, 28–29; III, 373–76; and VI, 267–84.

prologues he printed in *Poems &c.* One other prologue printed in *Ostella* is called *A Prologue spoken at the Red-Bull to a Play called the Whisperer, or what you please.*

Of the many printed inductions[32] the great majority are really a part of the play with which they were published, though not always essential to it. Less occasional than the pieces written by Brome and Randolph and the unknown author of "An Induction for the House" or John Tatham's two prologues, but partially divorced from their plays and essentially theatrical in character, are the inductions for Goffe's *Careless Shepherdess*, Marston's *Malcontent*, and the anonymous *Lady Alimony*. In the last what is really an induction has been printed as act 1 in the text of 1659. Obviously none was written by the author of the play, and all make much of theatrical affairs.

Irregular pieces like these would normally have been productions of the theatre's ordinary poet, for they were much concerned with the affairs of the theatre and the company.

Publication

The plaintiffs in their complaint of 12 February 1639/40 say that one of the clauses in the second contract of August 1638 prohibited publication:

> And that he should not suffer any play made or to be made or composed by him for your subjects or their successors in the said company in Salisbury Court to be printed by his consent or knowledge, privity, or direction without the license from the said company or the major part of them.[33]

This clause too appears to have been conventional. Brome does not mention it, but his publication record shows that he observed it; the printing of his plays is not an issue

---

32. There is a convenient list of 56 of them published by Stephen C. Young in *Philological Quarterly*, XLVIII (January 1969), 131–34.
33. Haaker transcript, p. 298.

in the suit. This subject of the publication of plays, 1590–1642, has involved so much heated controversy over the last century, and it is so complex, that it requires an independent discussion. The subject will be considered at length in Chapter X.

CHAPTER VII

Regulation and Censorship

ALL PLAYS presented in the London theatres throughout the period required approval by the Master of the Revels, whose censorship seldom admitted of any appeal. Every dramatist knew this, every manager, every player, and every factotem of the company. One important stage in the intricate progression of every play from an idea in the playwright's head to first performance was the submission of the manuscript to the Master of the Revels for his official permission to proceed. Normally his permission was set down in his own autograph at the end of the manuscript. Several of these autograph official statements have been preserved. The manuscript of *The Second Maiden's Tragedy* (British Museum MS Lansdowne 807) carries on the verso of the last leaf the autograph statement

> This second Maydens tragedy (for it hath no name inscribed) may wth the reformations bee acted publikely, 31 octob^r 1611   By me G. Buc

Sir Henry Herbert, successor to George Buc's successor as Master of the Revels, was using approximately the same form 22 years later. Another British Museum play manuscript (Egerton 1994) carries his license on the last page:

> This play, called the Seaman's Honest wife, all the oaths left out in the action as they are crossed in the book, and all other reformations strictly observed may be acted, not otherwise. This 27 June 1633. Henry Herbert. I command your bookkeeper to present me with a fair copy hereafter and to leave out all oaths, profaneness, and public ribaldry, as he will answer it at his peril. Herbert.[1]

A third play in the same manuscript volume at the British Museum (Egerton 1994) bears an autograph license at the end. This time the Master has evidently assigned the censorship of the play to his deputy.

> This play called the Lady-mother (the Reformations observed) may be acted. October 15. 1635 Will. Blagrave deputy to the master of the Revels.

Even the printed texts of plays in one or two instances bear testimony to the customary form and position of the Master of the Revels's license for acting. The quarto of Thomas Jordan's very popular *Walks of Islington and Hogsdon*, said to have been "Acted 19 days together," is an example. Evidently the compositor set the play from the theatre's prompt copy, for when he came to the end he set up Herbert's acting license from the manuscript before him. On H₄, after the epilogue, he set up

> This Comedy, called, *The Walks of Islington and Hogsdon, With the Humours of Woodstreet-Compter*, may be Acted: This 2 August, 1641.
> *Henry Herbert.*

Even in extant play manuscripts which no longer bear the license statement of the Master of the Revels there is

---

1. J. Q. Adams, ed., *The Dramatic Records of Sir Henry Herbert*, New Haven, 1917, pp. 34–35.

sometimes evidence that it once was there. Massinger's *Parliament of Love* was licensed, according to the office book, for the Cockpit company on 3 November 1624, though it was never printed in the seventeenth century. The manuscript of the play, now in the Victoria and Albert Museum, is rather badly mutilated by damp and carelessness, but there has also been deliberate vandalism, as Edmond Malone and successive editors have noted. At the end of the manuscript, where the Master normally wrote his allowance, a strip of paper 5⅞ by 1⅝ has been neatly cut out of the page.[2]

These licenses to act are Jacobean and Caroline examples of the workings of a system gradually developed in the entertainment world. Edmund Tilney, George Buc, John Astley, and Henry Herbert were the successive Elizabethan, Jacobean, and Caroline Masters of an office set up in the reign of Henry VIII to regularize the supervision of court entertainment, which had previously had *ad hoc* direction.

The Office of the Revels was originally established to select, organize, and supervise all entertainment of the sovereign, wherever the court might be. Such supervision would cover masques, shows, plays, exhibitions, contests, and all the equipment they required, so that costumes, properties, sets, and weapons accumulated in great store in the London Office of the Revels. At first the Masters of the Revels and their subordinates confined their activities to the selection of entertainment for the sovereign and the complex supervision of its presentation. But gradually the power of general dramatic censorship came into the hands of the Master of the Revels. After a good deal of jockeying for position between the authorities of the City of London (generally hostile to the theatre) and the representatives of the generally sympathetic royal authority, usually exercised through the Privy Council of the sovereign, a

2. See K. M. Lea's edition for the Malone Society, Oxford, 1928, pp. v–xiii.

new patent was issued to the Master of the Revels, Edmund Tilney, in 1581. This patent was intended to centralize the regulation of "all and every player or players, with their playmakers," and it was reissued to Sir George Buc in 1603 and to Sir John Astley in 1622.

. . . we have and do by these presents authorize and command our said servant, Edmund Tilney, Master of our said Revels, by himself, or his sufficient deputy or deputies, to warn, command, and appoint, in all places within this our realm of England, as well within franchises and liberties as without, all and every player or players, with their playmakers, either belonging to any nobleman, or otherwise bearing the name or names of using the faculty of playmakers or players of comedies, tragedies, interludes, or what other shows soever, from time to time, and at all times, to appear before him with all such plays, tragedies, comedies, or shows as they shall have in readiness, or mean to set forth; and them to present and recite before our said servant, or his sufficient deputy, whom we ordain, appoint, and authorize by these presents, of all shows, plays, players, and playmakers, together with their playing places, to order and reform, authorize and put down, as shall be thought meet or unmeet unto himself, or his said deputy in that behalf.

And also likewise we have by these presents authorized and commanded the said Edmund Tilney that in case if any of them, whatsoever they be, will obstinately refuse upon warning unto them given by the said Edmund, or his sufficient deputy, to accomplish and obey our commandment in this behalf, then it shall be lawful to the said Edmund, or his sufficient deputy, to attach the party or parties so offending, and him or them to commit to ward, to remain without bail or mainprise until such time as the said Edmund Tilney, or his sufficient deputy, shall think the time of his or their imprisonment to be punishment sufficient for his or their said offences in that behalf; and that done, to enlarge him or them so being imprisoned at their plain liberty, without any loss, penalty, or forfeiture, or other danger in this behalf to be sustained or borne by the said Edmund Tilney, or his deputy, any act, statute, ordinance, or provision heretofore had or made to the contrary hereof in any wise notwithstanding.[3]

Though there was uncertainty for several years in the application of these powers, and though the Lord Mayor and Corporation never ceased to express their hostility, generally through letters and petitions to the Privy Council, nevertheless these are the powers which had to be recognized and accommodated by Shakespeare, Henslowe, Heywood, Heminges, Webster, Alleyn, Chapman, Burbage, Brome, Beeston, and all other dramatists, actors, and managers from 1581 to 1642. The hypotheses so often and so solemnly advanced by many critics and readers of Tudor and Stuart plays about the dramatist's "advice to the Queen" or "protests against the law" or "assertions of his religious dissent" must be made either in ignorance of the powers of the Master of the Revels or in assumption of his incompetence or his venality.

By 1590 the procedures in the Revels office were pretty well established, though Sir Henry Herbert later made them more explicit and rigorous. As theatres, companies, and dramatists became more numerous in the 1580s and 1590s, the demands upon the initiative of the Master became too great for him to "warn, command, and appoint" the players "to appear before him with all such plays, tragedies, comedies, or shows as they shall have in readiness, or mean to set forth; and them to present and recite before our said servant." Instead, all companies were required voluntarily to bring in for inspection all play manuscripts before the plays were acted. This system of individual licenses for individual plays before performance was

---

3. Albert Feuillerat, *Documents Relating to the Office of the Revels in the Time of Queen Elizabeth*, Louvain, 1908, p. 52.

already in effect in 1574. On 10 May 1574 Queen Elizabeth issued a royal patent to James Burbage and the other
members of the Earl of Leicester's men. They were allowed to act in London and the provinces, and provincial
officials in towns and boroughs throughout the realm were
ordered to permit their performances, "provided that the
said comedies, tragedies, interludes and stage plays be by
the Master of our Revels for the time being before seen
and allowed."[4] The same provision stated in another form
is found in the license of another company nearly ten years
later. In March 1583/84 a company of players visited the
town of Leicester and requested permission to act. In proof
of their legitimacy they showed their credentials, dated
6 February 1582/83, and the warrant was copied into the
town records at Leicester. One sentence in this warrant for
the players reads: "No play is to be played, but such as is
allowed by the said Edmund Tilney and his hand at the
latter end of the said book they do play."[5]

Ten years later Henslowe's diary shows that he was making regular payments to the Master of the Revels in behalf of the companies he financed for the allowance of
their new plays; he was also making payments on his own
behalf for the licensing of his theatres while acting was in
progress. In early 1592 he was paying the Master five shillings a week for permission to operate his theatre, and
later in the year he was paying 6s 8d; in the later nineties
and the first two years of the seventeenth century he was
paying 40s and later £3 a month.

A Note what I have laid out about the house . . .

.   .   .   .

Item paid unto Mr. Tilney's man 26 of February 1591
   5s

4. *Elizabethan Stage*, ii, 87–88.
5. William Kelly, *Notices Illustrative of the Drama and Other
Popular Amusements*, Leicester, 1865, p. 212.

Item paid unto Mr. Tilney's man 4 of March 1591
5*s*

Item paid unto Mr. Tilney's man 10 of March 1591
5*s*

.   .   .   .

Item paid unto Mr. Tilney's man the 20 of May 1592
6*s* 8*d*

Item paid unto Mr. Tilney's man the 9 of June 1592
6*s* 8*d*

Item paid unto Mr. Tilney's man the 14 of June 1592
6*s* 8*d*[6]

Later, in the year 1601, increased fees for the operation of the theatres were shown in a different form of record.

Received of Mr. Henslowe the 9 of June £3 which he is to pay for the month's pay for the Fortune, and due unto the Master of Revels

Robte Hassard

Received from Mr. Henslowe by me William Plaistowe to the use of my master, Master Edmond Tilney Master of Her Majesty's Revels for one month's pay due unto him the day and year above written [31 July 1601] the sum of £3, I say . . . £3.[7]

Such payments for licenses for their theatres were ordinarily made by the theatre owners, and not by the players, except in those rare cases where the actors also owned the theatres—as Shakespeare, Burbage, Heminges, Condell, Phillips, and Kempe owned the Globe, and later Shakespeare, Burbage, Heminges, Condell, and Sly the Blackfriars.

Of greater significance for most dramatists were the activities of the Master of the Revels in licensing their plays for performance in those theatres which he had already allowed. Again, Henslowe's records show the sys-

6. Foakes and Rickert, pp. 14–15.
7. Ibid., 194, 164.

tem. These payments to the Master of the Revels for inspecting and allowing their plays Henslowe, as financial agent, charged against the acting companies, whereas the payments for the Fortune and his other theatres were Henslowe's own expense as owner of the theatres.

> Laid out for my Lord Admiral's men as followeth, 1597
> Lent unto Thomas Downton for the company to pay to the Master of the Revels for licensing of 2 books 14 shillings, abated to Downton 5 shillings and so rest . . . 9s.
> Paid unto the Master of the Revels's man for the licensing of a book called the Four Kings . . . 7s.
> Paid unto the Master of the Revels's man for licensing of a book called Beech's Tragedy the sum of . . . 7s.
> Paid unto the Master of the Revels's man for licensing of a book called Damon and Pithias the 16 of May, 1600, the sum of . . . 7s.[8]

These records show clearly enough that Henslowe had to pay a fee in behalf of his companies for the allowance of each of the plays they acted at his theatres, and they show what he paid the Master for his trouble. Such records do not show, however, very much about what the Master did. Such knowledge comes mostly from the records of a later successor of Edmund Tilney, Sir Henry Herbert.

Tilney was succeeded in his office by Sir George Buc, who served from 1597 as his deputy, taking over many of his duties; after 1607 he seems to have performed all the duties of the office. In May 1622 Sir John Astley took over, but he functioned in the office for only a little over a year and in July 1623 turned over to Henry Herbert. Herbert served until the closing of the theatres and tried, with only partial success, to reestablish his right to the office after the Restoration of Charles II.

8. Ibid., 86, 106, 130, 134.

Scattered bits from the records of all these Masters are extant, but the only one whose office book is known to have been preserved well beyond his own time is Henry Herbert. Until the end of the eighteenth century it was extant and was examined by Edmund Malone and George Chalmers and by an unidentified transcriber, perhaps Craven Ord. Since then the manuscript has disappeared, and we must rely on the transcriptions of these scholars. Fortunately their notes are extensive enough to illustrate the Master's customary treatment of dramatists' manuscripts, though it must always be remembered that these three scholars did not copy everything, but tended to concentrate on well-known plays and dramatists. Insofar as we can tell from these extant notes, Sir Henry followed the pattern of his predecessors, though one gets the impression that he was more efficient than Buc or Astley.

The simplest and commonest action of the Master when he was brought a manuscript, usually by the manager of the theatre in which it was to be acted, was to read the script, find nothing objectionable, and write his allowance at the end, like the one at the end of the British Museum manuscript (Egerton 2828) of *Believe as You List* which Philip Massinger had prepared for performance by the King's company: "This Play, called Believe as you list may be acted this 6 of May 1631 Henry Herbert."

These official licenses were recorded by the Master or his clerk in the lost office book whence they were transcribed by the eighteenth- and nineteenth-century scholars mentioned. The form of entry in the office book varies a little with the passage of time—or possibly only with the degree of interest of Chalmers or Malone.

1622, 10 May A new Play, called *The Black Lady* was allowed to be acted by the Lady Elizabeth's Servants.

1623, 30 July For the Prince's Players, A French Tragedy of *the Bellman of Paris*, written by Thomas Dekker and John Day, for the company of the Red Bull.

1623, 29 October For the Palsgrave's Players; a new Comedy, called, *Hardshift for Husbands, or Bilboes the best blade*. Written by Samuel Rowley.

1624, 17 April For the Fortune; *The way to content all women, or how a Man may please his Wife*: Written by Mr. Gunnel.[9]

23 June 1641. Recd for the licensing a book for the Fortune comp. called the Doge and the Dragon . . . £2.[10]

It will be noted that the fee for allowance of a new play had risen from the 7 shillings Henslowe's companies paid in the 1590s to £1, which seems to have been the standard fee for the Master in the 1620s; sometime in the 1630s the fee was doubled to £2.

These licenses are all perfectly straightforward allowances for the company to act plays in which the Master of the Revels found nothing objectionable. But in a number of instances the Herbert memorandum of allowance shows that some alteration in the dramatist's manuscript was required of the company, and that the Master had indicated on the manuscript what was to be changed.

> 1624/25, 25 January For the Prince's Company; A new Play called, *The Widow's Prize*; which containing much abusive matter, was allowed of by me, on condition, that my reformations were observed.

And more specific objections were noted a few years later when Queen Henrietta's company sent in a better-known play by a famous dramatist.

> R. for allowing of *The Tale of the Tub*, Vitru Hoop's part wholly struck out, and the motion of the tub, by command from my Lord Chamberlain; exceptions being taken against it by Inigo Jones surveyor of the king's

9. Adams, Herbert, pp. 23, 24, 26, 28.
10. *Jacobean and Caroline Stage*, v, 1321.

works, as a personal injury unto him. May 7, 1633 . . .
£2.[11]

Not only did the Master require that the dramatist or
the company bookkeeper make alterations in manuscripts,
but he sometimes refused to allow the play at all. This he
did when a representative of the King's company brought
him a play written for them by Philip Massinger: "This
day being the 11 of Janu. 1630, I did refuse to allow of a
play of Massinger's because it did contain dangerous
matter. . . ."[12] On another occasion he sent a messenger to
stop the performance of a play after the bills had been
posted and the actors were ready to begin. The play was
at least twenty years old, and there must have been con-
sternation at the Blackfriars when Sir Henry's warrant was
delivered.

> On Friday the nineteenth [actually eighteenth] of Octo-
> ber, 1633, I sent a warrant by a messenger of the
> chamber to suppress *The Tamer Tamed*, to the King's
> players, for that afternoon, and it was obeyed; upon com-
> plaints of foul and offensive matters contained therein.
>   They acted *The Scornful Lady* instead of it; I have
> entered the warrant here:
>   These are to will and require you to forbear the act-
> ing of your play called *The Tamer Tamed, or the Tam-
> ing of the Tamer* this afternoon, or any more till you
> have leave from me: and this at your peril. On Friday
> morning the 18 October 1633.
>   To Mr. Taylor, Mr. Lowins, or any of the King's
> players at the Blackfryers.
>   On Saturday morning following the book was brought
> me, and at my Lord of Hollands request I returned it
> to the players the Monday morning after, purged of
> oaths, profaneness, and ribaldry, being the 21 of October
> 1633.[13]

11. Adams, *Herbert*, pp. 30, 34.
12. Ibid., p. 19.   13. Ibid., p. 20.

When Herbert returned the manuscript of their play to the King's men he added a note to the company bookkeeper which throws a little more light on the vicissitudes of a dramatist's manuscript in the playhouse before the first performance. Fortunately he copied this note into his office book.

> Mr. Knight,
> In many things you have saved me labor; yet where your judgment or pen failed you, I have made bold to use mine. Purge their parts, as I have the book. And I hope every hearer and player will think that I have done God good service, and the quality no wrong; who hath no greater enemies than oaths, profaneness, and public ribaldry, which for the future I do absolutely forbid to be presented to me in any playbook, as you will answer it at your peril. 21 October 1633.
> This was subscribed to their play of *The Tamer Tamed*, and directed to Knight, their bookkeeper.[14]

One must sympathize with the harassed bookkeeper, who was only an employee of the company, hired to take care of the manuscripts, prepare parts, and adjust the texts for prompt use. Now the Master of the Revels was expecting part of the censoring to be done for him by the poor bookkeeper before the manuscript was submitted for official approval. How would his bosses, the sharers of the company, take to this presumption? Or even the regular dramatist, Philip Massinger? Backstage life is never serene, but Herbert's demands in 1633 seem calculated to produce even more friction. Altogether, there must have been a series of crises within the company over *The Tamer Tamed* business. The indignation of the actors does not need to be imagined; the Master himself attests to it. Not only did he comment in his note of 21 October that his action "hath raised some discourse in the players, though no disobedience," but at the end of the whole affair, nearly a week

14. Ibid., p. 21.

after his sudden cancellation of the Blackfriars performance, he recorded a final step in the imbroglio: "The 24
October 1633, Lowins and Swanston were sorry for their
ill manners, and craved my pardon, which I gave them in
the presence of Mr. Taylor and Mr. Benfeilde."[15] These
four men were the top brass in the King's company in
1633; no other record in the office book reveals the presence of such a large company representation. One would
guess that John Lowin and Eyllaerdt Swanston had lost
their tempers with the Master over his proscription of an
already advertised and rehearsed play, and that Benfield
and Taylor, horrified at the contemplation of the endless
trouble that an estranged Master of the Revels could cause
them, had prevailed upon their hot-tempered fellows to
make a formal apology to the Master. Since it took nearly
a week to persuade them, one must suspect that the original outburst was rather more than "some discourse in the
players," which Herbert admitted.

This example of the sudden proscription of a once allowed play may appear to set the limits of the arbitrary
power which the Master of the Revels could exercise over
the affairs of players and playwrights. But the King's men
were more fortunate than most; they had powerful friends
throughout the reigns of James and Charles, and what the
Earl of Holland (Henry Rich) did for them on this occasion other noblemen did earlier and later. At any rate they
got their manuscript back, and they presented the "purged"
play at court a little over a month later.

Herbert's disapproval of play manuscripts could be more
arbitrary and final than it was in the case of *The Tamer
Tamed*. On 8 June 1642 a manuscript was brought into
the Revels office by Mr. Kirke, who was probably the
manager of the Red Bull theatre. It did not please Sir
Henry: "Received of Mr. Kirke for a new play which I

15. Ibid., pp. 20, 21.

157

burnt for the ribaldry and offense that was in it . . . £2."[16]
Though the Master of the Revels often marked parts of a
manuscript for alteration or deletion, this is the most dras-
tic reaction to a script that is known. The Red Bull theatre
had the lowest reputation of any in London at this time,
and it may be that Herbert thought they needed a lesson,
but his action evidently did not reflect a permanent disapproval of Kirke, for the last extant record from the office
book, made apparently on the same day, is, "Received of
Mr. Kirke for another new play called *The Irish Rebellion*, the 8 June, 1642 . . . £2."[17]

As Master of the Revels, Sir Henry Herbert took his
responsibility very seriously and he exercised some control
over revivals at the theatres as well as over new plays being performed for the first time. Not long after he had
come into office, he made the entry:

> For the king's players, An old play called *Winter's Tale*,
> formerly allowed of by Sir George Bucke, and likewise
> by me on Mr. Hemmings his word that there was noth-
> ing profane added or reformed, though the allowed
> book was missing; and therefore I returned it without
> a fee, this 19 of August, 1623.[18]

Evidently John Heminges, who was the active and trusted
manager of the King's company at this time, was sufficiently aware of Sir Henry's meticulousness to take pre-
cautions because the manuscript of Shakespeare's play which
the company was using was not the one with Buc's holograph allowance at the end. Since the dramatist was Shakespeare, there has been much speculation about what happened to the allowed manuscript and which one was used
as copy for the first folio. Nobody knows, but the revival
for which Heminges was preparing was obviously successful, for the company presented the play at court five
months later.

16. Ibid., p. 39.   17. Ibid., p. 39.   18. Ibid., p. 25.

On the same day that John Heminges brought in a manuscript of Shakespeare's *Winter's Tale*, a representative of Prince Charles's company appeared with the manuscript of an old play in their repertory. This transcription of the allowances is the one made by Craven Ord, and is somewhat more complete than the one made by George Chalmers.

> For the Prince's servants of the Rede Bull; an oulde playe called the Peacable King or the lord Mendall formerly allowed of by Sir George Bucke (likewise by mee) because itt was free from addition or reformation I tooke no fee this 19th August, 1623.[19]

However favored the King's company was at this time, their manuscript of *The Winter's Tale* received from the Master of the Revels the same treatment as the Red Bull manuscript of *The Peaceable King or The Lord Mendall*.

The manuscript of *The Winter's Tale* bearing the official allowance of Sir George Buc was not the only one that the King's company lost, and the same situation which Heminges had handled with the Master of the Revels was managed some eighteen months later by another leading actor of the royal company, Joseph Taylor. At this time Taylor, in conjunction with John Lowin, was gradually taking over the company representative's chores which had been handled so long and so ably by the now aging Heminges and Condell. Herbert recorded Taylor's visit and also noted one of the ways in which the company representatives were accustomed to facilitate their constant dealings with the Master of the Revels. "For the King's company. An old play called *The Honest Man's Fortune*, the original being lost, was reallowed by me at Mr. Taylor's intreaty, and on condition to give me a book this 8 February 1624[/25]."[20]

19. *Jacobean and Caroline Stage*, v, 1393, from the Folger manuscript.
20. Adams, *Herbert*, p. 30.

Herbert's most explicit statement about the regulation
of revived plays is made in connection with the affair of
The Tamer Tamed, which has already been noted. By
1633, when he handled that case, he was settled in his
office and his procedures were clearly worked out in his
own mind. He made some precise statements about policy,
far more explicit than one usually finds from Stuart officials—at least as far as plays are concerned. To the statements already quoted Herbert added these remarks:

> Because the stopping of this play for that afternoon,
> it being an old play hath raised some discourse in the
> players, though no disobedience, I have thought fit to
> insert here their submission upon a former disobedience,
> and to declare that it concerns the Master of the Revels
> to be careful of their old revived plays, as of their new,
> since they may contain offensive matter, which ought
> not to be allowed in any time.
>
> The Master ought to have copies of their new plays
> left with him, that he may be able to show what he
> hath allowed or disallowed.
>
> All old plays ought to be brought to the Master of
> the Revels, and have his allowance to them, for which
> he should have his fee, since they may be full of offen-
> sive things against church and state; rather that in
> former time the poets took greater liberty than is al-
> lowed them by me.
>
> The players ought not to study their parts till I have
> allowed of the book.[21]

Herbert was a conscientious Master, probably more conscientious, or at least better organized, than his predecessors, as he implies in his statement "rather that in former time the poets took greater liberty than is allowed
them by me," but what he was looking for in old plays
was generally the same as what Buc and Tilney had sought:

21. *Ibid.*, pp. 20–21.

"offensive things against church and state." All the Masters occasionally dozed, as Herbert himself sometimes did, but no matter how alert Tilney and Buc may have been they could not have been expected to anticipate political change. The Statute of Oaths did not become law until 1606, and expressions of simple realistic vigor to Tilney were censorable to Herbert. In the same way international relations changed, and statements about Spain which could be applauded in 1595 offended the government in 1623. And of course the sensitivity of the Privy Council and the Master of the Revels to comments on church government was much greater in 1633 than it had been in 1605.

The policy which the Master had been at such pains to set down in the case of *The Tamer Tamed* was accepted and followed by the King's men, and no doubt by the other London companies. Their conformity, and Herbert's care to remove lines which had once been acceptable, is shown in the record of the submission of another old play by the company at Blackfriars a month later.

> The King's players sent me an old book of Fletchers called *The Loyal Subject*, formerly allowed of by Sir George Bucke, the 16 November 1618, which according to their desire and agreement I did peruse, and with some reformations allowed of, the 23 November 1633, for which they sent me according to their promise . . . £1.[22]

But however uneasy Herbert may have been about the possibility of offensive matter in revived plays, he not only sanctioned revivals, but licensed revisions made in preparation for the revivals, as various of his office book entries show.

Often Sir Henry is vague about what the dramatist has done in his preparation of the old play for revival, but

22. Ibid., p. 22.

several times he is more particular. In January 1631/32 his statement about the revived play is quite vague: "For allowing of an old play, new written or furbished by Mr. Biston, the 12th of January, 1631 . . . £1."[23] "Mr. Biston" was Christopher Beeston, manager of Queen Henrietta's company and principal owner of their playhouse, the Phoenix or Cockpit in Drury Lane. The fee charged implies that the revisions must have been considerable. Beeston, though a very well-known theatre figure, is not otherwise known as a dramatist, and the fact that he "furbished" this play suggests that the function of "play doctor" may sometimes have been performed by an experienced man of the theatre who was not the company dramatist.

In an entry two years earlier Herbert was more specific about what had been done in revising the play, though less specific concerning by whom and for whom the additions were made: "For allowing of a new act in an old play, this 13th of May 1629 . . . 10s."[24] At this time his fees had not yet been increased and the charge of 10 shillings indicates the earlier rate, not that the new act was only half as extensive as Christopher Beeston's refurbishings.

The powers of the Master of the Revels over players, playwrights, and theatres were so great that one tends to think of him as omnipotent in theatrical matters, but this was not the case: the Master had a master. And on occasion Sir Henry Herbert and Sir John Astley are known to have been overruled. Their superior was the Lord Chamberlain, and now and then he interfered in the licensing of plays. Before Herbert took over the office, Sir John Astley wrote in the office book:

Item 6 Sept. 1622, for perusing and allowing of a new play called *Osmond the Great Turk*, which Mr. Hemmings and Mr. Rice affirmed to me that the Lord Chamberlain gave order to allow of it because I refused to

23. *Jacobean and Caroline Stage*, III, 17.
24. Adams, *Herbert*, p. 32.

allow at first, containing 22 leaves and a page. Acted by the King's players . . . 20s.[25]

And even the Lord Chamberlain had a superior who sometimes intervened to get approval for the manuscript of a playwright with influential friends. The affair of Davenant's comedy, *The Wits*, discussed later, gives an amusing picture of such intervention.

These numerous records of the control exercised by Tilney, Buc, Astley, and Herbert over the play manuscripts which the dramatists had sold to the players leave no room for uncertainty about the extent of their powers. But most players in any time are by temperament a reckless lot, otherwise they would not be in such an always risky profession. In spite of all the checks and regulations, the London companies did sometimes stage plays or parts of plays which were not acceptable. Two examples from Sir Henry Herbert's accounts will illustrate.

In December of 1624 the King's company actually staged a play which the Master of the Revels had never licensed at all. This folly is known from the letter of apology which they wrote, and which Sir Henry copied into his office book nine years later at the time of *The Tamer Tamed* affair for the reason which he noted in the margin: " 'Tis entered here for a remembrance against their disorders." The letter reads:

To Sir Henry Herbert, Kt. master of his Majesty's Revels. After our humble service remembered unto your good worship, whereas not long since we acted a play called *The Spanish Viceroy*, not being licensed under your worship's hand, nor allowed of: we do confess and hereby acknowledge that we have offended, and that it is in your power to punish this offence, and are very sorry for it; and do likewise promise hereby that we will not act any play without your hand or substitute's hereafter,

25. *Jacobean and Caroline Stage*, III, 119.

nor do anything that may prejudice the authority of your office. So hoping that this humble submission of ours may be accepted, we have thereunto set our hands. This twentieth of December, 1624.

Joseph Taylor	John Lowin
Richard Robinson	John Shancke
Elyard Swanston	John Rice
Thomas Pollard	Will. Rowley
Robert Benfeilde	Richard Sharpe
George Burght[26]	

Most interesting is the fact that this letter is an official document, for it is signed by every one of the patented members of the company except John Heminges and Henry Condell. They were the oldest and most experienced of the sharers—though by no means the most distinguished actors. One wonders if they had had the foresight somehow to dissociate themselves from the company's folly.

Another device which indiscreet actors sometimes used to circumvent the Master of the Revels is recorded in the accounts of Jonson's comedy *The Magnetic Lady*. The play had been licensed regularly enough, as the office book allowance shows: "Received of Knight, for allowing of Ben Jonson's play called *Humours Reconciled, or the Magnetic Lady* to be acted this 12 October, 1632 . . . £2."[27] But after the play was performed, troubles arose. There was offensive matter in the lines spoken by the players, who were evidently hauled up before the Court of High Commission. This fact, and the device the players had used to get their lines past the censor, is revealed in another memorandum which Sir Henry set down in the official records of his office:

Upon a second petition of the players to the High Commission court, wherein they did me right in my care to

26. Adams, *Herbert*, p. 21.   27. Ibid., p. 34.

purge their plays of all offense, my lords Grace of Canterbury bestowed many words upon me, and discharged
me of any blame and laid the whole fault of their play,
called *The Magnetic Lady*, upon the players. This happened the 24 of October, 1633, at Lambeth. In their
first petition they would have excused themselves on me
and the poet.[28]

Herbert's statement that in their first petition to the court
the players of the King's company "would have excused
themselves on me and the poet" means that they told the
court they had acted only what Jonson had written and
Herbert had licensed for performance. Evidently Herbert
somehow proved that he had not licensed objectionable
lines, and in their second petition the players admitted that
Jonson and Herbert were not at fault, and the Archbishop,
as spokesman for the court, "laid the whole fault . . . upon
the players." That is, the players in their performances
had added offensive lines not to be found in Jonson's manuscript which Herbert had read. Now and again dramatists in jeopardy had accused actors of such enlivening of
their texts, but I can recall no other instance in which the
players are known to have admitted the charge.

Before passing on to an attempt to classify the grounds
on which plays were censored in these years, it is relevant
to note one period of what appears to have been excessive
violation. Anyone conversant with the history of the Jacobean stage has probably observed that the infringement of
the standards and regulations of the Master of the Revels
and the Privy Council appear to have been violated with
excessive frequency by the boy companies in the first decade
of the reign of James I. Of course we may be misled by
the comparative paucity of direct theatre records in the
absence of Henslowe's diary and Herbert's office book in
these years, but Heywood's statement in his *An Apology
for Actors*, published in 1612, suggests that the impression

28. Ibid., pp. 21–22.

is not false. He wrote at the end of his defense of his profession:

> Now to speak of some abuse lately crept into the quality, as an inveighing against the State, the Court, the Law, the City and their governments, with the particularizing of private men's humors (yet alive) Noblemen and others. I know it distastes many; neither do I anyway approve it, nor dare I by any means excuse it. The liberty which some arrogate to themselves, committing their bitterness and liberal invectives against all estates to the mouths of children, supposing their juniority to be a privilege for any railing, be it never so violent. I could advise all such to curb and limit this presumed liberty within the bands of discretion and government. But wise and judicial censurers, before whom such complaints shall at any time hereafter come, will not (I hope) impute these abuses to any transgression in us, who have ever been careful and provident to shun the like. I surcease to prosecute this any further, lest my good meaning be (by some) misconstrued; and fearing likewise lest with tediousness I tire the patience of the favorable reader, here, though abruptly, I conclude my third and last treatise.

It should be borne in mind that Heywood wrote as both an attached professional playwright and a patented member of Queen Anne's company. He clearly intends to distinguish between "children" like the company of the Queen's Revels at Blackfriars, the Children of the King's Revels at Whitefriars, and Paul's Boys, on the one hand, and the adult companies like the King's men, Prince Henry's company, the Duke of York's company, and his own troupe of Queen Anne's men on the other. He refers to the former as "the mouths of children" and to the latter as "us, who have ever been careful and provident to shun the like." He appears to impute these distasteful violations to the irresponsibility of the managers and playwrights of the boy companies. It is notable that he tries to disassociate them from the responsible members of the profession.

Grounds for the Censorship of Plays

These quoted records of their activities show clearly enough that the Masters of the Revels regularly examined the dramatists' manuscripts in the hands of the London companies and frequently ordered deletions from them. But most of the examples so far quoted do not make very clear just what the Masters sought to suppress, or what was found objectionable by superior authorities though the Master had missed it when he first censored the manuscript.

An analysis of the scattered surviving records of censorship, reprimand, and punishment of the players for offenses in their plays shows that most of the censoring activities were intended to eliminate from the stage five general types of lines or scenes.

1. Critical comments on the policies or conduct of the government
2. Unfavorable presentations of *friendly* foreign powers or their sovereigns, great nobles, or subjects
3. Comment on religious controversy
4. Profanity (after 1606)
5. Personal satire of *influential* people

Some of these classes are, of course, overlapping. The unfavorable presentations of foreign powers or their leaders is obviously entangled with criticism of the government; it could get the King and his ministers into difficulties with the ambassadors of the friendly powers, as in the cases of Chapman's *Byron* and Middleton's *A Game at Chess*. Similarly, the influential person satirized might also be an official of a friendly foreign power, like Count Gondomar. Of course the Masters of the Revels did not have before them such a list of offenses as I have made, but most of their known repressive actions can be classified under these heads.

The most seriously objectionable lines in plays were those making political comments which were critical (or implied criticism) of the government. Such criticism was very seldom direct: more often it was the dramatization of a scene which might be thought analogous to some current political situation, or lines, which, though spoken by a foreigner about a foreign government, might be thought applicable to policies of Elizabeth or James or Charles; or it was an attack on a foreign power or foreign sovereign at the moment friendly to England or whose friendship the government was trying to cultivate.

The best-known example of the analogous scene is the deposition scene in Shakespeare's *Richard II*. Elizabeth and some of her ministers saw an analogy—or rather thought many people fancied an analogy—between Elizabeth and Richard II. Therefore the staging of a scene showing the deposition of Richard might be thought to hint at similar actions against Elizabeth. The Essex conspirators evidently thought so when they bribed the Lord Chamberlain's company to revive the play on the eve of the Essex rebellion. That the deposition scene was thought censorable by someone is demonstrated by its deletion from the first three quarto editions of the play in 1597, 1598, and again in 1598; it does not appear in print until the fourth quarto of 1608, five years after Elizabeth's death. Whether the scene was cut before the play was ever staged or only deleted from later performances and from the early printed texts is not material at the moment. The significant fact is that the deposition scene is the sort of material which someone in authority found censorable in 1597 and 1598.

For similar reasons Samuel Daniel's play *Philotas* made trouble for the author and the actors in 1605. There had been a good deal of murmuring after the trial and execution of the popular Earl of Essex in February 1600/1601, and for several years thereafter the Privy Council was acutely aware of disaffection among the former partisans of Essex. Daniel's play, which was acted by the Children of the Queen's Revels, dramatized the classic story of Alexander and Philotas; in acts 4 and 5 he handled the trial and punishment of Philotas, which seemed to the Privy Council too much like the affairs of the Earl of Essex. In protesting his innocence to the Earl of Devonshire, whom he seems to have implicated, Daniel wrote:

> And therefore I beseech you to understand all this great error I have committed. First I told the Lords I had written three acts of this tragedy the Christmas before my Lord of Essex's troubles, as divers in the city could witness. I said the Master of the Revels had perused it. I said I had read parts of it to your honor, and this I said having none else of power to grace me now in Court and hoping that you out of your knowledge of books and favor of letters and me might answer that there was nothing in it disagreeing nor anything as I protest there is not but out of universal notions of ambition and envy, the perpetual arguments of books and tragedies. I did not say you encouraged me to the presenting of it, if I should I had been a villain, for that when I showed it to your honor I was not resolved to have had it acted, nor should it have been had not my necessities overmastered me. . . .[29]

Whether Daniel was as innocent of perception of the analogy between the affairs of Philotas and of Essex as he protested is not significant here. The significant fact for understanding the principles of Jacobean censorship is that there *was* an analogy whether the author had had it in mind when he wrote or not, and therefore the play was dangerous and required suppression by authority.

29. Laurence Michel, ed., *The Tragedy of Philotas by Samuel Daniel*, New Haven, 1949, p. 38.

Almost as well known as the affair of *Richard II* is that of *A Game at Chess*, which Thomas Middleton wrote for the King's company in 1624. The censorable matter in this play is clear enough, and its allowance by Sir Henry Herbert on 12 June 1624 was probably a matter of collusion between the Master of the Revels and certain members of the Privy Council. The political situation the play exploited was most unusual. For several years King James had been cultivating Spain and deferring to the skillful Spanish Ambassador, Count Gondomar, in spite of the increasingly violent anti-Catholic and anti-Spanish feeling in the nation. In 1623 the King had gone so far as to try to arrange a marriage between his heir, Prince Charles, and the Spanish Infanta, and when the Prince and the Duke of Buckingham returned, foiled and angered from Madrid, the general popular rejoicing was so great that their return had been celebrated with bonfires in the streets. In this instance popular sentiment was overwhelmingly against the King and the pro-Spanish faction at court, and Middleton and the King's players seized the opportunity to capitalize.

The topical play was *A Game at Chess*, produced (by design?) when the King and most of the Privy Council were out of town, at the Globe in August 1624. It ran for nine days, the greatest hit of the first quarter of the century, before the Privy Council intervened, closed down the theatre entirely, arrested the players, and tried to jail Middleton. The collusion which was necessary to get the play licensed in the first place and to run so long without suppression is not relevant here, but the material which made the play so objectionable to those not on the popular side is. The play was partly an allegory of recent affairs, partly a dissemination of scandals against the Catholics, and especially the Jesuits. The characters—all chessmen—are the White King (James I), the White Knight (Prince Charles), the Black King (Philip IV of Spain), the Black Bishop (the Father General of the Jesuits), the Black

Knight (Gondomar), and so on. Obviously this was political comment with a vengeance, and Middleton and the fellows of the King's company must have thought either that it was past history and all national policy was now reversed, or that they had friends powerful enough to protect them. In the latter assumption they appear to have been correct, for though they had to post a bond of £300 and were restrained from acting at all for about ten days, the sums they were reputed by contemporaries to have made out of the play more than compensated. For a time the Master of the Revels was in serious trouble for having allowed *A Game at Chess*, but he was functioning regularly in his office in the next month. However the licensing and performance of *A Game at Chess* are accounted for, the play is clearly an example of the sort of dramatic work the Master of Revels was expected to suppress.[30]

Sometimes the writer of the offending lines could be more innocent in his intentions than Middleton was in *A Game at Chess*. The manuscript of Walter Mountfort's play, *The Launching of the Mary, or the Seaman's Honest Wife*, bears on the last page the allowance of the Master of the Revels with the qualification that all oaths "as they are crossed in the book and all other reformations strictly observed." Herbert has crossed out all references to the Amboyna massacres, a total of seventy-five or eighty lines at different places in the play.

Now Walter Mountfort, an employee of the East India Company for at least twenty years, had written his play, as he notes on his manuscript, during a long voyage from India to England. The Amboyna massacre had taken place in 1623 on the island of that name in the Southern Moluccas, when the Dutch garrison tried, tortured, and executed about eighteen Englishmen, agents of the East India Company. There was a good deal of excitement when the news

30. See *Jacobean and Caroline Stage*, IV, 870–79.

reached England, but for political reasons and in spite of popular indignation, no significant retaliatory action was ever taken, and the massacre rankled in the popular mind in England. It was inflammatory, therefore, when Mountfort had a shipbuilder describe the tortures and name several of the Dutchmen involved. Clearly Mountfort hated the Dutch as did many Englishmen, especially in the East India Company. He probably did not know as he wrote during his long voyage home that he was writing during a time of complex maneuvering with the French, the Dutch, and the Spanish about affairs in the Low Countries, and that in such a time the English government was anxious that no overt public hostility toward the Dutch should be reported back to the States by the Dutch ambassador. Whether Mountfort was aware of anything more than the hatred of his company and his friends for the Dutch or not, it is clear that Herbert suppressed the inflammatory Amboyna material in the play because it might have embarrassed the government in its dealings with supposedly friendly foreign powers.

Another play written by Philip Massinger for the King's company shows the kind of lines which seemed, by analogy, to be comments on current English political controversy. In 1638 when the country was becoming more incensed by King Charles's desperate taxation measures, Sir Henry not only quoted some of the lines he had censored in a play, but proudly indicated that King Charles concurred in his judgment:

> Received of Mr. Lowin for my pains about Massinger's play called *The King and the Subject*, 2 June, 1638 . . . £1.

> The name of *The King and the Subject* is altered, and I allowed the play to be acted, the reformations most strictly observed, and not otherwise, the 5th June, 1638.

At Greenwich the 4 of June, Mr. W. Murray gave me power from the King to allow of the play, and told me that he would warrant it.

Moneys? We'll raise supplies what ways we please
And force you to subscribe to blanks, in which
We'll mulct you as we think fit. The Caesars
In Rome were wise, acknowledging no laws
But what their swords did ratify, the wives
And daughters of the senators bowing to
Their wills as deities, . . .

This is a piece taken out of Philip Massinger's play called *The King and the Subject*, and entered here forever to be remembered by my son and those that cast their eyes upon it, in honor of my master King Charles, who reading over the play at Newmarket, set his mark upon the place with his own hand, and in these words: "This is too insolent, and to be changed." Note, that the poet makes it the speech of a king, Don Pedro, King of Spain, and spoken to his subjects.[31]

In the light of the fact that these lines were written in the time of the protests about ship money and corporate monopolies and other forms of alleged royal tyranny, Massinger must have been naïve to think that they would be approved by the Master of the Revels. Such lines, which could easily be thought to express criticism of current actions or policies of the government, are just what the Master of the Revels was appointed to eliminate from plays performed in the London theatres.

The second type of officially offensive material was the unfavorable presentation of friendly foreign powers or their sovereigns, great nobles, or subjects. As has been suggested, this second type of material was very closely related to the first, for the friendly foreign powers attacked were friendly because of the current policy of the govern-

31. Adams, *Herbert*, pp. 22–23.

ment. An example of censorship for this reason is to be found in Sir Edmund Tilney's deletions in *Sir Thomas More* at some unascertained date in the 1590s. It was the play's sympathetic treatment of English riots against arrogant foreign merchants and artisans in London that was the source of Sir Edmund's severe treatment. This play is extant in a mutilated and much revised manuscript in the British Museum (Harley 7368). One of the several revisers of the manuscript is often thought to have been William Shakespeare, hence the numerous studies of the play. But the names of the collaborators and revisers—three of whom were Anthony Munday, Henry Chettle, and Thomas Dekker—are not so relevant here as the objections of the Master of the Revels. On the first page of the manuscript he has written:

> Leave out the insurrection wholly and the cause thereof and begin with Sir Thomas More at the Mayor's sessions, with a report afterwards of his good service done being sheriff of London upon a mutiny against the Lombards only by a short report and not otherwise at your own perils.
>
> E. Tilney[32]

These objections would eliminate a good part of the play, and it is not clear that the manuscript was ever thoroughly rewritten as suggested or that the play ever reached performance. In any case the fears of the Master of the Revels that the objectionable scenes might stimulate new attacks on the foreigners whom the government allowed to work in London is clearly implied in his signed statement.

Also offensive to a friendly power was Chapman's two-part play, *The Conspiracy and Tragedy of Charles, Duke of Byron, Marshall of France*, published in 1608 after having been acted at Blackfriars earlier in the same year. The published text shows heavy cuts: the fourth act of

32. Chambers, *William Shakespeare,* i, 503.

The Conspiracy has been drastically cut, leaving it only about half as long as the other four acts; in *The Tragedy* at the end of act 1 and the beginning of act 2 one or more episodes have been expurgated. Chapman himself alluded to the expurgations when he spoke of "these poor dismembered poems" in his dedication of the 1608 quarto to Sir Thomas Walsingham and his son. Though the official records of the censorship of this play are lost—as are most of the records from the incumbency of Sir George Buc—a letter preserved in the Bibliothèque nationale shows what happened. The letter was written by the French Ambassador in London to the Marquis de Sillery. A translation of the relevant part reads:

> April 8, 1608, I caused certain players to be forbid from acting the history of the Duke of Byron; when, however, they saw that the whole Court had left the town, they persisted in acting it; nay, they brought upon the stage the Queen of France and Mademoiselle de Verneuil. The former, having accosted the latter with very hard words, gave her a box on the ear. At my suit three of them [i.e., the players] were arrested, but the principal person, the author, escaped.[33]

The scene mentioned does not appear in the printed play and is clearly one of the long passages cut out; this scene was offensive to a friendly power and the players suffered for staging it. Possibly the French ambassador slightly exaggerated his power and influence in his letter to his friend in France, but there is no need to doubt the essential facts he records. The Queen of France was unfavorably presented in a play and the objections of the French Ambassador led to censorship, and, in this case, contributed to the suppression of the guilty company.

The dramatists' awareness of the stern opposition of

33. Thomas Marc Parrott, *The Plays and Poems of George Chapman: The Tragedies*, New York, 1910, p. 591.

authority to the presentation in the theatres of critical por-
traits of friendly foreign powers or their nobles is evi-
denced in the prologue printed in the 1615 quarto of *The
Hector of Germany, or the Palsgrave, Prime Elector*. The
author wants to make sure that everyone understands that
the Palsgrave of his play is *not* Frederick IV, Count Pala-
tine of the Rhine, who had married James's daughter,
Elizabeth, with many royal and national celebrations on
14 February 1612/13. The speaker of the prologue an-
nounces to the audience:

> Our author, for himself, this bade me say,
> Although the *Palsgrave* be the name of th' Play,
> 'Tis not that Prince which in this kingdom late
> Married the maiden-glory of our state:
> What pen dares be so bold in this strict age
> To bring him while he lives upon the stage?
> And though he would, Authority's stern brow
> Such a presumptuous deed will not allow:
> And he must not offend Authority. . . .

A couple of years later an unknown author of an unknown play was not so careful. At their regular sitting on
22 June 1617, the Privy Council sent an order to the official in charge of the regulation of plays, players, and
playwrights:

> A letter to Sir George Buck, Knight
>   Master of the Revels.

> We are informed that there are certain players or come-
> dians, we know not of what company, that go about to
> play some interlude concerning the late Marquesse d'
> Ancre, which for many respects we think not fit to be
> suffered. We do therefore require you upon your peril
> to take order that the same be not represented or played
> in any place about this city or elsewhere where you have
> authority. And hereof have you a special care.[34]

34. *Malone Society Collections*, Oxford, 1911, I, parts 4 and 5,
376.

The Marquesse d'Ancre, the favorite of the French Queen, had been murdered in Paris less than two months before, and some company was evidently trying to capitalize on a current sensation, as the King's company did with Fletcher and Massinger's play, *Sir John van Olden Barnavelt*, two years later. Since the councillors say "go about to play," they apparently had advance notice from some interested party—possibly the French Ambassador.

In 1630/31 the Master of the Revels refused to license a play for the King's company because it came into this same class of objection. In this case the Master was gratifyingly explicit:

> This day being the 11 of January, 1630, I did refuse to allow of a play of Massinger's because it did contain dangerous matter, as the deposing of Sebastian King of Portugal, by Philip the Second and there being a peace sworn betwixt the Kings of England and Spain. I had my fee notwithstanding which belongs to me for reading it over, and ought to be brought always with the book.[35]

The third type of material which the Master was alert to expunge from the dramatists' manuscripts was that bearing on religious controversy. Essentially such material was political too, since it concerned the state church and the attempts of the government to suppress dissent, one phase of which was ridicule of persons or practices in the established church. Obviously such instances of conflict were tempting to players and playwrights, and they could assume a good deal of public interest if they could succeed in getting a dramatization of them past the censor. There are various records of their occasional success in the first stage—a performance license—but suppression after the play was on the stage.

35. Adams, *Herbert*, p. 19. Massinger's revisions to make this suppressed play acceptable will be discussed in Chapter IX.

In 1619 there was a good deal of London interest in political affairs in the Netherlands involving the conflict which was echoed in English church–state difficulties of the time. One climax in the Dutch struggle was the downfall, trial, and execution of the Dutch patriot, Sir John van Olden Barnavelt, in the spring and early summer of 1619. The King's company saw an opportunity to exploit the London interest in these events, and their regular dramatist, John Fletcher, probably with the assistance of Philip Massinger, prepared for them a play on the subject. They must have worked with great dispatch, since their play was rehearsed and ready for the stage on 14 August 1619, though it included an event not known in London until 14 July. The manuscript was allowed by Sir George Buc, whose initials are signed to one correction on the prompt manuscript. But at the last moment religious authority stepped in. A letter written from London on 14 August 1619 to Sir Dudley Carleton, King James's Ambassador at The Hague, reports that, "The players here were bringing of Barnavelt upon the stage, and had bestowed a great deal of money to prepare all things for the purpose, but at the instant were prohibited by my Lord of London." The Bishop of London was not normally directly concerned with the performance of plays, but he was the director of censorship of printed matter and a member of the Privy Council, and his authority was great. What alterations he required in the performance are not known, but his objections were satisfied, for Sir Dudley received another letter from the same correspondent dated 27 August 1619, in which he said, "Our players have found the means to go through with the play of Barnavelt and it hath had many spectators and received applause."

One suspects that players and printers may have been uneasy about this play: there are no records of its performance after those original Globe afternoons; it did not appear in the company's list of unprinted plays in their repertory in 1641; though its later interest to the company must have been slight, it was never printed in quarto; it was omitted from both the first and the second Beaumont and Fletcher folios in 1647 and 1679; indeed, it was never published at all until A. H. Bullen printed it from the British Museum manuscript in his *Collection of Old English Plays* in 1883. The ever-increasing virulence of the religious conflict from 1619 to 1642 certainly did nothing to make the religious implications of *Sir John van Olden Barnavelt* less dangerous.[36]

One of the problems of the Master of the Revels in his endeavors to keep controversial religious implications out of performances in the London theatres lay in the very nature of the theatre: impressions on audiences are made visually as well as orally. The normal meanings or implications of words can be changed by the action and spectacle which accompanies them. Something of the sort must have happened on the stage of the Salisbury Court theatre when the King's Revels company produced an unnamed play in February 1634/35. In his office book Sir Henry records only his stern action on the occasion.

> I committed Cromes, a broker in Long Lane, the 16th of February, 1634, to the Marshalsea for lending a church robe with the name of JESUS upon it to the players in Salisbury Court to present Flamen, a priest of the heathens. Upon his petition of submission, and acknowledgment of his fault, I released him the 17 February, 1634.[37]

If Herbert said anything about his punishment of the players who performed this play, Malone and Chalmers failed to copy it. The employment of such a robe for "a priest of the heathens" cannot have been innocent in intent.

A clearer example of the defiance of religious censor-

---

36. See Wilhelmina Frijlinck, *The Tragedy of Sir John van Olden Barnavelt*, Amsterdam, 1922, pp. i–clviii.

37. Adams, *Herbert*, p. 64.

ship by the players occurred four years later. By this time the controversy over religious ceremonial was in its later stages of violence, and the approach of civil war was apparent to many. Our knowledge of this event comes not from Herbert—though his lost office book must have carried some reference to it—but from correspondence printed in the *Calendar of State Papers, Domestic*. In a letter of 8 May 1639 Edmund Rossingham wrote to Viscount Conway:

> Thursday last [2 May] the players of the Fortune were fined £1,000 for setting up an altar, a bason, and two candlesticks, and bowing down before it upon the stage, and although they allege it was an old play revived, and an altar to the heathen gods, yet it was apparent that this play was revived on purpose in contempt of the ceremonies of the Church; if my paper were not at an end I should enlarge myself upon this subject, to show what was said of altars.

There is another account of this affair over a year later. It appears in an antiepiscopal propaganda pamphlet, and its details are therefore suspect. Certainly it dishonestly implies a date much nearer the end of 1640 than the facts warrant, and I suspect the propagandist patness of some of the details, such as the name of the play and other insinuations of the common Puritan charge that Archbishop Laud expected to be made Roman Catholic cardinal of England. Nevertheless this account in *Vox Borealis*, though not trustworthy in all its details, shows why the authorities had good reason to fear such plays as the one produced at the Fortune.

> In the meantime let me tell ye a lamentable Tragedy, acted by the Prelacy against the poor players of the Fortune Playhouse which made them sing
>> *Fortune my foe, why dost thou*
>> *frown on me? &c*

for they having gotten a new old play, called *The Cardinal's Conspiracy*, whom they brought upon the *stage* in as great *state* as they could, with *Altars*, *Images*, *Crosses*, *Crucifixes*, and the like, to set forth his pomp and pride. But woeful was the sight to see how in the midst of all their *mirth*, the Pursuivants came and seized upon the poor cardinal, and all his consorts, and carried them away. And when they were questioned for it in the High Commission Court, they pleaded *Ignorance*, and told the Archbishop *that they took those* examples of their *Altars*, *Images*, and the like from *Heathen Authors*. This did somewhat assuage his anger, that they did not bring him on the stage. But yet they were fined for it, and after a little imprisonment got their liberty. And having nothing left them but a few old swords and bucklers, they fell to act *The Valiant Scot*, which they played five days with great applause, which vexed the bishops worse than the other, insomuch as they were forbidden playing it any more, and some of them prohibited ever playing again.[38]

Vox Borealis is much too gleeful in his account of the discomfiture of the hated bishops to be fully trusted, especially in his selection of the title *The Valiant Scot* so as to bring slyly to the minds of his nonconformist readers the salutary drubbing which the noble Scottish Presbyterians had given to the Episcopalians in the Bishops' Wars, actually much later than the players' fine of 4 May 1639.

Such bringing of religious controversy onto the stage as these examples have illustrated was one of the major offenses which the Master of the Revels was trying to detect and eliminate as he read over play manuscripts. Of course he had not been appointed to read without prejudice; it is noteworthy that all these punished offenses involved attacks on the established church, not on the dissenters. Sneers at Puritans and Brownists and Presbyterians are

38. See *Jacobean and Caroline Stage*, vi, 167–68.

common enough in the allowed plays, as all readers of Jonson, Middleton, and Shirley know.

The fourth of the principal offenses which the censor was looking for was profanity. Unlike the previously discussed offenses this one was defined during the period. Also different was the fact that enforcement was more dependent upon the personal ideas of the Master, as some of the examples will show. From 1590 to 1606 there is very little evidence as to what was thought profane or what was done in the way of restricting it. But in 1606 Parliament passed an act which was intended to purify the language in plays.

An Act to Restrain Abuses of Players

For the preventing and avoiding of the great abuse of the holy name of God in stage plays, interludes, May-games, shows, and such like; be it enacted by our sovereign Lord the King's majesty and by the Lords spiritual and temporal, and Commons in this present Parliament assembled and by the authority of the same, that if at any time or times, after the end of this present session of Parliament, any person or persons do or shall in any stage play, interlude, show, May-game or pageant jestingly or profanely speak or use the name of God or of Christ Jesus, or of the Holy Ghost or of the Trinity, which are not to be spoken but with fear and reverence, shall forfeit for every such offense by him or them committed ten pounds, the one moiety thereof to the King's majesty, his heirs and successors, the other moiety thereof to him or them that will sue for the same in any court of record at Westminster, wherein no essoigne, protection, or wager of law shall be allowed.[39]

This statute, with its legal provision for rewards to informers, set up the possibility that any member of a theatre audience might make himself £5 by tattling in a court of law about what he had heard. A careful bookkeeper in the theatre might be well advised to regularize any casual

39. Chambers, *Elizabethan Stage*, IV, 338–39. Transcribed from *Statutes of the Realm, 1101–1713.*

exclamations he found in a play manuscript even before he sent it to the Master of the Revels. Probably this often happened, for certain texts are extant which show more meticulous expurgation than it is easy to imagine the Master performing. An eloquent example is the folio text of *Othello*. A collation of this 1623 edition with the first quarto of 1622 shows scores of petty revisions. Since the play is known to have been performed at court by the King's company eighteen months before the profanity statute was passed, the folio revisions may be assumed to be due in part to fear of the penalties of the law. A few examples of these changes show what was involved.

	1622	1623
1.2.35	And I, God blesse the marke	And I (blesse the marke)
1.1.94	Zounds [God's wounds] sir you are robd.	Sir, y'are rob'd
2.2.91	Fore God an excellent song	Fore Heaven: an excellent song
2.2.167	Zouns, you rogue, you rascal	You rogue; you rascal
3.3.180	Zouns	What dost thou mean?
3.3.203	Good God, the souls of all	Good Heaven, the souls of all
3.4.92	Then would to God	Then would to Heaven
4.3.114	God me such usage send	Heaven me such uses send
5.2.105	O Lord, Lord, Lord.	[Line omitted]
5.2.148	O Lord, what cry is that?	Alas! what cry is that?
5.2.270	O God, O heavenly God. Zouns, hold your peace.	Oh Heaven! O heavenly Powers! Come, hold your peace.

The manuscript of Walter Mountford's play, *The Launching of the Mary, or the Seaman's Honest Wife*, which is preserved in the British Museum (Egerton 1994), carries on the last page the autograph allowance of Sir Henry Herbert, and the text of the play shows the Master's marks of disapproval at several points. Some, as we have observed, require the deletion of politically offensive material, but others indicate offensive oaths, as the Master explicitly states in his license "all the oaths left out in the action as they are crossed in the book. . . ." Sir Henry most frequently required the omission of the comparatively inoffensive "faith," which he marked for deletion at least nineteen times. He also marked "Troth" and " 'Slife" and "by the lord."

On the same grounds he marked for omission in act 2, scene 1, the third line of Captain Fitz John's exclamation:

O happy above many happy man
Born and brought up in Time's full happiness
Next to the sole redeemer of my soul
How I am bound, obliged, engaged, devoted
to my much honored masters.

Evidently Sir Henry Herbert found the profanity still used in Fletcher's *The Tamer Tamed* offensive in 1633, though the play had been duly licensed by his predecessor long before. After he had stopped the revival performance of the play, he returned the manuscript to the King's men, as he says, "I returned it to the players the Monday morning after purged of oaths, profaneness, and ribaldry."

In January 1633/34 Sir Henry recorded an unusual series of events which illuminate the problem of defining censorable profanity. William Davenant, who had previously prepared two or three plays for the King's company, had another manuscript ready late in 1633. We first hear of it after Herbert had recently rejected or perhaps only heavily censored it, and Davenant's friend and patron,

Endymion Porter, had interfered on behalf of the play-wright. Sir Henry says:

> This morning, being the 9th of January, 1633[/34] the King was pleased to call me into his withdrawing chamber to the window, where he went over all that I had crossed in Davenant's playbook and allowing of *faith* and *slight* to be asseverations only and no oaths, marked them to stand and some other few things, but in the greater part allowed of my reformations. This was done upon a complaint of Endymion Porters in December.
>
> The King is pleased to take *faith, death, slight,* for asseverations and no oaths, to which I do humbly submit as my master's judgment; but, under favor, conceive them to be oaths, and enter them here to declare my opinion and submission.
>
> The 10 of January, 1633[/34], I returned unto Mr. Davenant his play-book of *The Wits* corrected by the King.
>
> The King would not take the book at Mr. Porter's hands, but commanded him to bring it to me, which he did, and likewise commanded Davenant to come to me for it, as I believe; otherwise he would not have been so civil.[40]

Either this manuscript was not the final one produced by the company at Blackfriars (possibly because Davenant wanted to treasure it as a royal memento) or else more time than usual was spent in incorporating the corrections, for the final official license which Malone noted in the Revels manuscript but did not copy was dated 19 January. At any rate the company went into immediate production at Blackfriars, for Sir Humphry Mildmay saw the play there on the 22nd.

This affair was a most unusual one on several counts, most notably because of the overriding of the Master of

40. Adams, *Herbert,* p. 22.

185

the Revels by King Charles, who was not accustomed to concern himself with such petty details of Revels office business. But Endymion Porter was a favorite, and Davenant was his protégé. Secondly it was unusual for anyone but the producing company to have the manuscript. How Davenant got his manuscript back from the bookkeeper at Blackfriars can only be guessed, but somehow this was all a personal matter—witness the fact that Herbert gave the manuscript back to Davenant and not to the representative of the King's company.

Finally it is unusual for a Master to be so specific about his objections and to record significant differences of opinion. Herbert thought of *faith*, *death*, and *slight* as being obvious corruptions of "God's faith," "God's death," and "God's light" and therefore forbidden by the statute which set punishments for players who "jestingly or profanely speak or use the name of God. . . ." The King thought the old corruptions had passed into common usage and lost their original denotations. Herbert was not convinced.

It is easy to think of the Master of the Revels as an enemy to dramatic genius and the stern foe of the players, for most of his recorded activities are inhibitive. But he did not think of himself this way, and some understanding of his position between the Puritan bitter enemies of players and playwrights and the overindulgent Cavalier audiences can be seen in the compliments he paid to a play James Shirley wrote for Queen Henrietta's men. These comments were written in July 1633, six months before Davenant's troubles with *The Wits* and just at the time when William Prynne's virulent *Histriomastix, The Players' Scourge and the Actors' Tragedy* was rallying the antitheatrical forces in London. When he licensed the play on 3 July 1633, Herbert wrote this most unusual comment:

> The comedy called *The Young Admiral*, being free from oaths, profaneness, or obsceneness, hath given me much delight and satisfaction in the reading, and may

serve for a pattern to other poets, not only for the better-
ing of manners and language, but for the improvement
of the quality, which hath received some brushings of
late.

When Mr. Shirley hath read this approbation, I know
it will encourage him to pursue this beneficial and clean-
ly way of poetry, and when other poets hear and see his
good success, I am confident they will imitate the original for their own credit, and make such copies in this
harmless way, as shall speak them masters in their art,
at the first sight, to all judicious spectators. It may be
acted this 3 July, 1633.

I have entered this allowance for direction to my successor, and for example to all poets that shall write after
the date hereof.[41]

These comments on *The Young Admiral*, a rather foolish
tragicomedy, may not place Sir Henry very high in the
ranks of dramatic critics—especially modern ones—but
they do demonstrate that in his own mind he was not
simply the watchdog for the King's prerogative, the bishops' hegemony, and the tender sensibilities of the ambassadors of friendly foreign powers, but the promoter of the
best interests of the national theatrical enterprise. Though
he could not foresee that in nine years the enemies of the
theatre would triumph and abolish the enterprise, he could
see the strength of Prynne and his sympathizers in the London of 1633, and he could appreciate some of the theatrical
customs which gained them adherents. When he says that
plays free from oaths, profaneness, and obsceneness like
The Young Admiral will serve "for the improvement of
the quality [i.e., the profession of players and playwrights]
which hath received some brushings of late" he is not
thinking of the freedom of the artist—actor and dramatist—to observe and to comment, but of the preservation
of their joint enterprise. However narrow-minded he may

41. Adams, *Herbert*, pp. 19–20.

have been in his censorship, he had clearly before him those antitheatrical sentiments so frequently expressed in the city parishes, the London corporation, and in parliamentary debates, to say nothing of the 1,100 pages of *Histriomastix*. The quality had indeed received some brushings of late.

The final classification of the censoring activities of the Master of the Revels was the suppression of personal satire on the stages in London. This was a very tricky chore. The Master had, essentially, two problems: first, was there satire in the performance which had not been apparent in the text? and second, was the person or persons ridiculed sufficiently influential to count? Because of the first difficulty, the records we have of suppression for personal satire come mostly from actions taken after performance: most of the plays had scraped past the Master. Because of the second, the Master had to make nice estimates of prominence and influence, and modern critics are sometimes fooled into imagining satire of the King or members of the Privy Council because they have seen allowed satire of nonentities like Thomas Dekker and Captain Hannam and Ben Jonson in 1601, or Agnes Howe or Ann Elsdon, or enemies of the establishment like William Prynne. It was the favored and the influential whom the Master of the Revels and the Privy Council tried to protect, not just anyone whom the players chose to ridicule.

This distinction between impersonation of ordinary Londoners and impersonation of gentlemen of good desert and quality is exemplified in the minute of a letter sent to certain Justices of the Peace in Middlesex by the Privy Council on 10 May 1601:

> We do understand that certain players that use to recite their plays at the Curtain in Moorfields do represent upon the stage in their interludes the persons of gentlemen of good desert and quality that are yet alive under obscure manner, but yet in such sort as all the hearers may take notice both of the matter and the per-

sons that are meant thereby. This being a thing very un-fit, offensive, and contrary to such direction as have been heretofore taken that no plays should be openly showed but such as first were perused and allowed and that might minister no occasion of offense or scandal we do hereby require you that you do forthwith forbid those players to whomsoever they appertain, that do play at the Curtain in Moorfields to represent any such play and that you will examine them who made that play and to show the same unto you, and as you in your discretion shall think the same unfit to be publicly showed to forbid them from henceforth to play the same either privately or publicly, and if upon view of the said play you shall find the subject so odious and inconvenient as is informed, we require you to take bond of the chiefest of them to answer their rash and indiscreet behavior before us.[42]

Even the favored and influential might be impersonated, it would appear, if the impersonation were complimentary. An instance of such a presentation is recorded in a letter of 1599. On 26 October of that year Rowland Whyte wrote from the Strand in London to Sir Robert Sydney:

Two days ago, the overthrow of *Turnholt* [Turnhout] was acted upon a stage, and all your names used that were at it; especially Sir *Fra.Veres*, and he that played that part got a beard resembling his, and a watchet Satin Doublet, with Hose trimmed with silver lace. You was also introduced, killing, slaying, and overthrowing the *Spaniards*, and honorable mention made of your service, in seconding Sir *Francis Vere*, being engaged."[43]

42. Chambers, *Elizabethan Stage*, IV, 332, from *The Acts of the Privy Council of England.*
43. Arthur Collins, *Letters and Memorials of State*, London, 1746, II, 136. Rowland Whyte's interest in the actor's attempt to suggest the person of Sir Francis Vere was probably characteristic of the gossip of London audiences about plays. Twenty-five years later John Chamberlain reported the gossip about a less innocent play, *A Game at Chess* (which he had not seen himself). He reports the

But innocent or admiring impersonation was not the concern of the Master of the Revels as he read the play manuscript, nor of the other officials who took action later after a libelous piece had been performed.

In Herbert's time, it was probably personal satire which the Master had in mind when he cut the anonymous lost play called *The Widow's Prize* on 25 January, 1624/25. "For the Prince's company, a new play called *The Widow's Prize*, which containing much abusive matter was allowed of by me on condition that my reformations were observed."[44]

He was more explicit and more severe in the case of the comedy called *The Ball* written by James Shirley, regular playwright for Queen Henrietta's company, and he expressed his disapproval to Christopher Beeston, manager of the company and owner of their theatre, the Phoenix.

18 November 1632. In the play of *The Ball*, written by Shirley and acted by the Queen's players, there were divers personated so naturally, both of lords and others of the court, that I took it ill, and would have forbidden the play, but that Beeston promised many things which I found fault withall should be left out and that he would not suffer it to be done by the poet any more, who deserves to be punished; and the first that offends in this kind of poets or players shall be sure of public punishment.[45]

Edmund Malone, in his notes from the original manuscript of the office book, recorded that this play had been

---

talk about the impersonation of Count Gondomer, the hated Spanish ambassador, "They counterfeited his person to the life, with all his graces and faces, and had gotten (they say) a cast suit of his apparel for the purpose, and his litter, wherein the world says lacked nothing but a couple of asses to carry it, and Sir G. Peter or Sir T. Mathew to bear him company" (N. E. McClure, ed., *The Letters of John Chamberlain*, Philadelphia, 1939, ii, 578).

44. Adams, *Herbert*, pp. 18–19.
45. Ibid., p. 19.

licensed to be acted two days earlier, on the 16th. Both the dates and the phrase "personated so naturally" suggest that Herbert had not recognized the personal satire in the manuscript, but it was brought out by the actors, and this interpretation is also consonant with his threat of future punishment of "poets or players." In these notes on his action Herbert makes it clear when he says that those who were so naturally personated were "both of lords and others of the court" that it was the rank and influence of those impersonated which made the satire of poet and players culpable.

The importance to the Master of considering the standing and influence of the individual satirized is illustrated in his allowance of another play for Queen Henrietta's company six months later. He wrote,

> Received for allowing of *The Tale of the Tub*, Vitru Hoop's part wholly struck out, and the motion of the tub, by command from my lord chamberlain; exceptions being taken against it by Inigo Jones, Surveyor of the King's Works as a personal injury unto him. May 7, 1633 . . . £2.[46]

The Lord Chamberlain, Sir Henry's superior, did not intercede for just anyone; Inigo Jones stood high at this time as architect of the principal Whitehall buildings, including the Banqueting Hall, designer of Court masques, and one of the authorities in art matters for the art-loving King Charles. He was in the category of "lords and others of the court" in *The Ball*, not of William Prynne and Henry Burton.

Sometimes the weight of authority came down on players and playwrights for their mixture of individual satire and political satire of projects favored by the government in which those individuals were involved. Such a mixture was found in the lost anonymous play called *The Whore*

46. Ibid., *Herbert*, p. 19.

New Vamped, which must have evaded the vigilance of
Sir Henry, though neither Malone nor Chalmers copied
his license. At any rate Prince Charles's [II] company was
already performing the play in the troubled autumn of
1639 when the Privy Council heard about it and took steps
against all concerned. Their action is recorded in the min-
utes of the meeting of 29 September 1639. The "Cain"
mentioned in the account of the performance was Andrew
Cane, the leader of the company, and at the time the most
talked about comedian in London.

> Order of the King in Council. Complaint was this day
> made that the stage-players of the Red Bull [have for]
> many days together acted a scandalous and libelous [play
> in which] they have audaciously reproached and in a
> libel [represented] and personated not only some of the
> aldermen of the [city of London] and some other per-
> sons of quality, but also scandalized and libeled the
> whole profession of proctors belonging to the Court of
> [Probate], and reflected upon the present Government.
> Ordered that the Attorney-General be hereby prayed
> forthwith to call before him, not only the poet who
> made the play and the actors that played the same, but
> also the person that licensed it, and having diligently
> examined the truth of the said complaint, to proceed
> roundly against such of them as he shall find have been
> faulty, and to use such effectual ex[pedition] to bring
> them to sentence, as that their exemplary punishment
> may [check] such insolencies betimes.
>
> Exceptions taken to the play above referred to. In the
> play called "The Whore New Vamped" where there
> was mention of the new duty on wines, one personating
> a justice of the peace says to Cain, "Sirrah, I'll have you
> before the alderman"; whereto Cain replies, "The alder-
> man, the alderman is a base, drunken, sottish knave, I
> care not for the alderman, I say the alderman is a base,
> drunken, sottish knave." Another says, "How now Sir-
> rah, what alderman do you speak of?" Then Cain says,
> "I mean alderman [William Abell], the blacksmith in

Holborn"; says the other, "Was not he a Vintner?" Cain answers, "I know no other." In another part of the play one speaking of projects and patents that he had got, mentions among others "a patent of 12d a piece upon every proctor and proctor's man who was not a knave." Said another, "Was there ever known any proctor but he was an arrant knave?"[47]

The Privy Council is refreshingly explicit in stating the grounds for objecting to the popular play at the Red Bull. *The Whore New Vamped* was offensive not because *somebody* was impersonated, but because it had "personated . . . some of the aldermen of the city of London and some other *persons of quality*." It was doubly censorable because it had also "scandalized and libeled the whole profession of proctors belonging to the Court of Probate, and *reflected upon the present government*." If it had been regularly licensed, the Master of the Revels ("the person that licensed it") was also culpable.

The character of the quotations from *The Whore New Vamped*, naming no characters but using the name of the best-known actor in the company, strongly suggests that the Privy Council did not have the manuscript but were taking testimony from a member of the audience at the Red Bull, perhaps an informer of the type authorized by the 1606 Statute of Oaths. The offense seems serious, and certainly the prompt and sweeping action of the Privy Council indicates that they thought so, but there is no further record of the play. The company was not disgraced, for a few weeks later, in the month of November, they performed three plays at court, for which the accused Andrew Cane received payment in the following May. But even supposing that the report was exaggerated or that the informer was a liar, the reaction of the Council and the

47. William Douglas Hamilton, ed., *Calendar of State Papers, Domestic, Series of the Reign of Charles I, 1639,* London, 1873, pp. 529–30.

nature of the report on which they acted show clearly what this high authority considered to be "scandalous and libelous."

All these examples of the activities and the power of the Master of the Revels were well known to the dramatists preparing plays for the London companies. They were themselves in personal danger if their plays violated the standard restrictions, as shown in the cases of Nashe and *The Isle of Dogs*, Jonson, Chapman, and Marston in *Eastward Ho*, and Middleton in *A Game at Chess*. But the threat of inconvenience, financial loss, and actual imprisonment to the managers and players was even more constant. As we have seen, there were various degrees of severity in the actions taken against offenders in the theatres. Least severe were the inconvenient required alterations in the text of the play which the company had bought. This requirement is seen in the cited examples of *The Seaman's Honest Wife*, *The Widow's Prize*, *The Tamer Tamed*, *The King and the Subject*, and *The Tale of the Tub*. More severe and inconvenient for the players were the Master's orders that the performance of the play be stopped, as in the instances of *The Loyal Subject* and *The Tamer Tamed*. Still more severe was the requirement that the play be stopped and the theatre closed, as in the case of *The Isle of Dogs* and *A Game at Chess*. And in extreme cases the Master went so far as to stop the play, confiscate the manuscript, close the theatre, send actors or dramatist or both to prison, and appoint a new manager for the company. The clearest example of such extreme punishment is the case of William Beeston and the actors of the King and Queen's Young company at the Cockpit in Drury Lane in the spring of 1640.

William Beeston had succeeded his father, Christopher, as manager of the company at the Phoenix in October 1638, and in the spring of 1640 his company had produced a play commenting on current political affairs and not licensed by the Master of the Revels. At this time many people were deeply disturbed by the King's military expedition to Berwick to suppress the Scottish revolt against the Prayer Book and the bishops, and by the failure of the expedition. This was the situation very foolishly dealt with in the play William Beeston had staged at the Phoenix. Herbert recorded his actions in his office book.

> On Monday the 4 May 1640 William Beeston was taken by a messenger and committed to the Marshalsea by my Lord Chamberlain's warrant for playing a play without license. The same day the company at the Cockpit was commanded by my Lord Chamberlain's warrant to forbear playing, for playing when they were forbidden by me and for other disobedience, and lay still Monday, Tuesday, and Wednesday. On Thursday, at my Lord Chamberlain's entreaty I gave them their liberty and upon their petition of submission subscribed by the players I restored them to their liberty on Thursday.
> The play I called for and, forbidding the playing of it, keep the book because it had relation to the passages of the King's journey into the North and was complained of by his Majesty to me with command to punish the offenders.[48]

The two warrants from the Lord Chamberlain mentioned by Herbert are recorded in the warrant books of the Lord Chamberlain's office, the first ordering the suppression of this play and all other plays at the Cockpit, and the second ordering the imprisonment of the leaders of the company: "A warrant of apprehension and commitment to the Marshalsea of William Beeston, George Estotville, and [Michael] Moon [or Mohun] upon the above specified occasion."[49] Severe as this punishment sounds, there was more for William Beeston, who was probably the principal culprit. It is not known how long he was allowed to pine

48. Adams, *Herbert*, p. 66.
49. *Malone Society Collection*, II, part 3, 394.

in the Marshalsea, but he was ousted from his position as manager of the King and Queen's Young company, and before the end of the next month William Davenant was officially appointed by the Lord Chamberlain to take his place, and the members of the company were ordered "that they obey the said Mr. Davenant and follow his orders and directions as they will answer the contrary."[50]

Probably only a few managers and dramatists suffered punishments as severe as William Beeston's, but they all knew that such punishments were within the Master's powers. The inhibitions which such knowledge produced are not difficult to imagine. They affected what the professional dramatists wrote for the companies; they affected what the managers and the sharing members of the company were willing to accept; and they affected what the bookkeeper did to the manuscript as he worked on the prompt copy and the players' sides. The number of recorded plays which nevertheless dared to transgress the standards of the Master of the Revels may seem to be large. But when the number is considered in the light of the two thousand or so plays which were probably written in England between 1590 and 1642, it is evident that players and playwrights ordinarily took pains to avoid those words, subjects, and attitudes proscribed by the Master of the Revels.

50. Ibid., 395.

CHAPTER VIII

Collaboration

COLLABORATION AND REVISION were related activities of the professional dramatists since each required one author to accommodate his writing to that of another. But since the analysis of each activity must be complicated, it is expedient to consider them in consecutive chapters rather than in a single discussion.

The two assignments are frequently entangled in the printed texts which have come down to us. This entanglement is most familiar in the plays of the Beaumont and Fletcher folios of 1647 and 1679 in which Massinger evidently had a hand. The evidence is overwhelming that Beaumont had nothing to do with most of the plays in these two collections; there is no doubt that Massinger and Fletcher several times collaborated, and no doubt that Massinger sometimes revised the work of Fletcher. But for several plays it is doubtful whether Philip Massinger collaborated or revised or did both.

Collaboration is inevitably a common expedient in such

a cooperative enterprise as the production of a play. Every performance in the commercial theatres from 1590 to 1642 was itself essentially a collaboration: it was the joint accomplishment of dramatists, actors, musicians, costumers, prompters (who made alterations in the original manuscript) and—at least in the later theatres—of managers.

To the professional dramatist all this cooperation was very familiar; he had it in mind when he began to write. Even amateurs like Lodowick Carlell and Thomas Goffe knew a good deal about it. In an enterprise which could get nowhere without the give and take of joint efforts, collaboration between two or more writers on the original script was to be expected. Long before 1590 it had begun.

Even before the appearance of the regular commercial theatres in London collaboration was a well-known phenomenon in the drama, and all students know of the joint work of Norton and Sackville on *Gorboduc*, of Gascoigne and Kinwelmershe on *Jocasta*, and of Wilmot, Stafford, Hatton, Noel, and "G. Al." on *Gismond of Salerne*. A similar collaboration just before the beginning of our period was that of Hughes, Bacon, Trotte, Fulbeck, Lancaster, Yelverton, Penroodock, and Flower on *The Misfortunes of Arthur*.

All these compositions were prepared for amateur production, but before 1590 comparatively little is known of the men who wrote plays for the professional companies: the large majority of all English plays before the reign of Elizabeth are anonymous, and even from 1558 to 1590 the authors of most plays are unknown. In such circumstances it is not surprising that most of the early Elizabethan plays by named writers—extant or lost—were prepared for production at an Oxford or Cambridge college, at a public school, at one of the inns of court, at some company hall, or in some private house.

When we come to the period of the professional theatre

in the reigns of Elizabeth and James, collaboration has become one of the notable features of the activities of the professional dramatists; in the days of Charles I it falls off somewhat.

Since records of authorship are so sparse for the period as a whole, we can only guess at the precise amount of collaboration involved in the plays, but the evidence still extant shows that it must have been large. We know the titles (often no more) of about 1,500 plays from 1590 to 1642. For about 370 we know nothing at all about authorship. For the remaining 1,100 or so, we have evidence that between 1/5 and 1/6 contained the work of more than one man as either collaborator, reviser, or provider of additional matter. If we consider the professional dramatists only, this proportion is much too low, for the total includes over 200 amateur plays, which after 1590 were seldom collaborated, and it includes many plays about whose authorship we have only a title-page statement, which tended, as a number of known examples show, to simplify the actual circumstances of composition. Altogether the evidence suggests that it would be reasonable to guess that as many as half of the plays by professional dramatists in the period incorporated the writing at some date of more than one man. In the case of the 282 plays mentioned in Henslowe's diary (far and away the most detailed record of authorship that has come down to us) nearly two-thirds are the work of more than one man.

The first recorded collaboration in our period was *A Looking Glass for London and England,* the joint work of Robert Greene and Thomas Lodge, acted in or about 1590 probably for the Queen's company. The play was published in 1594 and a number of times thereafter, and both the title pages and the entry in the Stationers' Register assert that it was the work of Greene and Lodge. This collaboration evidently remained viable for a long time:

not only are there five editions extant, but the play was still in repertory from twenty to thirty years after it was written.[1]

Probably acted about the same time as *A Looking Glass for London and England,* and certainly first published in the same year as that play, was *Dido, Queen of Carthage,* whose 1594 title page says, "Played by the Children of Her Majesty's Chapel. Written by Christopher Marlowe and Thomas Nash. Gent." The play had nothing like the extended stage life of *A Looking Glass,* and there have been suggestions by Marlowe enthusiasts that Nashe's contribution may have been that of continuator or editor rather than collaborator. In the present state of style-identification studies the extent or timing of Nashe's work cannot be determined.

But these collaborations are known only from chance recordings on title pages (many title pages in this decade name no author at all) and the chance preservation of a theatre manuscript. It is not until we get to Henslowe's detailed records of his payments for plays that the full evidence of the extent of joint authorship is revealed. The change is striking: for 1597 *The Annals of English Drama* lists 23 plays, six with single authors, one collaboration, and 16 of unknown authorship; for 1598 the full details of Henslowe's accounts are available in addition to the publication and allusion testimony, and together they give a much more complete account of what was actually going on in the London theatres. For 1598 the same *Annals* lists 46 plays, 16 by single named playwrights, 20 collaborations by two or more, and only ten whose author or authors are unknown. Theatres and writers did not change in 1598; the proportion of records preserved changed. There is no reason to think that the true situation in 1597 was different from that in 1598.

1. See *Modern Philology,* xxx (August 1932), 29–51, and the Malone Society reprint of the play.

A few of Henslowe's many payments for collaborations will illustrate the prevalence of this method of play-writing; they also illustrate the frequency with which these records reveal the existence of plays not known from any other sources and the activities of dramatists inadequately known from printed texts and occasional allusions.

In August 1598 Henslowe bought a finished play for the Lord Admiral's company: "Lent unto the company the 18 of August 1598 to buy a book called Hot Anger Soon Cold of Mr. Porter, Mr. Chettle, and Benjamin Jonson in full payment the sum of . . . £6."[2] Ben Jonson, who has more to say about himself and who published his plays with greater care than any other dramatist of his time, carefully avoided all mention of this play, and it would be unknown without this record.

The very next day Henslowe was making payments on another otherwise unknown play for the Lord Admiral's men.

Lent unto the company the 19 of August 1598 to pay unto Mr. Wilson, Munday, and Dekker in part of payment of a book called Chance Medley the sum of £4 5s in this manner Wilson 30 shillings, Chettle 30 shillings, Munday 25 shillings. I say . . . £4 5s.

But there was still another collaborator involved in *Chance Medley*, for five days later a further payment was entered: "Paid unto Mr. Drayton the 24 of August 1598 in full payment of a book called Chance Medley the sum of . . . 35s."[3] A somewhat more common method of payment to the company's dramatists is illustrated in the accounts for the lost and otherwise unknown play called *Robert II, or the Scot's Tragedy.*

Lent unto Thomas Downton the 3 of September 1599 to lend unto Thomas Dekker, Benjamin Jonson, Harry

2. Foakes and Rickert, p. 96.
3. Ibid., pp. 96 and 97.

Chettle and other gentleman in earnest of a play called Robert the second King of Scot's Tragedy, the sum of . . . 40s.

Lent unto Samuel Rowley and Robert Shaw the 15 of September 1599 to lend in earnest of a book called The Scot's Tragedy unto Thomas Dekker and Harry Chettle, the sum of . . . 20s.

Lent unto Harry Chettle the 16 of September in earnest of a book called The Scot's Tragedy, the sum of . . . 10s.

Lent unto William Borne the 27 of September 1599 to lend unto Benjamin Jonson in earnest of a book called The Scot's Tragedy, the sum of . . . 20s.[4]

Robert II, or the Scot's Tragedy, like *Hot Anger Soon Cold*, is a dramatic effort of which the redoubtable Ben did not choose to inform posterity, and these payments are the only records of its existence.

Seven months later in March 1599/1600 another cooperating group of dramatists were paid for their work on a play, but the entry forms are somewhat different. The first entry is written not in Henslowe's hand, but in that of William Birde, one of the leading members of the Lord Admiral's company, who signed the acknowledgment. The second is the usual form of entry in Henslowe's hand; the third is also in Henslowe's hand, but it is signed by the actor-dramatist Samuel Rowley, another leading sharer in the company, who authorized the payment and apparently took charge of the money.

Received of Mr. Henslowe the one of March to pay to Henry Chettle, Thomas Dekker, William Haughton, and John Day for a book called The Seven Wise Masters the sum of . . . 40s.

W. Birde

Lent unto Samuel Rowley the 8 of March 1599 to pay unto Harry Chettle and John Day in full payment for

4. Ibid., p. 124.

a book called The Seven Wise Masters the sum of . . . 50*s*.

Samuel Rowley

Lent unto Harry Chettle the 2 of March in earnest of a book called The Seven Wise Masters the sum of . . . 30*s*.[5]

Other collaborations for which Henslowe paid involved plays which made their way into print and are now available in various editions. But the diary sometimes gives information which significantly alters the statements on the original title pages. In 1607 *The Famous History of Sir Thomas Wyatt* was published. The play concerns the development of the Lady Jane Gray faction, the Wyatt Rebellion, and the suppression and punishment of those concerned, and the title page of the 1607 quarto gives the information, "As it was played by the Queen's Majesty's Servants. Written by Thomas Dekker and John Webster." But Henslowe's payments show that the title page gives only part of the truth. Henslowe did make his payments in behalf of the Earl of Worcester's company (the troupe whose name was changed on the accession of James to Queen Anne's company or Her Majesty's Servants) and Dekker and Webster were indeed concerned with the composition, but there were others unnamed on the title page:

Lent unto John Thare the 15 of October 1602 to give unto Harry Chettle, Thomas Dekker, Thomas Heywood, and Mr. Smith and Mr. Webster in earnest of a play called Lady Jane the sum of . . . 50*s*.

Lent unto Thomas Heywood the 21 of October 1602 to pay unto Mr. Dekker, Chettle, Smith, Webster, and Heywood in full payment of their play of Lady Jane the sum of . . . £5 10*s*.

5. Ibid., p. 131.

> Lent unto John Duke the 27 of October 1602 to give
> unto Thomas Dekker in earnest of the second part of
> Lady Jane the sum of . . . 5s.

> Lent unto John Duke the 6 of November 1602 for to
> make a suit of satin of _____ for the play of the Over
> Throw of the Rebels, the sum of . . . £5.[6]

The payment of five poets for collaborating on the same
play is not unusual in the diary, nor is the use of two different titles for the same piece. Six months earlier in the same
year a group of five playwrights, including two of the
authors of *Lady Jane*, were paid on behalf of another company, the Lord Admiral's men, for another collaboration.

> Lent unto the company the 22 of May 1602 to give unto
> Anthony Munday and Michaell Drayton, Webster and
> the rest, Middleton, in earnest of a book called Caesar's
> Fall the sum of . . . £5.

> Lent unto Thomas Downton the 29 of May 1602 to pay
> Thomas Dekker, Drayton, Middleton, and Webster and
> Munday in full payment for their play called Two
> Shapes, the sum of . . . £3.[7]

In a modern impresario's books the two different titles
would strongly suggest two plays, but in Shakespeare's
time this variation in names was not unusual before the
play had been acted—or sometimes (as in the cases of
Othello, *Henry IV*, *Twelfth Night* and *Much Ado*) even
after. The proximity of the two dates, the identity of the
five names, and the fact that the first payment was "in
earnest" and the second "in full payment" demonstrate
that *Caesar's Fall* and *The Two Shapes* were one play.

Most of the plays of joint authorship so far noted are
no longer extant, and several would have been totally unknown without Henslowe's diary. But collaboration was a
common phenomenon of the period, and well-known plays

6. Ibid., pp. 218 and 219.
7. Ibid., pp. 201 and 202.

were also collaborations, though sometimes this would never have been known from their title pages alone.

Dekker's play, *The Honest Whore*, was rather popular, at least with readers, for it went through five early quarto editions—more than most of the plays of Shakespeare. The title page of the 1604 quarto reads:

> The Honest Whore, With the Humours of the Patient Man and the Longing Wife.
> Tho: Dekker.

The later editions of 1605, 1615, 1616, and the undated one all display the same statement of authorship on their title pages, but a diary payment shows that Dekker did not work alone.

> Lent unto the company to give unto Thomas Dekker and Middleton in earnest of their play called The Patient Man and The Honest Whore the sum of . . . £5.[8]

The number of collaborations attested by Henslowe's records is very great. Indeed they show that the majority of the plays he bought for both the Lord Admiral's company and for the Earl of Worcester's men were not individual compositions but collaborations. This troublesome fact has inclined a number of critics to assert that collaboration was a peculiar feature of Henslowe's policy and imposed by him upon the companies he financed. Such a distinction is highly improbable; the significant difference among the companies is rather that for the other London troupes there are almost no records at all, outside government and legal documents, literary allusions, and play publications. If the theatrical archives now preserved at Dulwich College had been destroyed, as the financial records of all *non*-Henslowe companies have been, then we would know as little of the repertories and purchasing policies of the Lord Admiral's men and the Earl of Worcester's company as we do of those of the Lord Chamberlain's.

8. Ibid., p. 209.

But joint composition was common in the repertories of the other London troupes of actors, though the surviving evidence is scanty in the total absence of their own financial records.

Shortly after Henslowe advanced money for Prince Henry's company (the new Jacobean name for the old Lord Admiral's troupe) to pay for Dekker and Middleton's collaboration on *The Honest Whore*, Ben Jonson was working with George Chapman and John Marston on a play for the Queen's Revels company at Blackfriars. Jonson's arrogance and belligerence would appear to have made him one of the most unlikely collaborators among the Elizabethan dramatists, but he had been involved in joint authorship for Henslowe in *Hot Anger Soon Cold*, *Robert II, or The Scot's Tragedy*, and *The Page of Plymouth*, and he had worked on another man's play when he wrote additions to *The Spanish Tragedy* for the Admiral's men in 1602.

The play he created with Chapman and Marston was *Eastward Ho!* whose production got the company and the authors into trouble. Jonson himself spoke of this collaboration and of the consequent dangers to the authors. In his conversations with William Drummond years later, he told his host that

> He was dilated by Sir James Murray to the King for writing something against the Scots in a play, Eastward Ho, and voluntarily imprisoned himself with Chapman and Marston, who had written it amongst them. The report was that they should then [have] had their ears cut and noses.[9]

Jonson evidently took collaboration for granted as a common method of composition in his time and felt no shame or hesitancy in acknowledging his participation to

9. C. H. Herford and Percy and Evelyn Simpson, *Ben Jonson*, Oxford, 1925–1953, I, 140.

Drummond. In his address "To the Readers," prepared for the first quarto of *Sejanus* a couple of years after its performance by the King's company at the Globe with William Shakespeare in the cast, he wrote:

> Lastly I would inform you that this book, in all its numbers, is not the same with that which was acted on the public stage, wherein a second pen had good show: in place of which I have rather chosen to put weaker (and no doubt less pleasing) of mine own, than to defraud so happy a genius of his own right by my loathed usurpation.

Perhaps only Jonson, with his growing preoccupation with posterity, would have gone so far as painstakingly to weed out of his text all the words of his collaborator, whoever he was, and to replace them with his own. This meticulous effort is quite like that which he expended on the 1601 text of *Every Man in his Humour* to transform it into the version published in 1616. These examples are widely known, but it is often not observed that in textual concern with his plays Jonson was unique. He is the only active dramatist among Shakespeare's contemporaries who expended anything remotely approaching this effort on his play texts.

But though Jonson was not typical in his concern for his text, he was normal enough in his familiarity with collaboration. Not only had he himself been involved in five or more collaborations, but he took the prevalence of collaboration sufficiently for granted to make him think it worthwhile to point out specifically that *Volpone*, which the King's men had acted in 1606, was *not* a collaboration. In the prologue to this play he wrote:

> 'Tis known, five weeks fully penned it
> From his own hand, without a coadjutor,
> Novice, journeyman, or tutor.

It is tempting to speculate on the varieties of collaboration which a meticulous writer like Jonson intended to imply in the words "coadjutor," "novice," "journeyman," "tutor." But it is safer to be content to note Jonson's obvious assumption that the Globe audience would think it likely enough that more than one dramatist had been involved in the writing of *Volpone*.

By the time Jonson published his prologue for *Volpone*, the mostly widely advertised collaborators in Elizabethan drama had begun writing plays for the London theatres. Whether Fletcher had a hand in the preparation of *The Woman Hater* for the Children of Paul's or *The Knight of the Burning Pestle* for the Queen's Revels at Blackfriars may be doubted by some, as is Beaumont's participation in *The Woman's Prize*. But by 1608 or 1609, when the King's company performed *Philaster*, this writing partnership was established and these collaborating dramatists were producing for the King's men in the last years of Shakespeare's active participation in the affairs of the company *The Captain, The Coxcomb, Cupid's Revenge, Philaster, A King and No King,* and *The Maid's Tragedy,* and others.

This most famous collaboration must have come to an end in 1613 or 1614 when Beaumont married an heiress and apparently retired to her estates in Kent, but Fletcher wrote regularly for the King's company until his death in August 1625. The title of the 1647 folio *Comedies and Tragedies Written by Francis Beaumont and John Fletcher, Gentlemen* has long been recognized as grossly misleading, since at least thirty of the plays were written after Beaumont's death. About the time of the publication of the 1647 folio, Sir Aston Cokayne wrote a verse letter to his cousin Charles Cotton protesting that

> Had *Beaumont* lived when this edition came
> Forth, and beheld his ever living name
> Before plays that he never writ, how he

Had frown'd and blushed at such impiety!

　　·　　　　·　　　　·　　　　·　　　　·

And my good friend old *Philip Massinger*
With *Fletcher* writ in some that we see there.[10]

In the same volume Cokayne printed another set of protesting verses to the publishers of the folio, Moseley and Robinson, and finally a third set making even greater claims for the collaboration of Massinger with Fletcher.

> An Epitaph on Mr. John Fletcher, and Mr. Philip Massinger, who lie buried both in one Grave in St. Mary Overies Church in Southwark.
>
> In the same grave Fletcher was buried here
> Lies the stage-poet Philip Massinger:
> Plays they did write together, were great friends
> And now one grave includes them at their ends:
> So whom on earth nothing did part, beneath
> Here (in their fames) they lie, in spight of death.

All Fletcher's plays written after 1616 were, so far as we can tell now, the property of the King's men, and this powerful company succeeded in withholding all but one of them from publication until after the closing of the theatres in 1642. For these plays there are no quartos which might have acknowledged Massinger's work on their title pages, only the blanket and false attribution of the folio of 1647. Many analyses of these folio plays have been made in the last century, and though they by no means show unanimity in their findings, the best of them presents reasonable evidence that Massinger's work is to be found in 19 plays of the folios.

Even more suggestive of the importance of collaboration for the leading Jacobean company is the fact that *most* of the plays published at one time or another under Fletcher's name show evidence of the writing of another man, whether Massinger, Beaumont, Field, Rowley, or

10. *A Chair of Golden Poems*, London, 1658, pp. 91–93.

209

Shirley.[11] Such evidence is much too extensive and complex for consideration here, but it gives overwhelming support to the view that joint authorship was a commonplace in the repertory of the King's company, at least from 1616 to 1642. In this period, 46 plays of the Beaumont and Fletcher folios can be shown to have been performed by the King's men (compared with 16 from the Shakespeare folio).[12]

The vogue of these collaborated plays at court was equally great. The majority of the records of the performances of selected plays before members of the royal family and the court do not give the name of the play acted, but there remain a number of records of such performances by the King's company between 1616 and 1642 that do give play titles. Of the performances at court of plays listed by name, 42 performances (including repetitions) are of plays from the Beaumont and Fletcher folios, compared to 18 performances of plays written by Shakespeare, and 7 performances of plays written by Jonson. The not uncommon notion that collaborated plays were inferior and probably notable only in the Henslowe companies is thoroughly exploded by these records of the productions of the most distinguished and powerful company in London in the reigns of James I and Charles I.

At the same time other less familiar collaborations were being offered in various London theatres. In most instances the fact that the plays were collaborations is known only from the title pages, and the examples of *Sir Thomas Wyatt*, *The Honest Whore*, and *Sejanus* have shown that the information on single-author title pages is often incomplete. Nevertheless on the title pages or in the printed

11. See Cyrus Hoy, "The Shares of Fletcher and His Collaborators in the Beaumont and Fletcher Canon," *Studies in Bibliography, Papers of the Bibliographical Society of the University of Virginia,* vols. VIII-XV, Charlottesville, Va., 1956–1962.

12. See *Jacobean and Caroline Stage,* I, 108–34.

epistles the publishers indicate that in the first decade of King James's reign John Day, William Rowley, and George Wilkins were collaborating on *The Travels of the Three English Brothers* for Queen Anne's company; Dekker and Middleton on *The Roaring Girl* for Prince Henry's men at the Fortune; Beaumont and Fletcher on *Cupid's Revenge* for the Children of the Queen's Revels; Heywood and William Rowley on *Fortune by Land and Sea* for Queen Anne's men at the Red Bull; and Beaumont and Fletcher on *The Scornful Lady* for the Queen's Revels company.

One of the most active collaborators in this decade and a little later was a man whose dramatic compositions have not yet been noticed, the actor-dramatist Nathan Field. Because of their intimate association with the company and its needs, such men who were both players and playwrights had special contributions to make in joint compositions, and there is a notably high proportion of collaboration in the known work of Samuel Rowley, William Rowley, Heywood, and Field.

Nathan Field, the son of a Puritan and the brother of a bishop, began his stage career at the age of twelve or thirteen when he became one of the boy actors in the Queen's Revels troupe at Blackfriars, and until his early death at the age of thirty-three or thereabouts he was conspicuous on the London stage; Ben Jonson and several later writers pair him with Richard Burbage as one of the great actors of his time. His plays published as by Field alone are *Woman is a Weathercock* and *Amends for Ladies*, the first for his boy company and the second for the Lady Elizabeth's company, of which Field became one of the principals. In this company he was both a leading actor and a dramatist, as he was later in the King's company. Some of his correspondence with Philip Henslowe in both capacities has been preserved. At the end of June 1613, Field was writing a play with Robert Daborne for his company. The name of the play is unknown. Field wrote to Henslowe:

> Mr. Daborne and I have spent a great deal of time in conference about this plot which will make as beneficial a play as hath come these seven years. It is out of his love he detains it for us, only £10 is desired in hand, for which we will be bound to bring you in the play finished upon the first day of August. . . .

The collaborated play about which Robert Daborne later wrote to Henslowe on 30 July 1613 was probably this same lost work with Field. Daborne was, as usual, trying to get another advance from Henslowe on an unfinished play. He said, in part: ". . . I pray, sir, of your much friendship do me one courtesy more till Thursday when we deliver in our play to you as to lend me twenty shillings. . . ."[13]

About the same year Field was involved in another collaboration for the Lady Elizabeth's company. The letter is undated, and the play, as usual, unnamed; it may have been a totally unknown play, and it may have been—as the name of Fletcher suggests—one of the pieces (possibly *The Honest Man's Fortune*) published together in the 1647 Beaumont and Fletcher folio. The vaguely allusive letter to Henslowe is written from jail by Field, with postscripts by Philip Massinger and Robert Daborne. At the moment of writing, the need for bail was more important to these dramatists than the name of their play.

> Mr. Henslowe:
> You understand our unfortunate extremity, and I do not think you so void of Christianity but that you would throw so much money into the Thames as we request now of you rather than endanger so many innocent lives. You know there is £10 more at least to be received of

13. W. W. Greg, ed., *Henslowe Papers*, London, 1907, pp. 84 and 74–75.

you for the play. We desire you to lend us £5 of that, which shall be allowed to you, without which we cannot be bailed, nor I play any more till this be dispatched. It will lose you £20 ere the end of next week besides the hinderance of the next new play. Pray, sir, consider our cases with humanity, and now give us cause to acknowledge you our true friend in time of need. We have intreated Mr. Davison to deliver this note, as well to witness your love as our promises and always acknowledgment to be ever

Your most thankful and loving friends,
Nat: Field

The money shall be abated out of the money remains for the play of Mr. Fletcher and ours.

Rob: Daborne

I have ever found you a true loving friend to me and in so small a suit it being honest I hope you will not fail us.

Philip Massinger

The letter was effective, for at the end appears the receipt, written in another hand:

Received by me Robert Davison of Mr. Henslowe for the use of Mr. Daborne, Mr. Field, Mr. Massinger the sum of £5.

Robert Davison.[14]

It is likely that during the years of his membership in the Lady Elizabeth's company Field was engaged in joint work on several plays with other writers for the company such as Massinger, Fletcher, Beaumont, Daborne, Tourneur, or Middleton.

In or about 1616 Field was taken into the premier London company, King James's men, in which he was prominent for the four or five remaining years of his life. T. W. Baldwin thinks that he succeeded to Shakespeare's shares

14. Ibid., pp. 65–67.

in the company,[15] and he certainly became a leading actor, several plays of this period showing that they were composed for dual male leads, a young man and an older man—almost certainly Nathan Field and Richard Burbage.

There is no doubt that he collaborated on certain of the company's plays and a very strong probability that he made some contribution to others. He certainly worked with Massinger on *The Fatal Dowry*, which was acted by the King's men at court in February 1631/32 and published later in the year, "As it hath been often Acted at the private house in Blackfriars, by His Majesty's servants. Written by P. M. and N. F."

Another collaboration for his company was the play about the notorious murder of the Dutch jeweler, John de Wely, in the household of Prince Maurice in 1616. It was probably written soon after the event, as was the similar timely play about Dutch affairs, *Sir John van Olden Barnavelt*, composed by Fletcher and Massinger and acted by the King's men at the Globe in August 1619. Nathan Field's similarly topical play for the company is lost—as was *Sir John van Olden Barnavelt* until the manuscript was discovered in the late nineteenth century. The manuscript of Field's collaboration was still extant in 1654, when it was entered by Humphrey Moseley in the Stationers' Register: "A play called The Jeweler of Amsterdam or The Hague. By Mr. John Fletcher. Nathan Field, and Philip Massinger."

Other plays in which the collaborating hand of Nathan Field has been seen with some show of evidence by various scholars are *Four Plays in One*, *The Knight of Malta*, *The Laws of Candy*, *The Queen of Corinth*. Final demonstration of Field's contribution to these plays in the Beaumont and Fletcher folio is not yet possible, and it is unlikely that he would have made *major* contributions to all

15. T. W. Baldwin, *The Organization and Personnel of the Shakespearean Company*, Princeton, 1927, p. 51.

of them in the years when he was involved in his *known* collaborations and in developing his reputation as a leading London actor. There is no doubt, however, that he was a steady collaborator while he was a leading player in one or the other of his companies.

Another actor-dramatist-collaborator whose career was similar to Field's was William Rowley. They were writing in much the same years, but Rowley published a good deal more because his first known play appeared two years before Field's, and he lived five or six years longer. Both were more famous as actors than Shakespeare, Heywood, or Samuel Rowley. Field was known as a "juvenile" lead and Rowley as a comedian who specialized in the part of the fat clown. Indeed Rowley sometimes recorded his type roles himself, signing the address to the reader "Simplici-tie," the name of the clown in the piece, in his collaboration *The World Tossed at Tennis*, and listing in the dramatis personnae of *All's Lost by Lust* "Jaques, a simple clownish Gentleman, his sonne, personated by the Poet." Rowley also represented his company several times at court when he signed the receipt for payment for their performances before royalty.

Both Field and Rowley are known to have worked mostly in collaboration; both wrote nearly always for the companies in which they acted; both spent the last few years of their lives as patented members of the leading London company, King James's men; and finally both were collaborators with John Fletcher, the principal dramatist of the royal company.

For most of his acting career, however, Rowley was a member of Prince Charles's company, which had been known as the Duke of York's men before its patron became the heir apparent on the death of his elder brother, Henry, in November 1612. Rowley was one of the leaders of this company from before March 1610, when his name appeared second in the royal charter of the company, until about 1623, when he became a patented member of the King's company. It is not unlikely that he had had some early attachment to Queen Anne's troupe, for inexperienced actors were not normally made chartered members of prominent companies, as Rowley was in 1610. His two earliest compositions, both collaborations, were *The Travels of Three English Brothers*, acted by Queen Anne's men in 1607, and *Fortune by Land and Sea*, written with a patented member of the Queen's company, Thomas Heywood, and acted by that group a year or so later. One of his three unassisted plays, *A Shoemaker a Gentleman*, was probably also written for this same troupe about this time, but the evidence is not conclusive.

The largest group of plays by this actor-dramatist consists of those he wrote for the company he belonged to for the longest time, Prince Charles's men, who performed variously at the Curtain, the Phoenix, and the Red Bull. Rowley's earliest known work for them was his unassisted comedy, *Hymen's Holiday or Cupid's Vagaries*, which he and his fellows performed at court on 24 February 1611/12 and which was revived in another court performance 22 years later before the King and Queen, a performance which Sir Henry Herbert says was "Likte."

A few years later Rowley worked with Thomas Middleton on another play for his company, *A Fair Quarrell*, which was also acted before the King. The second issue of the play has three additional pages of comic material which are probably Rowley's. In his next collaboration Rowley brought in Philip Massinger as well as Middleton. The piece was called *The Old Law, or a New Way to Please You*, and though there is no clear indication of the company for which it was prepared, it may have been the Prince's men again.

In 1621 Rowley collaborated with John Ford and Thomas Dekker on a topical play for Prince Charles's company called *The Witch of Edmonton*. In fact there may have been other collaborators, for the title page of the only edition says "A known true story. Composed into a Tragi-Comedy by divers well-esteemed Poets; *William Rowley, Thomas Dekker, John Ford &c.*" This play too attained a performance before royalty in December 1621.

There are three plays by Rowley in the early twenties which were eventually acted by the Lady Elizabeth's company at the Phoenix. It is not entirely clear for which company Rowley originally wrote them, but since Lady Elizabeth's company succeeded Prince Charles's men at the Phoenix, since Christopher Beeston financed both companies in the early twenties, and since, for a short time at least, there seems to have been some sort of cooperation between them, it may have been that Rowley's break from his acting company in these three compositions was only apparent and not real. The three plays are his unaided composition, *All's Lost by Lust,* and the two collaborations with Thomas Middleton, *The Changeling* and *The Spanish Gypsy*. The first, though later acted by Lady Elizabeth's men, was written before that company was reorganized for its London career at the Phoenix, and in the dramatis personnae of the play Rowley identifies himself as the actor who created the role of Jaques. *The Changeling* is probably Rowley's best-known play, and the serious parts of the tragedy have impressed many critics, but it was the comic parts—probably Rowley's portion—which seemed most memorable to contemporaries. It was the comic material that gave the play its title, and the actors mentioned especially in seventeenth-century performances, William Robbins, Timothy Reade, and Thomas Sheppy, were all comedians.

The Spanish Gypsy, the latest of Rowley's six known collaborations with Thomas Middleton, was another successful play which was kept in the repertory of the Phoenix for at least sixteen years and was revived more than once after the Restoration.

In the late summer of 1624 Rowley was working with John Ford, Thomas Dekker, and John Webster, preparing for the stage a dramatization of two recent scandalous events in London, a matricide and a seduction. The play is unfortunately lost, but a good deal is known about it from the lawsuit brought by the son-in-law of the slandered woman. The piece was called *The Late Murder of the Son upon the Mother, or Keep the Widow Waking*, and it was acted at the Red Bull, probably by Prince Charles's company. If so, this was Rowley's last composition for his old company, with which he appears to have retained some sort of ambiguous connection.[16]

He became a member of the King's company and in the summer of 1623 collaborated with the company's principal dramatist, John Fletcher, on *The Maid in the Mill*, a play in which Rowley again acted one of the chief roles. He is also known to have created the role of the Archbishop of Spolato in Middleton's sensational hit, *A Game at Chess*, which ran for an unprecedented nine days at the Globe in August 1624.

It is likely that Rowley was involved in other compositions for his new company in 1624 and 1625, but the evidence is very confused. *A New Wonder, A Woman Never Vexed* was published six years after his death, in 1632, with a title page saying "Written by William Rowley, one of his Maiesties Servants," but with no indication of company and little of date. There are several other plays, mostly lost, which have been dubiously attributed to him in the Stationers' Register after the closing of the theatres or on Restoration title pages.

In the years in which Rowley was working with Middleton on plays for the Phoenix and then with Fletcher on plays for the King's men at Blackfriars and the Globe, other London theatres were commissioning plays for joint

16. See *Jacobean and Caroline Stage*, ii, 556.

authorship. For the company playing at the Fortune, Sir Henry Herbert, Master of the Revels, licensed on 22 October 1624 "For the Palsgrave's Company, a new play called *The Bristow Merchant*, written by Ford and Dekker." The play is lost, and nothing beyond this official license to be acted is known of it.

Probably also at the Red Bull, in addition to the sensational *Late Murder of the Son upon the Mother, or Keep the Widow Waking* by Dekker, Ford, Rowley, and Webster there was the collaboration of John Ford and Thomas Dekker on the lost play called *The Fairy Knight*. It was licensed for performance by Sir Henry Herbert on 11 June 1624, and though he did not mention the theatre, it is likely to have been the Red Bull.

Another Red Bull collaboration was a lost play written by Thomas Dekker and John Day. The entry in Sir Henry Herbert's office book in a version somewhat fuller than the one usually printed reads: "The Princes Players—A French tragedy of *The Bellman of Paris*, containing 40 sheets written by Thomas Dekker and John Day for the company of the Red Bull this 30 July 1623 . . . £1."[17] Of the five plays whose manuscript length is noted by Sir Henry, this is so much the longest that one wonders why. Is it caused by extra songs? Extra prologues or epilogues or an induction? Extensive revisions? General sprawl?

Also at the Red Bull they performed the joint composition of William Sampson and Gervase Markham called *Herod and Antipater*. Though Sampson wrote two other plays and Gervase Markham one, these two men were not professional dramatists, and *Herod and Antipater*, an otherwise unremarkable production, is one of the few collaborations known to have been written by amateurs for the professional acting companies in London.

17. From an independent transcript, probably made by Craven Ord, and now pasted into Halliwell-Phillipps's scrapbooks at the Folger Shakespeare Library.

At the Phoenix or Cockpit in Drury Lane, several collaborations are known to have been acted during these four or five years. Middleton and Rowley's *Changeling* in 1622, their *Spanish Gypsy* in 1623, and Rowley's further collaboration for his company with Dekker and Ford on *The Witch of Edmonton* have already been noticed. In addition the company had licensed on 2 October 1623 "A new comedy called *A Fault in Friendship* Written by Young Johnson and Brome." The play is lost, and Herbert's odd designation "Young Johnson" has given rise in the writings of the impressionable to a mythical play-writing son for Ben Jonson. The laureate had no son who survived to manhood; Herbert's designation makes an implication about the age of Richard Brome's collaborator, but not about his parentage.

A fifth joint composition known to have been prepared for a Phoenix production in these years was a curious piece called *The Sun's Darling*. When the Master of the Revels licensed it on 3 March 1623/24, he wrote: "For the Cockpit company *The Sun's Darling* in the nature of a masque by Dekker and Ford." And when a revision was published in 1656 the title page read *The Sun's Darling: A Moral Masque*. It is not a regular court masque, though the same title page adds the statement: "As it hath often been presented at Whitehall by their Majestys' Servants; and after at the Cock-pit in Drury Lane with great Applause." And it is not a simple moral allegory, though it has many of the features ordinarily found in such writings. Some of the planned stage effects would surely have overtaxed the resources of the Phoenix. However puzzling Dekker and Ford's composition may be, the Master of the Revels's license makes it clear enough that it was planned for regular production in Drury Lane.

After the death of Fletcher and the accession of Charles I, there appears to have been a decline in the number of collaborated plays prepared for the London stage. One must always be chary of such generalizations, for one can be perfectly certain that most of the evidence of theatrical activities has disappeared. Nevertheless it is clear enough that certain changed conditions in the London theatre world made collaboration less necessary.

Most obvious is the existence of large repertories of actable old plays. We know the titles of approximately 835 plays written between 1590 and 1625 inclusive; and at least 400 of them were presumably available to Caroline companies, since they are still available in print or in manuscript in the twentieth century.[18] Of the now well-known "Elizabethan" plays the great majority were written before 1626.

A rather striking piece of evidence that in the reign of Charles I the better London companies not only could have but actually did live in large part on their old repertories and did not commission new plays at anything like the old rate is to be found in the records of performances at court of the King's company, the troupe whose prestige in the time of Charles I was unrivaled. From the year 1625 to 6 January 1641/42 (the last recorded appearance of the company at court before the wars) there are records of 256 performances of the King's men before royalty. Usually these command affairs are known only from payment for blocks of performances without the names of the individual plays, but on 88 occasions the play is named. Now the Caroline court was certainly avid for new thrills in the theatre—as elsewhere—and one would expect most of the plays selected for the court in these 17 years to have been the newest acquisitions of the company. But they were not. Sixty-four of the 88 named plays were old ones, and only 24 were plays first produced within a year of the court performances. Not only were the majority of the plays not new, but many were twenty or more years old;

18. See Alfred Harbage and S. Schoenbaum, *Annals of English Drama*, 975–1700, London, 1964, pp. 54–122.

plays such as *A Midsummer Night's Dream, Volpone, The Maid's Tragedy, A King and No King, Philaster, Henry IV, The Duchess of Malfi, Everyman in his Humour, Richard III, The Taming of the Shrew, The Faithful Shepherdess, Cymbeline, Bussy D'Ambois, Catiline, Epicoene, The Beggar's Bush, The Loyal Subject, Othello, Hamlet, Julius Caesar, The Merry Wives of Windsor, The Chances, The Coxcomb, Rollo, Duke of Normandy.*

This tendency to rely on a classic repertory accumulated through the longest period of successful operation (1594 to 1625–1642) of any known company is a suggestive feature of the operation of the King's men at the Blackfriars and the Globe in the reign of Charles I. Edmund Malone, who examined at length and made random excerpts from the now lost records of the Master of the Revels, 1622–1642, said that in these years the King's men licensed only about four new plays a year. The company's reliance in Charles's time on a classic repertory is also made apparent by the terms in which James Shirley, regular dramatist for the company between 1640 and 1642, complained, in the prologue to his comedy, *The Sisters*, about the slim attendance at Blackfriars in the ominous spring of 1642.

> Does this look like a Term? I cannot tell,
> Our Poet thinks the whole town is not well,
>
> .   .   .   .   .
>
> What audience we have, what company
> "To Shakespeare comes, whose mirth did once beguile
> Dull hours, and buskined made even sorrow smile,
> So lovely were the wounds that men would say
> They could endure the bleeding a whole day":
> He has but few friends lately, think o' that,
> He'll come no more, and others have his fate.
> "Fletcher, the Muses' darling, and choice love
> Of Phoebus, the delight of every grove;
> Upon whose head the laurel grew, whose wit
> Was the time's wonder and example yet,"

'Tis within memory, trees did not throng
As once the story said to Orpheus' song.
"Jonson t' whose name wise art did bow, and wit
Is only justified by honoring it:
To hear whose touch, how would the learned choir
With silence stoop? And when he took his lyre,
Apollo dropped his lute, ashamed to see
A rival to the God of Harmony."
You do forsake him too, we must deplore
This fate, for we do know it by our door.

Their selection of a repertory for court performances
and Shirley's complaint of the sparce attendance in 1642
at performances of the customary favorites both show how
the Caroline King's company was relying on its glorious
past. But this was not the pattern for other times in this
company, nor necessarily for this time in all London companies. Not even the Phoenix had such a repertory, to say
nothing of the Red Bull, the Fortune, and Salisbury Court.

In the 1590s and the first decade of the seventeenth century new plays, especially collaborations, had been required
at a great rate because no acceptable inherited repertory
was available. The expedients necessary in this situation are
made clear from Henslowe's records of payments for new
play manuscripts in the years 1598 to 1602. Suppose Henslowe and the Burbages and Alleyn had tried to rely on
plays twenty to thirty years old, as their heirs did in the
1630s? What was available to them? Those still extant
from the accession of Queen Elizabeth to 1580 are Wager's
Life and Repentance of Mary Magdalene, *The Longer
Thou Livest the More Fool Thou Art*, and *Trial of Treasure*; Philip's *Patient and Meek Grisel*; Heywood's *Thyestes*; Sackville and Norton's *Gorboduc*; Bower's *Appius
and Virginia*; Edwards's *Damon and Pithias*; Gascoigne's
Supposes, *Jocasta*, and *Glass of Government*; Wilmot's
Gismund of Salerne; Pickering's *Horestes*; Fulwell's *Like
Will to Like*; Garter's *Most Virtuous and Godly Queen*

Hester; Woodes's *Conflict of Conscience*; Walpull's *Tide Tarrieth No Man*; Lupton's *All for Money*; and Merbury's *Marriage between Wit and Wisdom*. However interesting these plays may be to historians of the drama, the Burbages and Henslowe needed no prescience to guess that they would never draw spectators to the Curtain, the Globe, the Rose, the Fortune, or Blackfriars.

But however much the production of new plays and especially of collaborations fell off in the reign of Charles I, joint authorship did not entirely cease to be practiced. Thomas Randolph alluded to the situation in his play *The Jealous Lovers*, produced in the spring of 1632 after he had spent a period as regular playwright for the King's Revels company at the Salisbury Court.[19] Randolph makes his character Asotus, who has just crowned Charylus and Bromolochus poets laureate, say to them:

> I will not have you henceforth . . .
>
> . . . nor work journey work
> Under some playhouse poet, that deals in
> Wit by retail.

Two other plays, one of which was acted in the same year as Randolph's *Jealous Lovers*, were later published as collaborations, but they were not. In 1639 Andrew Crooke and William Cooke published *The Ball* and *Chabot, Admiral of France* with the same statement on both title pages:

> As it was presented by her Majesty's Servants at the private house in Drury Lane
>
> Written by   George Chapman
> and
> James Shirley

Neither is a collaboration. *Chabot* is an old play of Chapman's written about 1621 but apparently never acted for political reasons. Shirley revised it for the production at

19. See *Jacobean and Caroline Stage*, v, 966–67.

his theatre, the Phoenix or Cockpit in Drury Lane, in 1635 when Chapman was dead. There is reason for confusion here, for the play clearly contains work by both men, though there is no likelihood that they worked together. *The Ball* was wholly by Shirley, as the license of the Master of the Revels and his severe comment in censoring the play shows. The publishers simply used the same setting of type for the performance and authorship statements about each play. Probably they were simply confused.

Even the King's company, with a repertory as large and distinguished as we have seen, still sometimes commissioned collaborations. In the summer of 1634 Richard Brome and Thomas Heywood worked together to produce *The Late Lancashire Witches* for the Globe. This was a timely play, rushed through to capitalize the popular interest in the Lancashire women accused of witchcraft and brought to London for trial in 1634. Other London companies were interested in exploiting this sensation and the urgency of the need felt by the King's men to get their play on the Globe stage is documented in a petition they made to the Master of the Revels, a petition which was recorded in the warrant books of the Lord Chamberlain's office:

> A petition of the King's players complaining of intermingling some passages of witches in old plays to the prejudices of their designed comedy of the Lancashire Witches and desiring a prohibition of any other till theirs be allowed and acted. Answered per reference to Blagrave in the absence of Sir Henry Herbert. July 20, 1634.[20]

There were two other collaborations by Brome and Heywood which are now lost and known only from an entry of the manuscripts in the Stationers' Register by the great

20. See *Malone Society Collections*, II, part 3, p. 410, and *Jacobean and Caroline Stage*, III, 73.

dramatic publisher Humphrey Moseley. The entry, on 8 April 1654, reads: "Mr. Moseley. Entered for his copies two plays called The Life and Death of Sir Martin Skink, with the wars of the Low Countries, by Richard Brome and Thomas Heywood. And the Apprentice's Prize &." The entry gives no hint as to the date at which the plays were written nor of the company for which they were prepared. The collaboration of the same two men on *The Late Lancashire Witches* might suggest that they too were prepared for the King's company about 1634, but this is by no means certain. Indeed, the form of the entry would not necessarily mean that *The Apprentice's Prize* had the same authorship as *Sir Martin Skink*.

A couple of plays acted at Blackfriars in the last three years before the outbreak of the wars are often asserted (probably with reason) to have been joint compositions. The two are *The Country Captain* and *The Variety*, published together in 1649 as "Written by a person of honor. Lately presented by his Majesty's Servants at the Blackfriars." The person of honor was the famous Duke of Newcastle, then Earl of Newcastle and Baron Ogle. After he had become a Royalist general, his Puritan enemies frequently sneered at him as a playwright, "one that in time of peace tired the stage in Blackfriars with his comedies," "A great pretender of wit, a member of the Blackfriars College, a stage player," "At best but a playwright, one of Apollo's whirligigs, one that when he should be fighting would be fornicating with the Nine Muses or the Dean of York's daughters."

When it is remembered that the noble lord, who was a patron of many literary men, was engaged in numerous activities in the last three years before the wars, that during most of this time James Shirley was the regular dramatist, probably under contract, for the company at Blackfriars, and that later Newcastle was a patron of Shirley, who followed him to the wars, some association seems not unlikely. Anthony à Wood in his *Athenæ Oxoniensis* is very specific about it: "Our author Shirley did also much assist his generous patron, William, Duke of Newcastle, in the composition of certain plays which the Duke afterwards published."[21]

Methods of Collaborating

These records of plays of joint authorship should have made it abundantly clear that a good proportion of the pieces prepared for performance in the London theatres between 1590 and 1642 were the work of more than one author. Since collaboration was so common there is likely to have been a normal method of procedure when more than one man was assigned to prepare a new piece for the stage of the Rose or the Fortune, the Red Bull or the Globe.

Methods of cooperation are much more difficult to discover than the mere fact of joint authorship: printed title pages and Henslowe payments and occasional nondramatic statements have furnished copious evidence that dramatists *did* work together, but very few of them give hints as to *how* they worked together. In the modern theatre where joint authorship (at least acknowledged joint authorship) is not so common, most accounts indicate a sort of blending of the writing of two or more men who often spend time working in the same room jointly developing scenes or even lines. Such a method seems natural enough.

Considering how incomplete, scattered, and contradictory is our evidence of the ways in which Elizabethan, Jacobean, and Caroline dramatists worked together, no one can be dogmatic about their methods. An analysis of collaborated manuscripts like *Sir Thomas More* and a comparison with results of examinations of the various styles in the collaborated plays in the Beaumont and Fletcher

21. 1721 edition, London, II, 378.

folios would reveal a good deal of variety in the apparent division of the work. Moreover, a few playwrights—notably William Rowley—appear to have specialized in certain types of scenes or characters. A complete consideration of types of joint effort displayed in the extant plays of the time would require hundreds of pages.

But there is one method of collaboration used by the playwrights in these years which is most frequently referred to and which was evidently so much more generally practiced then than now that it deserves discussion. Separate composition of individual acts is a division of labor which was quite common from 1590 to 1642.

Very early in the period Robert Wilmot testified that this method of collaboration by separate acts was old. When he revised *Tancred and Gismund* for publication in 1591, he stated on the title page that the play was "Compiled by the Gentlemen of the Inner Temple, and by them presented before her Majesty." And at the end of each act he indicated the name of the author: *"Rod. Staff."* (Stafford?), *"Hen. No."* (Henry Noel), *"G. Al."*(?), *"Chr. Hat."* (Christopher Hatton). The epilogue he signs *"R. W."* (Robert Wilmot, the editor) and presumably he means that he was the author of the preceding act 5, as well. Since the original play had been acted before Queen Elizabeth in 1566 or 1567, composition by acts was not new in 1591.

The many entries about payment for plays in Henslowe's diary are never explicit in assigning individual acts to the different collaborators, but most of his serial payments are compatible with such composition, especially in the several instances where he pays one or two writers for a play in his early payments and adds others in his final payments.

The composition of the notorious lost play, *The Isle of Dogs*, for which dramatists and players were imprisoned, bringing all acting temporarily to a halt, was by acts, if the statement of Thomas Nashe, one of the authors, is to be trusted. A couple of years after the sensational suppression of July 1597, Thomas Nashe, who had fled at the time of the difficulties about his play, wrote in his pamphlet, *Nashe's Lenten Stuffe*, that the play was:

An imperfect Embrion I may well call it, for I having begun but the induction and first act of it, the other four acts without my consent, or the least guess of my drift or scope, by the players were supplied, which bred both their trouble and mine too.[22]

Nashe seems to say that the last four acts were composed "by the players," which is at best something of a quibble, for one of them was Ben Jonson, who was imprisoned for his share. Perhaps by "supplied" he meant arranged for by the players.

Three entries concerning the work of Ben Jonson and George Chapman certainly show composition by acts, but it is not clear that only one play is involved or that Jonson and Chapman worked together. The first entry simply shows a payment to Jonson for initiating the work on a play: "Lent unto Benjamin Jonson the 3 of December 1597 upon a book which he was to write for us before Christmas next after the date hereof which he showed the plot unto the company. I say lent in ready money unto him . . . 20 shillings."[23] Presumably the second entry refers to this plot which Chapman had taken up, but there is no specific notation of Jonson's collaboration beyond the plot, and the delay seems rather long for compositions for Henslowe: "Lent unto Robert Shaw and Juby the 23 of October 1598 to lend unto Mr. Chapman on his play book and two acts of a tragedy of Benjamin's plot the sum of . . . £3." It is not clear whether the third entry belongs with these two, but it seems likely, for the acts correspond, though Jonson is not mentioned. "Lent unto Mr. Chapman the 4 of Janu-

22. R. B. McKerrow, ed., *The Works of Thomas Nashe*, Oxford, 1958, III, 153–54.
23. Foakes and Rickert, p. 73.

ary 1598/99 upon three acts of a tragedy which Thomas Downton bade me deliver him the sum of . . . £3."[24] In any event, whether these three entries represent one, two, or possibly even three different plays, the wording shows that composition was proceeding by acts.

In 1613 Daborne's correspondence with Henslowe shows that he was writing by acts and in at least one instance collaborating by acts. On 17 April 1613 Daborne signed an agreement about completing a play for Henslowe:

> Memorandum 'tis agreed between Philip Henslowe, Esquire, and Robert Daborne, gentleman, that the said Robert shall before the end of this Easter term deliver in his tragedy called *Machiavelli and the Devil* into the hands of the said Philip for the sum of £20, £6 whereof the said Robert acknowledgeth to have received in earnest of the said play this 17th of April and must have other £4 upon delivery in of three acts, and other £10 upon delivery in of the last scene, perfected. In witness hereof the said Robert Daborne hereunto hath set his hand this 17th of April, 1613
>
> per me Rob: Daborne[25]

A fortnight later Daborne needed more money before it was due, but he still spoke in terms of composition by acts when he wrote a letter to his creditor.

> Mr. Henslowe:
> I am inforced to make bold with you for one 20 shillings more of the £10, and on Friday night I will deliver in the three acts fair written and then receive the other 40 shillings, and if you please to have some papers now you shall, but my promise shall be as good as bond to you. . . . At your command
>
> Rob: Daborne[26]

24. Ibid., pp. 100 and 103.
25. Greg, *Henslowe Papers*, p. 67.
26. Ibid., p. 69.

On another play, *The Owl*, Daborne was again working by acts, as a letter written about the end of December 1613 or the beginning of January 1614 indicates:

> Mr. Henslowe I acquainted you with my necessity which I know you did in part supply, but if you do not help me to 10 shillings by this bearer, by the living God I am utterly disgraced. On Friday night I will bring you papers to the value of three acts. Sir, my occasion is not ordinary that this suddenly I write to you. Wherefore I beseech you do this for me as ever you wished me well, which if I requite not, heaven forget me
>
> Yours at command,
Rob: Daborne[27]

In most of the correspondence of Robert Daborne making allusion to joint compositions in which he was engaged with Massinger, Field, or Fletcher he makes no mention of the method by which they collaborated. But in a letter concerning his work with Cyril Tourneur he does say how they were working. The statement implies that Henslowe did not know that Daborne had a collaborator, and it also implies that Henslowe would have no objections; indeed Daborne seems to feel that Henslowe ought to be pleased that he was taking intelligent steps to make haste.

> Mr. Henslowe:
>
> The company told me you were expected there yesterday to conclude about their coming over or going to Oxford. I have not only labored my own play [*Machiavelli and the Devil*] which shall be ready before they come over, but given Cyril Tourneur an act of *The Arraignment of London* to write that we may have that likewise ready for them. I wish you had spoken with them to know their resolution, for they depend upon your purpose. I have sent you two sheets more fair written. . . . 5 June 1613   At your command,
>
> Rob: Daborne[28]

27. Ibid., p. 81.   28. Ibid., p. 72.

Such evidence as we have, then, indicates that composition and collaboration on plays written for Henslowe companies was by acts. But the method was not confined to these troupes. The numerous scholars who have tried to disentangle the respective work of Beaumont, Fletcher, Field, Massinger, Rowley, and Middleton as printed in the Beaumont and Fletcher folios have generally found that joint composition was basically by acts—and this regardless of which playwrights were involved, and regardless of whether the play was prepared originally for the Queen's Revel's company, the Lady Elizabeth's company, or, in the case of the majority, for the King's men.[29]

The most explicit statement about collaboration methods comes from a lawsuit involving a play written for still another theatre, the Red Bull. In September 1624 the Master of the Revels licensed "A new tragedy called *A Late Murder of the Son upon the Mother*: Written by Ford and Webster." Like so many licenses, this one is incom-

29. The most satisfactory of the many attempts to break down the authorship of the plays in the two Beaumont and Fletcher folios is, of course, that of Cyrus Hoy. (*Studies in Bibliography, Papers of the Bibliographical Society of the University of Virginia*, vols. VIII–XV, 1956–1962.) Hoy simply identifies styles of two or more different dramatists in the plays and seldom tries to distinguish whether the writers other than Fletcher were collaborating or revising. In numerous instances there is external evidence of revision. As a consequence his stylistic analysis must inevitably show more multiple authorship within the acts of revised plays than was present in the version of a given play at first performance. Even so the plays on which both Fletcher and Massinger worked are highly suggestive. Massinger was not only Fletcher's most frequent collaborator, but the one whose linguistic habits are most sharply distinguished from Fletcher's. In these circumstances it is notable that in at least a dozen of the plays in which they worked together they obviously divided the first two acts between them, and the style of neither appears in the other's act. That this should still be apparent in the texts after many have been revised suggests that Fletcher and Massinger, the most productive collaborating partnership of the time, normally began their work by dividing up at least the two opening acts.

plete; the play was written for the company at the Red Bull theatre and it was a collaboration not of two playwrights, but of four. And the play had a subtitle, *Keep the Widow Waking*. The additional information comes from the testimony in a suit brought by Benjamin Garfield accusing a number of people of slandering his mother-in-law, the principal character in the subplot called *Keep the Widow Waking*. As one of the admitted authors of the play at the Red Bull, Thomas Dekker was called upon to testify. In his deposition he says:

> that John Webster . . . William Rowley, John Ford, and this defendant were privy consenting and acquainted with the making and contriving of the said play called Keep the Widow Waking and did make and contrive the same upon the instructions given them by one Ralph Savage. And this defendant sayeth that he this defendant did often see the said play or part thereof acted but how often he cannot depose. . . .[30]

More particular testimony as to how the four dramatists worked together on their play is given by Dekker in his answer as one of the defendants.

> . . . . and whereas in the said information mention is made of a play called by the name of Keep the Widow Waking, this defendant saith that true it is he wrote two sheets of paper containing the first act of a play called The Late Murder in Whitechapel, or Keep the Widow Waking and a speech in the last scene of the last act of the boy who had killed his mother. Which play (as all others are) was licensed by Sir Henry Herbert Master of His Majesty's Revels authorizing thereby both the writing and acting of the said play.[31]

Dekker testifies to the same kind of collaboration by acts which is implied in the other contemporary statements

30. *Library*, 4th series, VIII (1927), 258.
31. Ibid., p. 257.

noted. He does not testify as to the parts written by his three collaborators, and the only other one of the authors cited in the suit was William Rowley, who died before his testimony could be taken. An equable division would have been the division of acts two, three, and four among Ford, Webster, and Rowley, with each man writing a scene or a long speech in the last act.

COLLABORATION between two or more dramatists, especially professional dramatists, was a common method of composition in the greatest days of the English drama. It was more common in the reigns of Elizabeth and James, but it was not unusual in the time of Charles I. Well-known collaborations like those of Beaumont and Fletcher or Middleton and Rowley or Shakespeare and Fletcher should not be looked upon as oddities, but as common occurrences in the careers of professional dramatists of the time. Indeed, it is probable that a number of plays actually contain the work of more men than the first known records indicate. *The Honest Whore, Sir John Oldcastle, Sir Thomas Wyatt,* and *The Late Murder of the Son upon the Mother* are clear examples of a simplification of authorship on title pages and in official records which is likely to have occurred more frequently than we yet know.

CHAPTER IX

Revision

REVISION IS ASSOCIATED with collaboration both in the problems it presents to the modern scholar and in the activities of the professional playwright. For the scholar the two are often entangled: in a given text which appears to present the work of more than one man, is the second (or third or fourth) hand that of a collaborator, or of a reviser who may never have known the principal author? Several playwrights, like Philip Massinger, are known to have performed both functions on the work of one principal dramatist; in *The Little French Lawyer* he was almost certainly a collaborator; in *The Lovers' Progress or Cleander* he was the reviser. In fifteen or sixteen plays of the Beaumont and Fletcher folios, though it is almost certain that he was either collaborator or reviser, it is usually not clear which; in a few it seems likely that he was both. But Massinger's revising activities are only those best known; they are by no means peculiar.

There were two exceedingly common kinds of occasions

for revisions of a dramatist's completed manuscript, revisions which occurred regularly in the theatres of the time. The first must have affected almost all manuscripts for pieces which were accepted for performance; the other probably affected nearly all plays which attained *success* in performance.

The first kind of revisions consisted of those which the prompter or book-holder made in the manuscript his company had bought in order to prepare it for use by prompters in the playhouse. There are not many literary allusions to these practices, but the thirty or so extant play manuscripts which show alterations or additions written in the theatre make it abundantly clear that such work on the playwright's manuscript was apparently invariable.[1]

The few literary allusions to the treatment of a dramatist's manuscript in the playhouse are mostly printed complaints about cuts. John Webster, who certainly authorized the publication in 1623 of the ten-year-old *Duchess of Malfi*, since he wrote a dedication to Baron Barkeley and collected commendatory verses from Middleton, Ford, and Rowley, presumably authorized the statement on the title page, "The perfect and exact copy, with diverse things printed that the length of the play would not bear in the presentment."

This record of the cutting of the dramatist's original text is duplicated by Richard Brome nearly twenty years later. At the end of the 1640 edition of his popular play *The Antipodes*, Brome appended a curious note:

> Courteous Reader, you shall find in this book more than was presented upon the stage, and left out of presentation for superfluous length (as some of the players pretended). I thought good all should be inserted according to the allowed original and as it was, at first,

1. See W. W. Greg, *Dramatic Documents from the Elizabethan Playhouses*, passim, but esp. 1, 189–221. See also C. J. Sisson's edition of Massinger's *Believe as You List* in the Malone Society series.

intended for the Cockpit stage in the right of my most deserving friend, Mr. William Beeston, unto whom it properly appertained. And so I leave it to thy perusal, as it was generally applauded and well acted at Salisbury Court.

Farewell, Ri. Brome.

The confusion about companies in this note derives from Brome's troubles over his playwright's contract with the Salisbury Court players,[2] and the slight animosity in the phrase "as some of the players pretended" reflects his irritation at what he thought was his ill-usage. Nevertheless he records the fact that *The Antipodes*, like *The Duchess of Malfi*, was cut for performance in the theatre.

Rather more animosity about the players' treatment of his text is shown by Thomas Nabbes in his dedication of *The Bride* to the gentlemen of the Inns of Court. The play had been acted by Queen Henrietta's company at the Phoenix two years before Nabbes published it in 1640 with the dedication. He says that *The Bride* "is here dressed according to mine own desire and intention; without ought taken from her that myself thought ornament, nor supplied with anything which I valued but as rags." These allusions to the prompter's alterations made by Webster, Brome, and Nabbes are simply records of a few occasions in which the usual theatrical cuts seemed excessive to the dramatists.

The other type of revision of dramatists' manuscripts in the theatres occurred when the actors prepared the play for a revival. There are a great many records of one sort or another of this common practice; even the general public seems to have taken it for granted.

When Thomas Campion published his *Fourth Book of Ayres* about 1612, he said in his Address to the Reader:

You may find here some three or four songs that have been published before, but for them I refer you to the

2. The contract is discussed above, pp. 112–44.

players' bill that is styled, "Newly Revived with Additions" for you shall find all of them reformed either in
words or notes.

And even the players took it for granted that their audiences were familiar with the custom of revision, whether
it was admitted or not. The actor in the King's company
who delivered the prologue at the opening of *The False
One* about 1620 said:

> New titles warrant not a play for new,
> The subject being old; and 'tis as true,
> Fresh and neat matter may with ease be fram'd
> Out of their stories that have oft been nam'd
> With glory on the stage
>   ·   ·   ·   ·   ·   ·
> What we present and offer to your view
> Upon their faith, the stage yet never knew.

Of course the prime consideration of the King's company
here was that their audience should not think that this new
play of Fletcher and Massinger about Cleopatra was a revision of Daniel's *Tragedy of Cleopatra*, or Brandon's *The
Virtuous Octavia*, or Shakespeare's *Antony and Cleopatra*.
Thomas May's *Tragedy of Cleopatra, Queen of Egypt*
was not acted until five or six years later. Evidently they
could assume that a Blackfriars or Globe audience would
suspect a revised play when a familiar subject was dramatized. As Lupton said in his Character 20, entitled "Playhouses," in *London and the Country Carbonadoed and
Quartered into Several Characters*, 1632, "They [the ac-
tors] are as crafty with an old play as bawds with old
faces: the one puts on a new fresh color, the other a new
face and name."

Shakerley Marmion, who had a good deal more experience with actors and theatres than Lupton ever had, develops the same figure and expands it with more detail. In
act 2, scene 4 of *A Fine Companion*, acted by the Prince's

company at Salisbury Court in 1632 or 1633, he makes his character Littlegood say:

> Look you, here comes the old lecher! He looks as fresh as an old play new vampt. Pray see how trim he is, and how the authors have corrected him; how his tailor and his barber have set him forth; sure he has received another impression.

Thorough revision was sometimes frankly admitted rather than concealed. In 1634 Philip Massinger completely revised Fletcher's play, *The Lovers' Progress*, which had first been acted by the King's men in the winter of 1623. Massinger called the complete revision *Cleander*, but the prologue for the new version acted by the same company makes no attempt to conceal the fact that the play was an old one made over. The prologue actor says for Massinger:

> A story, and a known one, long since writ,
> Truth must take place, and by an able wit,
> Foul mouth'd detraction daring not deny
> To give so much to *Fletcher's* memory;
> If so, some may object, why then do you
> Present an old piece to us for a new?
> Or wherefore will your professed writer be
> (Not taxed of theft before) a plagiary?
> To this he answers in his just defence,
> And to maintain to all our innocence,
> Thus much, though he hath traveled the same way,
> Demanding, and receiving too the pay
> For a new poem, you may find it due,
> He having cheated neither us nor you;
> He vows, and deeply, that he did not spare
> The utmost of his strength and his best care
> In the reviving it, and though his powers
> Could not as he desired, in three short hours
> Contract the subject, and much less express
> The changes, and the various passages

> That will be looked for, you may hear this day
> Some scenes that will confirm it as a play,
> He being ambitious that it should be known
> What's good was *Fletcher's*, and what ill his own.

In the epilogue of this piece, along with the customary plea for applause, Massinger returns to the same undisguised discussion of aspects of the thorough revision of a Fletcher play and the presentation of it under a new title.

> Still doubtful, and perplexed too, whether he
> Hath done *Fletcher* right in this history,
> The Poet sits within, since he must know it,
> He with respect desires that you would show it
> By some accustomed sign, if from our action,
> Or his endeavors you meet satisfaction,
> With ours he hath his ends, we hope the best
> To make that certainty in you doth rest.

Such a prologue and epilogue show how misleading was Humphrey Moseley's publisher's blurb in the front matter of the 1647 Beaumont and Fletcher folio. Like so many publishers he claims a good deal more for the full and unaltered character of his texts than the facts warrant. Probably very few of the plays in the folio appear just as Beaumont and/or Fletcher wrote them. Revisions can be demonstrated in many of them, and Moseley himself had printed this revealing prologue and epilogue for *The Lovers' Progress*. Yet he said in his preface to "The Stationer":

> One thing I must answer before it be objected; 'tis this: when these *Comedies* and *Tragedies* were presented on the stage, the actors omitted some scenes and passages (with the authors' consent) as occasions led them; and when private friends desired a copy, they then (and justly too) transcribed what they acted. But now you have both all that was acted and all that was not; even the perfect and full originals without the least mutilation.

Moseley was trying to clear himself of the objections which some of his aristocratic readers who had manuscript copies of Beaumont and Fletcher plays might have made because of the differences between their copies and his printed texts. Fletcher plays were so popular that a number of such copies must have been in existence then, and several still are. Besides the two or three remaining playhouse manuscripts of these plays one can still examine private transcripts of just the sort Moseley mentioned: the Folger manuscript of *The Beggars' Bush*, Lord Harlech's manuscript of *The Humorous Lieutenant* entitled *Demetrius and Enanthe*, the Egerton manuscript of *The Elder Brother*, and the British Museum manuscript of *Sir John van Olden Barnavelt*.

Moseley covered himself against the protests of these owners of private transcripts, but his final statement about "the perfect and full originals without the least mutilations" is certainly untrue. It is doubtful that even the ten still living sharers of the King's company who signed the dedication to the Beaumont and Fletcher folio and who probably furnished Moseley with most of his texts had themselves ever seen "perfect full originals without the least mutilation" after the plays had been in active repertory for seventeen to thirty years.

In the reigns of Elizabeth, James, and Charles, only unacted or unsuccessful plays were likely to get into print in "the perfect full originals without the least mutilation." Probably we have one such—barring the usual printer's errors—in Samuel Harding's *Sicily and Naples, or the Fatal Union*. One of the writers of commendatory verses for this unacted play shows by his sneers not only his bias against theatres but what would have been expected had the text come from a playhouse. Nicholas Downey, after the usual comparison of his friend's work with that of the great Ben Jonson, says:

Thine is exposed to the world's large eye,
In its unchang'd and native infancy
Before some Players brain new drenched in sack
Does clap each term new fancies on its back.

Though Downey's phrase "unchang'd and native infancy"
is apt in more ways than he intended, his notion of what
happened to texts in the London theatres is not inaccurate
except in its implied frequency. "Does clap each term new
fancies on its back" alleges that for each of the three terms
of the law courts (seasons important in theatrical economy)
revisions of a popular play were made. This is surely an
exaggeration, but it does reveal the popular assumption
that plays regularly performed would be regularly revised.

Even the title pages of printed plays frequently give evidence that the following text certainly does not appear in
"its unchang'd and native infancy." On the title page of
the 1602 quarto of *The Spanish Tragedy* appears the statement, "Newly corrected, amended, and enlarged with new
additions of the Painters part, and others, as it hath of
late been divers times acted." Another revision of a popular play is announced on the title page of the third edition
of *Mucedorus* in 1610. William Jones "dwelling near Holborn Conduit at the sign of the Gun," who had also published the first two editions, has added to this title page
the statement "Amplified with new additions, as it was
acted before the King's Majesty at Whitehall on Shrove
Sunday night. By His Highness Servants usually playing
at the Globe." A rough collation of the texts shows that
this advertising statement is honest—there *are* additions
and alterations.

The third edition of *The Malcontent*, printed like the
first two editions in 1604, bears the title page statement,
"Augmented by Marston. With the additions played by
the King's Majesty's servants. Written by John Webster."
Again a little examination of the text shows that an induction as well as other less conspicuous additions have been

made to the text which had appeared in the two previous editions.

The frequently discussed additions to Marlowe's *Doctor Faustus* which were first printed in 1616 are not advertised in the edition of that year, but by the time he brought out his edition of 1619 John Wright had evidently concluded that the new material was worth advertising, and he added to the title page of that edition the statement, set off between rules, "With new Additions."

For the second edition of Chapman's *Bussy D'Ambois* in 1641, the publisher, Robert Lunne, had a title page printed with an unusually explicit statement: "Bussy D'Ambois: A Tragedy: As it hath been often acted with great applause. Being much corrected and amended by the Author before his death." The corrections and amendments do indeed appear in the text which Lunne had printed; whether the revisions had been made by Chapman, as asserted, is not quite so certain.

Early in the reign of James I, Thomas Heywood wrote for his company, Queen Anne's men, at the Red Bull, a successful play called *The Rape of Lucrece*. The play was printed five times, and evidently the songs were one of its popular features, for even the first edition carried an address to the reader which spoke of songs, "which were added by the stranger that lately acted Valerius his part." The fourth edition of 1630 contained various additions, including new songs, and the fifth edition of 1638 still more songs and more additions. This time Nathaniel Butter advertised the revisions on the title page, "The Rape of Lucrece. A True Roman Tragedy. With the several songs in their apt places, by Valerius the merry Lord among the Roman Peers. The Copy revised, and sundry songs before omitted, now inserted in their right places." One of the most explicit statements made by a Jacobean publisher about the revisions he found in his copy is that which John Trundle printed on the title page of the second issue of Middleton and Rowley's collaboration, *A Fair Quarrel*: "A Fair Quarrel. With new additions of Mr. Chaugh's and Tristram's Roaring, and the Bawd's song. Never before Printed. As it was acted by the Prince his Highness Servants." And he prints the new material as he has evidently received it, on additional pages bound in at the end and not distributed through the play, as it would have been when acted by Prince Charles's men before the King and on the public stage.

The majority of the plays of Beaumont and/or Fletcher were withheld from publication by the King's company which owned most of them until after the closing of the theatres, but a few were published in quarto, and two of the quartos advertise their revision. The second edition of *The Maid's Tragedy*, 1622, carried the title-page advertisement: "Newly perused, augmented, and enlarged. This second impression." A collation of this text with the previous one of 1619 shows a number of additions and alterations, as advertised.

A similar statement is found on the title page of the 1622 quarto of *Philaster*: "As it hath been diverse times acted at the Globe and Blackfriars by His Majesty's Servants. . . . The second impression, corrected and amended." And again collation verifies the advertisement, for the 1622 text shows a number of changes, including thorough revisions of the opening and the ending of the tragicomedy.

These sample statements of publishers on their title pages show the common knowledge that plays on the stage were regularly revised. And they show publishers frequently assuming that the reading public would be interested in buying the latest revisions which company dramatists had made for revivals of plays already in print. In those examples cited the advertisement of the publisher was honest, as a comparison of his text with the previous one shows. But the assumption of the publishers that readers with dramatic interests offered a better market for revised than for unrevised plays is equally demonstrated by the false advertisement of revisions. On the title page of the 1602 edition of Shakespeare's *Richard III*, Andrew Wise printed the claim, "Newly augmented." But he was lying in the hope of attracting new readers, for the edition was set up from his own 1598 text of the play. This dishonest tactic seems to have been successful, for Andrew Wise was only repeating what he had done before. In 1599 he had printed a third edition of *Henry IV*, part 1, with the title-page assertion, "Newly corrected by W. Shake-speare." Again there is no truth in his claim, for the text was set up from his own edition of the previous year.

Even after the closing of the theatres false claims about new texts were thought to be effective. In 1650 Francis Leake published another edition of *The Maid's Tragedy* with the statement on the title page, "The Sixth impression, Revised and Corrected exactly by the original." Though it is true, as we have seen, that *The Maid's Tragedy* had had a good deal of revision, as shown by a collation of the 1622 with the 1619 edition, Leake's text of 1650 does not differ from the two preceding editions.

As all readers of Shakespeare know, there are a good many plays which have come down to us in two or more editions, some of which, when collated, show extensive revisions. Yet the publisher either has not known about the revisions or has not chosen to advertise them. Examples can be seen in the 1633 (fourth) edition of Heywood's *The Second Part of If you know not me, You know nobody* and the 1616 edition of *Doctor Faustus*, which incorporated, but did not advertise, those revisions advertised on the 1619 title page.

Of course the great majority of plays acted in the London theatres between 1590 and 1642 were either not printed at all or appeared in only one edition, and we have no clue to the specific deletions, alterations, and additions they underwent during their years in repertory; but for a number some records of revision other than printed texts do exist. Generally the records clearly indicate that something was done to the play, but do not specify what it was. Henslowe several times speaks of "mending." On 15 February 1597/98 Anthony Munday had been paid £5 for his play *The First Part of Robinhood*, and the Master of the Revels had licensed both parts on 28 March following. Yet seven or eight months later the company decided that the play needed revision and Henslowe noted, "Lent unto Robert Shaw the 18 of November 1598 to lend unto Mr. Chettle upon the mending of the First part of Robinhood, the sum of . . . 10s."[3] Another play was handled similarly three years later. From July to November in 1601 William Haughton and John Day were paid £5 in four installments to write a play called *Friar Rush and the Proud Woman of Antwerp* for the Lord Admiral's company. After only two months, revisions were in order, and again Henry Chettle was paid for doing the work: "Lent unto Robert Shaw the 21 of January 1601/1602 to give to Henry Chettle for mending of the book called The Proud Woman, the sum of . . . 10s."[4] Sometimes we have evidence of more than one revision of a play. One of Henslowe's greatest outlays was on the two parts of *Cardinal Wolsey*, which he alternately called *The Rise of Cardinal Wolsey* and *The Life of Cardinal Wolsey*. The accounts for these plays seem to be confused in two or three instances, but from June to the middle of November 1601 Henslowe made at least 25 entries of payments for one or the other part of *Cardinal Wolsey*, and he laid out more than £60, mostly for new costumes. Two of these entries concern revisions; even such an expensive property as *Cardinal Wolsey* was expected to profit from further expenditures for revisions before it was a year old, and the Admiral's company authorized payments.

3. Foakes and Rickert, p. 101.
4. Ibid., p. 198.

Laid out at the appointment of my son and the company unto Harry Chettle for the altering of the book of Cardinal Wolsey the 28 of June 1601, the sum . . . 20s.

Lent unto Thomas Downton the 15 of May 1602 to pay Harry Chettle for the mending of the first part of Cardinal Wolsey, the sum of . . . 20s.[5]

The revisions of the anonymous *Tasso's Melancholy* come later in the play's existence than those Chettle made in *Cardinal Wolsey*. *Tasso* had been rather successful in the last half of 1594 and the first half of 1595 when Henslowe entered his part of the receipts at twelve performances. Evidently the leaders of the Admiral's company thought that the play might draw custom to the Fortune in 1602, and they authorized Henslowe to pay Dekker for two sets of alterations. It is suggestive that they were willing to invest in alterations about half what the play probably cost them in the first place.

Lent unto Thomas Dekker at the appointment of the company the 16 of January 1601[/1602] toward the altering of Tasso, the sum of . . . 20s.

Lent unto my son E. Alleyn the 3 of November 1602 to give unto Thomas Dekker for mending of the play of Tasso, the sum of . . . 40s.[6]

These four plays are lost and are now obscure, but a well-known and popular play like *Sir John Oldcastle*, which a publisher once tried to pass off as Shakespeare's, went through the same revisions. Philip Henslowe had paid Anthony Munday, Michael Drayton, Robert Wilson, and Richard Hathway the high price of £14 for the two parts of this play in October and December 1599. It started off so well in the theatre that the poets were presented with 10 shillings at the first performance. Yet within three years *Sir John Oldcastle* was being revised, as shown by

5. Ibid., pp. 175 and 200.   6. Ibid., pp. 187 and 206.

the entry: "Lent unto John Thare the 7 of September 1602 to give unto Thomas Dekker for his additions in Oldcastle, the sum of . . . 10s."[7]

Few plays have a record of greater success in the theatre than Marlowe's *Doctor Faustus*. Not only are there many allusions to it, but Henslowe's very incomplete performance records alone show that it was one of the best drawing pieces in the repertory. Yet, as is generally known, the play underwent extensive revisions. The diary has the entry: "Lent unto the company the 22 of November 1602 to pay unto William Bird and Samuel Rowley for additions in Doctor Faustus the sum of . . . £4."[8] When one recalls that many payments for "mending" or "additions" in these records were 10 shillings or 20 shillings and that at this time new plays brought £6 to £8, it is evident that Bird and Rowley must have revised rather extensively.

At least as popular as *Doctor Faustus* was *The Spanish Tragedy*, often called *Jeronimo*, yet it too underwent revisions probably more than once. Two entries in the accounts seem to indicate more than one stage in the alterations: "Lent unto Mr. Allen the 25 of September 1601 to lend unto Benjamin Jonson upon his writing of his additions in Jeronimo, the sum of . . . 40s." Nine months later there is a composite payment involving more changes in Kyd's play: "Lent unto Benjamin Jonson at the appointment of E. Alleyn and Wm. Bird the 22 of June 1602 in earnest of a book called Richard Crookback, and for new additions for Jeronimo, the sum of . . . £10."[9]

Even Jonson's own masterpieces, written after he had attained a great reputation and already in print, underwent the usual revisions in the theatre. *The Alchemist* had been part of the repertory of the King's company for nearly thirty years when Mrs. Ann Merricke wrote to her friend Mrs. Lydall: "I could wish myself with you, to ease you

7. Ibid., p. 216.   8. Ibid., p. 206.
9. Ibid., pp. 182 and 203.

of this trouble, and withall to see *The Alchemist*, which I hear this term is revised, and the new play a friend of mine sent to Mr. John Suckling and Tom. Carew (the best wits of the time) to correct. . . ."[10]

IN THESE QUOTED PAYMENTS to dramatists for alterations one cannot tell precisely what the revisers did to the plays in the repertories, but the word "additions" is the one which is most frequently used in reference to their activities. In the payments for *Doctor Faustus*, *The Spanish Tragedy*, and *Sir John Oldcastle* their work is called "additions," and elsewhere the term is common. "Paid unto Thomas Heywood the 20 of September [1602] for the new additions of Cutting Dick, sum of . . . 20s."[11]

In November and December 1602 and January and February 1602/1603 Henslowe had paid John Day, Richard Hathaway, Wentworth Smith "and the other poet," on behalf of the Earl of Worcester's men, for writing the two parts of *The Black Dog of Newgate*. A few months later, in February 1602/1603, part 2 was thought to need revisions. In this instance, contrary to the usual practice, the additions were made by the original authors of the play.

> Lent unto Thomas Blackwood the 21 of February 1602 [/1603] to give unto the four poets in earnest of their additions for the second part of The Black Dog, the sum of . . . 10s.

> Lent unto Thomas Blackwood the 24 of February 1602 [/1603] to give unto the four poets in part of payment for the additions in the second part of The Black Dog . . . 10s.

> Lent unto John Duke the 26 of February 1602 [/1603] to pay the poets in full payment for their additions for the second part of The Black Dog, the sum of . . . 20s.[12]

10. John Munro, ed., *The Shakespeare Allusion Book*, Oxford, 1932, I, 443.
11. Foakes and Rickert, p. 216.   12. Ibid., p. 224.

Even in the texts of their plays the dramatists sometimes alluded to this common practice of supplementing plays well known in the repertory. In the first scene of the fifth act of Middleton's *Hengist King of Kent, or the Mayor of Quinborough* a group of confidence men or cheaters are passing themselves off as strolling players, and they discuss with the mayor the plays they might perform for him:

1 Cheat. The Cheater and the Clown.
Symon. Is that come up again?
    That was a play when I was prentice first.
2 Cheat. Aye, but the cheater has learned more tricks since, sir
    And gulls the clown with new additions.

Plays could, of course, have even more extensive revisions than these examples indicate, and they could have been made by the original author for theatrical rather than literary reasons. On 11 January 1630/31 the Master of Revels recorded that "I did refuse to allow a play of Massinger's because it did contain dangerous matter, as the deposing of Sebastian King of Portugal by Philip the Second and there being a peace sworn twixt the Kings of England and Spain. . . ."[13] Massinger was at this time the regular dramatist for the King's company, and he completely revised and reset his play, as his extant manuscript shows. The original manuscript play concerned Sebastian, King of Portugal, who was supposed to have been killed in Africa in 1578, and whose throne was annexed by Philip II. Almost all evidences of this original setting and the names of the original characters have been excised by the dramatist for the King's company and the piece has been reset in Roman times and made to concern Antiochus the Great who was eventually defeated by the Romans in 191 B.C. The completely revised play was called *Believe as You*

13. J. Q. Adams, ed., *The Dramatic Records of Sir Henry Herbert*, New Haven, 1917, p. 19.

List; it was licensed for performance by the Master of the Revels on 6 May 1631 and was performed by the King's company. Like most plays of the time, it failed to attain print, and it is known from Massinger's most illuminating manuscript preserved in the British Museum.[14]

In the extant records of the Masters of the Revels there are also many accounts of the revisions of plays. But the interests of Henslowe and of the Masters in this constant play-doctoring were different. Henslowe needed to remember, primarily, how much money he had paid out in behalf of the company for the revisions. It was also helpful to him—though less important—to remember who had authorized the payments and who had done the revising. The Master of the Revels needed to remember first that he had passed on the revisions, and second how much he had been paid. Thus Henslowe always recorded the amount paid, usually the name of the reviser, though seldom what the reviser has done; whereas the Master of the Revels often set down what the revisions were, usually the fee paid him, but seldom the name of dramatists who had done the work for the acting company. As in all official or financial records, the bookkeeper was setting down the facts which might be useful for his own future reference, not, alas, those which would be most illuminating for posterity.

In 1624 Sir Henry entered his fee for allowing a revision of *The Virgin Martyr*. The play had been written four years before by Thomas Dekker and Philip Massinger for the company of the King's Revels acting at the Red Bull theatre. At that time there had been some trouble about censorable matter in the play, and Sir George Buc, Herbert's predecessor as Master of the Revels, had charged a double fee "for new reforming *The Virgin Martyr*." What Herbert allowed in 1624 was not the modification of censorable material, but an addition. "For the adding of

14. See the excellent edition of C. J. Sisson in the Malone Society Reprints, 1927.

a scene to *The Virgin Martyr*, this 7th July, 1624 . . .
10*s*."[15] This play had got into print two years before, probably because of the difficulties of the Queen Anne's–King's
Revels company, which was in a decline, and three plays
from its repertory were published in 1622. In 1624 the
company had declined to a provincial status, and it is not
known what organization paid the unknown dramatist—
and Sir Henry—for the additions to the play.

Five years later another extract from the office book of
the Masters of the Revels attests the addition of a full act
to an old play. Probably the Master had made a number
of such allowances in the five years, for it is difficult to
remember that we have only scattered extracts from Sir
Henry's accounts. The manuscript of his official records,
which was seen by Edmund Malone and George Chalmers
at the end of the eighteenth and the beginning of the nineteenth century, has since been lost, and we have only the
extracts these two scholars chose to make for illustrative
purposes; they were understandably interested mostly in
entries naming well-known plays or well-known dramatists. The following extract from the office book is not
characteristic of the usual interests Malone and Chalmers
displayed in the notes they published; in the original manuscript, however, it was probably more common. In this
entry Herbert mentions neither company nor dramatist,
but only the extent of the revision and the fee paid: "For
allowing of a new act in an old play this 13th of May
1629 . . . 10*s*."[16]

In another license for a revision four years later Sir
Henry is rather more informative. The play is Fletcher's
The Night Walker, whose date of original composition is
uncertain, perhaps about 1611. By 1633 it was in the hands
of Queen Henrietta's company, the owners of at least three
of Fletcher's plays, all first written for other Jacobean

15. Adams, *Herbert*, p. 29.
16. Ibid., p. 32.

companies before John Fletcher became the regular dramatist for the King's men. In 1633 *The Night Walker* was
revised, and the Master of the Revels in this instance
named the reviser as well as the allowance fee: "For a play
of Fletcher's corrected by Shirley called The Night Walk-
ers, the 11 May, 1633, £2. For the Queen's players."[17]
This revision must have been an extensive one, for Herbert's usual fee at this time for licensing alterations was
£1, and it was only for new plays that he was accustomed
to charge £2. Shirley had been for eight years the regular
dramatist for Queen Henrietta's company, and his revisions were very recent at the time of the license, for the
text of the play contains, in the third act, an allusion to
"the late Histriomastix," that is, William Prynne's sensational *Histriomastix, The Players' Scourge, or Actors'
Tragedy*, which was not published until 1633.

Three months later Christopher Beeston, the manager
of Queen Henrietta's company, was again in Herbert's
office on a double errand about another of the company's
old plays. This one was more than twenty years old, William Rowley's *Hymen's Holiday*. Herbert notes: "Received of Beeston for an old play called *Hymen's Holiday*,
newly revived at their house, being a play given unto him
for my use, this 15 August, 1633, £3. Received of him for
some alterations to it . . . £1."[18] In all likelihood the alterations were the work of the regular poet at the Phoenix in
Drury Lane, though Herbert does not name him as he had
done in *The Night Walker* entry three months before.
This revision was evidently a good job, for not only did
Sir Henry receive £3 as his share of the receipts, but the
company selected the play for a performance at court four
months later on 15 December, when it is said to have been
"Likte."

More informative than the records of the revision of
these plays in the 1630s are those for another one; this

17. Ibid., p. 34.   18. Ibid., p. 35.

time a play which was revised not *for* the King's company but for competition with them, "An old play with some new scenes, *Doctor Lambe and the Witches*, to Salisbury Court the 16th August, 1634 . . . £1."[19] Though the play is lost, this transaction is one which can be supplemented with other information. Doctor Lambe was a notorious London character, alleged to have been a conjurer, and widely hated and feared because he was an agent of the hated Duke of Buckingham. In June 1628 he had been attacked by a mob as he was leaving the Fortune theatre and stoned so mercilessly that he died of his injuries the next day. Because of his great notoriety (there are several accounts of his death, including a ballad on the subject) and because his patron and protector, the Duke of Buckingham, was assassinated two months later, Doctor Lambe was a prime subject for a topical play, like *Keep the Widow Waking*, or *The Old Joiner of Aldgate*, or *A Game at Chess*, or *The Whore New Vampt*. But the obvious time for such a play was late 1628 or 1629, not 1634. By 1634 Doctor Lambe was a stale subject, but there was a new popular scandal in the summer of that year which could be made to appear related to Doctor Lambe. This new scandal was that of the witches in Lancashire, who were brought to trial in London in the summer of 1634. The King's company at the Globe exploited this scandal in their play, *The Late Lancashire Witches*, written for them by Richard Brome and Thomas Heywood. The company at Salisbury Court had the same idea, but they were forestalled, as a petition in the Lord Chamberlain's warrant books makes clear.

> A petition of the King's players complaining of intermingling of some passages of witches in old plays to the prejudice of their designed comedy of the Lancashire witches, and desiring a prohibition of any others till

19. Ibid., p. 36.

theirs be allowed and acted. Answered per reference to Blagrave in absence of Sir H. Herbert. July 20, 1634.[20]

It seems very likely that the play the King's men complained of was *Doctor Lambe and the Witches*, revised from an old play about Doctor Lambe by an unknown dramatist at the order of the players of the Salisbury Court theatre. And Herbert's date, 16 August 1634, is near enough to one month after the petition of 20 July to show that the King's men's request of a month's delay had been granted.

It would be interesting to have the two versions of the Doctor Lambe play to compare as an example of revision techniques, but the extant evidence is enough to show one of the causes for revising plays, and the petition phrase "intermingling of some passages of witches" and Herbert's phrase "some new scenes" are enough to suggest something of the method of the unknown revising playwright.

Another allowance by Sir Henry in 1636 gives official confirmation of a charge often leveled against the actors: "bawds with old faces." This time Sir Henry gives the name of the man who brought in the manuscript, "old Cartwright." He is called "old" to distinguish him from his son and namesake, William Cartwright, who was also an actor at the Fortune. William Cartwright, senior, who had been a friend and associate of Edward Alleyn, was at this time a leading actor and probably the manager at the Fortune theatre in Golding Lane, in the parish of St. Giles-without-Cripplegate. Sir Henry's entry reads: "Received of old Cartwright for allowing the [Fortune] company to add scenes to an old play, and to give it out for a new one this 12th of May, 1636 . . . £1."[21] Unfortunately there is nothing in the entry to show what the Master of the Revels meant by "give it out for a new one"; he is not known

20. *Malone Society Collections*, II, part 3, 410.
21. Adams, *Herbert*, p. 37.

to have had any control over the playbill advertising of the company, nor over the admission prices charged at the theatres—generally double for a new play.

Sometimes the new additions or deletions in an old play are conspicuous in the text. A familiar example is the 1641 edition of Chapman's *Bussy D'Ambois*, published seven years after Chapman's death and thirty-three years after the last previous issue of 1608. Though the title page puffs the edition as "Being much corrected and amended by the Author before his death," there is some disagreement as to whether the 250-odd changes were made by Chapman or by another.[22] In any event there are extensive changes, and the prologue refers to at least three different productions, in one of which the lead was played by Nathan Field and in another probably by Eyllaerdt Swanston—at least he is known to have excelled in the role.

A better example of a quarto showing revisions of a text long after the original composition is the 1656 quarto of Thomas Goffe's pastoral comedy, *The Careless Shepherdess*, as produced at the Salisbury Court theatre about 1638. Though there are some obvious disturbances in its lines, the play proper reads like an academic production, perhaps for Christ Church, Oxford, where other of Goffe's plays were acted, but the long and interesting induction and the prologue were certainly not written by Goffe, for they are full of explicit and detailed references to conditions and practices at the Salisbury Court theatre. Goffe is not known to have had any experience of the London theatre, and the Salisbury Court, explicitly named as the setting for the induction, which refers to its actors, customs, rooms, and charges, was not yet built at the time of Goffe's death. In this case internal evidence in the play shows clearly enough that an old play by Thomas Goffe was revised for the

22. See Berta Sturman, *Huntington Library Quarterly*, xiv (February 1951), pp. 171–201, and Peter Ure, *Modern Language Review*, xlviii (July 1953), pp. 257–69.

Salisbury Court theatre about 1638 by the addition of an induction and a prologue, and probably by other changes in the body of the play which are less obvious now.

In the case of *The Careless Shepherdess* we have a strong suggestion, though not final proof, as to who the revising dramatist was. In July 1635 Richard Brome had signed a contract with the acting company at the Salisbury Court theatre to be the company dramatist. The contract was for three years and it was renewed in August 1638. In the suit which was brought against Brome in February 1639/40, alleging breach of contract, Brome replied by reciting some of his regular activities as contracted dramatist for the company during the previous four years. He says that in addition to the new plays which he had written for the company at Salisbury Court "he hath made divers scenes in old revived plays for them and many prologues and epilogues to such plays of theirs, songs, and one Introduction at their first playing after the ceasing of the plague."[23] This statement of Richard Brome's shows clearly that alterations of and additions to the revived plays in the repertory of a company were the usual work of the regular dramatist at the theatre. Consequently when the name of the attached dramatist for a company is known, we have a strong suggestion of the identity of the author of the revisions made in that company's plays during his incumbency. It would be a neat dovetailing of records if one could believe that the induction for *The Careless Shepherdess* was the very "Introduction at their first playing after the ceasing of the plague" to which Brome refers. Probably, however, it was not. There is nothing about the plague in the induction to *The Careless Shepherdess* as there is in Thomas Randolph's *Praeludium* for this theatre at its reopening after a previous plague in 1630. Moreover, the reopening Brome refers to was on 2 October 1637, and several allusions in

23. Ann Haaker, "The Plague, the Theater, and the Poet," *Renaissance Drama*, n.s. 1 (1968), p. 305.

the induction to *The Careless Shepherdess* seem to refer to events a few months after that. Nonetheless, that induction is one of those company dramatist's chores which Brome specifically says that he was carrying out for the Salisbury Court theatre from 1635 through 1638.

Another of the chores of the company dramatist mentioned by Richard Brome is to be seen in many texts and references. This is the writing of new prologues and epilogues for revivals and for special occasions. Several of Henslowe's payments are for such special new material in a play already acted. After he had paid Henry Chettle on 18 November 1598 for "mending of the first part of Robinhood," another payment one week later shows further additions to prepare the play for a special occasion: "Lent unto Harry Chettle at the request of Robert Shaw the 25 of November 1598 in earnest of his comedy called 'Tis No Deceit to Deceive the Deceiver [and] for mending of Robinhood for the court . . . 10*s*."[24] And the next year just before the court season Henslowe again recorded part of the company's preparation for a command performance, this time on their popular play *Fortunatus*, which had already been revised once a couple of weeks before: "Paid unto Mr. Dekker the 12 of December 1599 for the end of Fortunatus for the court at the appointment of Robert Shaw, the sum of . . . 40*s*."[25] And the same situation came up again in preparation for the court season of 1600–1601, when *Phaeton* seems to have required more work than *Robinhood* and *Fortunatus* did.

> Lent unto Samuel Rowley the 14 of December 1600 to give unto Thomas Dekker for his pains in Phaeton, the sum of . . . 10*s*.
>
> for the court

24. Foakes and Rickert, p. 102.
25. Ibid., p. 128.

258

Lent unto Samuel Rowley the 22 of December 1600 to give unto Thomas Dekker for altering Phaeton for the court . . . 30s.

Lent unto William Bird the 2 of January 1600[/1601] for divers things about the play of Phaeton for the court, the sum of . . . 20s.[26]

Even in the printed texts of plays there is much evidence of prologues and epilogues prepared not by the original dramatist for an opening performance, but by some other writer for a revival. Sometimes the new material is called "Prologue at the Reviving of this Play" or some such; sometimes there is only one prologue or epilogue printed, but that one refers to "some twenty years ago" or contains the lines

> This Comedy, long forgot, some thought dead,
> By us preserved, once more doth rise her head.

Now and then there is an even more explicit statement about the occasion of the revival for which the new prologue or epilogue has been written. A good example is the one for Fletcher's *Faithful Shepherdess*, which was first published in an undated quarto of about 1610. Various commendatory verses indicated that the play was a failure in its first production, but it had an elaborate revival twenty-three or -four years later when the Master of the Revels remarked that there "was presented at Denmark house, before the King and Queen Fletcher's pastoral called *The Faithful Shepherdess*, in the clothes the Queen had given Taylor the year before of her own pastoral."[27] And the new quarto of 1634 itself calls attention to some of the new material for the revival: "This Dialogue, newly added, was spoken by way of Prologue to both their Majes-

26. Ibid., pp. 137 and 138.
27. Adams, *Herbert*, p. 53.

ties at the first acting of this pastoral at Somersethouse on Twelfth Night, 1633."

There are other printed revival prologues and epilogues in the 1600 *Old Fortunatus*, the 1641 *Bussy D'Ambois*, the 1653 edition of Brome's *The City Wit*, as well as in the folio editions of *The Custom of the Country*, *The Elder Brother*, *The Noble Gentleman*, *The Coxcomb*, *Wit at Several Weapons*, *The Woman Hater*, *The Chances*, *Love's Cure*, and *The Nice Valor*, *or the Passionate Madman*. In his postscript for the 1647 folio, the publisher, Humphrey Moseley, who had been so insistent on the purity of his texts, even admits that "We forgot to tell the *Reader*, that some *Prologues* and *Epilogues* (here inserted) were not written by the *Authors* of this *Volume*; but made by others on the *Revival* of several *Plays*."

By far the most numerous and detailed studies of play revisions in the Elizabethan and Jacobean theatres are those of the texts of the plays of the principal dramatist of the Lord Chamberlain–King's company, William Shakespeare. Unfortunately for an understanding of the normal practices of professional dramatists in the time, these studies have an orientation not very helpful for the historian of the theatre. Dazzled by the genius of Shakespeare, scholars have inevitably concentrated on explications of his poetic achievements or on the misadventures of his creations in the printing houses. Both are rewarding and necessary; but, except for the often brash and generally discredited analyses of the disintegrators, most studies tend to take Shakespeare's plays out of the theatres for which they were created and to analyze them in the milieu of the lyric and philosophical poet and not in the milieu of the hard-working professional playwright devoted to the enterprise of the most successful and profitable London acting company of the time—or perhaps of any time.

Any detailed analysis of the demonstrable revisions of Shakespeare's plays before the closing of the theatres in

1642 would throw completely out of balance such a survey as this one, but the collations of his texts which have now gone on for more than two centuries are sufficiently familiar to make summarizing references intelligible.

Half the plays are known in one text only, since the King's men withheld them from publication until 1623, and they can furnish evidence of revision only through exacting and often not wholly satisfying analysis. The familiar fact of this single text, post-mortem publication of half Shakespeare's plays—a fact so mysterious to the anti-Stratfordians and to anachronistic critics—should be regarded as normal in the context of the Jacobean theatre with which Shakespeare was so intricately involved. The unusual event is the appearance of the first folio at all.

During Shakespeare's lifetime, under normal conditions —that is when the company was solvent, as the Lord Chamberlain–King's company always was, and the dramatist honest and modest—the acting company kept the manuscript which the playwright had sold to them in their own archives and out of the hands of the printers. Unsuccessful plays and plays too antiquated to revise were another matter; they could be sold to publishers as dead wood cleared out of the repertory. Publishers, of course, not infrequently secured play manuscripts in spite of the objections of the legal owners, through theft, dishonest dramatists, or private transcripts which the company had sanctioned in order to please important patrons. The fact, therefore, that half Shakespeare's known plays were first published in 1623 is evidence that these plays were successful at the Blackfriars and the Globe and therefore worth keeping exclusive in their repertories and also that they belonged to an acting company solvent enough to sell only what they did not want and powerful enough to discourage unfriendly publishers and unscrupulous rival theatres. It is illuminating to note in this context how the publication of Shakespeare's plays divides at about 1599. Before this date the company was pressed by competitors, especially the Lord Admiral's men. In 1599 the building of the new and handsome Globe signalized the new dominance of the company, which was seldom seriously challenged thereafter. And this new dominance was illustrated by their ability to withhold their plays from publication. By 1600 the King's men had influence enough to keep other companies from performing their plays even if they were in print, and the King's men themselves helped to arrange the publication of the first folio not for profit, but "onely to keepe the memory of so worthy a Friend & Fellow aliue, as was our SHAKESPEARE," as the leaders of the company, John Heminges and Henry Condell, say in their dedicatory epistle to the Earls of Pembroke and Montgomery.

But even in these limiting circumstances we have fairly clear evidence of revisions in the texts of the majority of Shakespeare's plays. The fact has been somewhat obscured because most Shakespearean scholars have been less interested in the clear evidence that the play has been revised at some time or other than in the much more difficult problem of who wrote what lines and when. For 25 of the plays in the canon we have some evidence that the text has undergone a revision. In eight or nine the evidence for revision is rather slight, as is the evidence for cutting in *All's Well* and *Measure for Measure* and for interpolation in the vision scene in *Cymbeline*—but in 16 of the plays there are clear differences in texts which go beyond printing-house variants, as in the added scene in *Titus*, the added lines in *Henry IV*, part 2, and *King Lear*, and the differences between the second quarto and the folio versions of *Hamlet*. The normal revision of plays kept in the repertory of a successful company is generally, though not invariably, exemplified in the extant texts of the plays of Shakespeare.

ALL THIS SCATTERED EVIDENCE makes it clear that if a play had sufficient theatrical appeal to be kept in the repertory of an Elizabethan, Jacobean, or Caroline acting company, it was normal for the text to be revised for at least one of the revivals. This revision would usually have been made—at least in the more settled Jacobean and Caroline days—by the regular dramatist for the company. In the only specific references to the contract of such a dramatist, he was required by the terms of his contract to doctor the old plays for revivals. Such a dramatist's knowledge of the personnel of the company made him the best-qualified writer for such a service, since a common change would have been the adjustment of lines or songs or scenes to any actors who may have succeeded those for whom the originals had been designed. Further changes to adjust to altered tastes or to exploit current scandals, as in *Doctor Lambe and the Witches*, or to delete political allusions which had become dangerous since the original appearance of the play, must have been frequent, but less invariable than adjustments to the company of actors.

On the basis of the extant evidence one can safely say that all the attached professional dramatists must have been involved in the revision of plays—their own as well as other men's—for the refurbishing of old plays in the repertory seems to have been the universal practice in the London theatres from 1590 to 1642. As a rough rule of thumb one might say that almost any play first printed more than ten years after composition and known to have been kept in active repertory by the company which owned it is most likely to contain later revisions by the author or, in many cases, by another playwright working for the same company.

CHAPTER X

Publication

SINCE THE PLAYS of the Elizabethan dramatists have customarily been read and analyzed as literary documents for the study rather than as working scripts for the theatres, the normal practices of those writers of plays who were the regular employees of the theatres—the group of attached professional dramatists—have been obscured by the publishing habits of unattached professionals like Ben Jonson, John Marston, John Ford, and William Davenant, or even amateurs like Lodowick Carlell or Jasper Mayne.

In general the attached professionals refrained from publication without the consent of the acting troupe for which the play had been written and whose property it was. Many circumstances could elicit the consent of the company, and others could frustrate its objections. Disbanded companies or bankrupt companies, or even financially hard-pressed companies either were in no position to object to the dramatist's sale of his script to a publisher or in their desperation sold it themselves. John Charlewood recorded one such occasion in the address to the reader which he printed with his edition of Lyly's *Endymion* in 1591:

> Since the plays in Paul's were dissolved, there are certain comedies come to my hands by chance, which were presented before her majesty at several times by the Children of Paul's. This is the first, and if in any place it shall displease, I will take more pains to perfect the next. I refer it to thy indifferent judgment to peruse, whom I would willingly please. And if this may pass with thy good liking, I will then go forward to publish the rest. . . .

Even more eloquent of a situation in which the company had to give up control of its plays is the publication in 1647, after all hope of the revival of the theatres had been abandoned, of 34 of the carefully guarded, twenty- to forty-year-old, unpublished manuscripts of Beaumont and Fletcher. This publication is most explicit in its evidence of official company consent, since the dedication of the collection is signed by all ten of the surviving actor-sharers of the King's company, which had so long and so successfully withheld them from publication, and the "Address to the Reader" was written by the last regular dramatist for the company, James Shirley.

Similarly indicative of the relaxation of company restraints in times of distress is the appearance in print of an unparalleled number of plays by professional dramatists during and immediately after the disastrous plague of 1636–1637, when the theatres were closed and the companies in distress for all but one week of 17 months. In the four years 1637, 1638, 1639, and 1640, 60 plays by the professional dramatists appeared on the London bookstalls, whereas in many of the previous years not a single one had been printed; and in no previous period of four years had so many as half this number of plays by professional dramatists come into print.

Even the attached professional dramatists themselves several times ushered into print the plays they had written for a particular company *after* their relations with that company had been broken. This phenomenon is apparent in the patterns of publication of Richard Brome and James Shirley, as will be noted presently. And in the canons of the regular professional playwrights there are several examples where company consent to publication appears to have been given for the printing of plays which had failed in the theatre or which had outlived their audience appeal. A consideration of the publication records of a few dramatists will support these generalizations.

The only contract so far discovered between an attached professional dramatist and the acting company and theatre owners who employed him is, as we have seen, the one which Richard Brome signed on 20 July 1635 and renewed for seven years in August 1638. In the suit against Brome the entire contract is not quoted, but both parties cite certain portions of it, including the section on publication. The company says that this part of the contract stipulated that Richard Brome

> should not suffer any play made or to be made or composed by him for your subjects or their successors in the said company in Salisbury Court to be printed by his consent or knowledge, privity, or direction without the license from the said company or the major part of them.[1]

1. Haaker transcript, p. 298. Explicit indications of the objections of other companies to the publication of the plays which had been written for them are to be seen in Henslowe's payment in March 1599/1600 of the large sum of 40 shillings to "staye the printinge" of *Patient Grissell*, which had been written for the company by Dekker, Chettle, and Haughton three or four months before. The sharers in the Whitefriars theatre had the same attitude toward publication a few years later when they made their agreement of 10 March 1607/1608, in which Item 8 stipulates:

> Item, it is also covenanted, granted, concluded and fully agreed between the said parties . . . that no man of the said company

In his reply to his employers Brome made no protest about this section of his contract; the company, which accused him of a number of other violations, never accused him of failure to observe this stipulation, and the records of his rather numerous publications show that he never did violate it. That is, during the period the contracts were in force, 1635–1639, he published no plays and no piece of his was entered in the Stationers' Register.

Brome's abstention is notable in the publishing records, for this period was a very active one for the printers of plays. During the full five years of his contracts, the London publishers entered nearly one hundred plays in the Stationers' Register, and well over forty written by professional dramatists appeared in print. And it is not that Brome was averse to publication, for in the three years *before* his contracts he had published two plays, and in the twenty years *after* his contracts, twenty of his plays were either entered in the Stationers' Register or printed or both. Not only this, but immediately after the abrogation of his contract Brome had three plays in the hands of the printer, Francis Constable, who entered them together in the Stationers' Register on 19 March 1639/40. Two of them, *The Antipodes* and *The Sparagus Garden*, were plays which had been written for the Salisbury Court under his contract,

shall at any time hereafter put into print . . . any manner of play book now in use, or that hereafter shall be sold unto them upon the penalty and forfeiture of £40 sterling or the loss of his place and share of all things amongst them, except the book of *Torrismount*, and that play not to be printed by any before twelve months be fully expired (*Transactions of the New Shakespeare Society*, 1887–1892, p. 276).

In later years the better companies themselves persuaded the Lord Chamberlain to forbid the publication of their plays without their consent, and that official wrote such letters for the King's men in 1619, and for the King's men and for the King and Queen's Young company in June 1637 (see *Malone Society Collections*, II, part 3, 384–85).

and they were published with Brome's consent and supervision, as signed dedications, commendatory verses, and an
address to the reader show. The third play, *Wit in a Mad-
ness*, probably had the same history, but one cannot be certain, since it was never published and the only references
to it are in the Stationers' Register.

These various facts add up to the conclusion that Richard Brome, an attached professional playwright not averse
to publication when not under contract to the contrary,
carefully refrained from giving the printers any of his plays
written under his contract to the Salisbury Court theatre
so long as that contract was in force, but that as soon as
the agreement was abrogated, he immediately gave the
manuscripts of two or three of those plays to Francis Constable for publication.

Finally, there is evidence that when Brome left the Salisbury Court for William Beeston's company at the Phoenix
or Cockpit in Drury Lane—the lawsuit says at a higher
salary than his previous pound a week—he similarly refrained from publication of the plays he wrote for his new
employers. Though Brome had seven plays in the hands
of the printers in 1640–1642 (the years he presumably
continued to write for Beeston) none of them was a Cockpit play. But after the closing of the theatres when all contracts of players and playwrights were in abeyance, at least
three of the plays he wrote for his new employers appeared
in print, *The Court Beggar*, *The Jovial Crew*, and *A Mad
Couple Well Matched*.[2]

Though Brome's contract is the only extant written record of an attached professional dramatist's agreement to
refrain from publishing those plays he wrote for them without the company's consent, there is a good deal of evidence
that other regular professionals were working under like
restrictions. James Shirley's writing and publication show
a similar pattern.

2. *Jacobean and Caroline Stage*, iii, 61–65, 70–73, 80–81.

In 1640, 1641, and 1642 Shirley regularly delivered an autumn play and a spring play to King Charles's company, presumably under contract. The plays were *Rosania or the Doubtful Heir*, *The Impostor*, *The Politic Father or the Brothers*, *The Cardinal*, *The Sisters*, and *The Court Secret*.[3] Now during the three years that Shirley wrote for the King's company at the Blackfriars and the Globe he certainly did not refrain from *any* publication. In the year 1640 alone, six of his own plays and one of Fletcher's, which Sir Henry Herbert had allowed with Shirley's revisions in 1633, were published, but all of them were plays he had written for his *former* companies, either Queen Henrietta's men at the Phoenix or the St. Werburgh Street theatre in Dublin. But none of the six plays he wrote for the King's men did he give to the printers while he was regular dramatist for the company.

All six plays did achieve print, but not until long after the King's men as a London troupe were no more. In 1653 Humphrey Robinson and Humphrey Moseley brought out *Six New Plays. . . . The First five were acted at the Private House in Black Fryers with great Applause. The last was never Acted. All Written by James Shirley*. Robinson and Moseley certainly printed with Shirley's cooperation, for each play has a separate address or dedication signed by the author. These are all the plays he wrote for the King's company, carefully withheld from publication until eleven years of suppression had killed all hope for a revival of the old days.

Before he left for Ireland during the long plague closing of 1636–1637, Shirley had been the ordinary poet for Queen Henrietta's company at the Phoenix since 1626. His writing and publication pattern in those years is similar, but not quite so clear.

During the eleven years he was attached to the Phoenix

3. Ibid., v, 1105–7, 1123–25, 1082–84, 1084–88, 1147–49, and 1100–2.

theatre, Shirley wrote 20 or 22 plays for them—20 were eventually published as performed by Queen Henrietta's men at this theatre, and two others, *Look to the Lady* and *The Tragedy of St. Albans*, were entered in the Stationers' Register in February and March 1639/40 but are now lost and may or may not have been written for Beeston's company. These plays constitute about half of all the new plays—i.e., not revivals inherited from previous companies—in the repertory of this prominent troupe in the years 1625–1636, and the spring and autumn regularity with which they were produced make Shirley's attachment to the company, probably contractual, quite clear.[4]

It is also clear that Shirley, a dramatist who saw to it that nearly all his plays eventually got into print, was exercising restraint during the years he was writing regularly for the Phoenix. The restraint was not total as it was during the three years he was attached to the King's men, but at least thirteen of Queen Henrietta's plays were kept out of the hands of the publishers until he had left the company and gone to Ireland, and then all thirteen were issued between 1637 and 1640, a clear indication of self-restraint during his term as ordinary poet for Queen Henrietta's company.

During these eleven years, seven of Shirley's plays did appear in print, but one of them, *The School of Compliment*, though later acted by Queen Henrietta's men, was originally licensed by the Master of the Revels in February 1624/25, before the company was formed, and was therefore evidently not subject to their agreement with Shirley. Another, *The Changes*, was written for a different troupe, His Majesty's Revels's company, and licensed in January 1631/32. This was Shirley's only play written for a company other than his own during the term of his attachment. I can only guess that there was some irregularity

4. See the company repertory, *Jacobean and Caroline Stage*, I, 250–59 and 226–27, n. 7.

(possibly the expiration of one seven-year contract and disagreement about the terms of a new one). At any rate, his regular sequence of plays for the Queen's company was only briefly broken, for his *Love's Cruelty* was licensed to be performed by them two months before *The Changes*, and *Hyde Park* three months after.

This leaves five of the 20 or 22 plays written for the Phoenix which were nevertheless published during Shirley's incumbency. They were *The Wedding*, published 1629, *The Grateful Servant*, 1630, *The Witty Fair One*, 1633, *The Bird in a Cage*, 1633, and *The Traitor*, 1635. None was surreptitiously printed, for each carries a dedication signed by the author; one, *The Wedding*, gives the cast of Queen Henrietta's men, and three contain sets of verses commending Shirley. Evidently the company allowed the publication of these five, though not of the other fifteen. One can only speculate as to what the reasons may have been.

Philip Massinger's attachment to the King's company from sometime after Fletcher's death in August 1625 to his own death in March 1639/40 shows a pattern of composition and publication similar to Shirley's, except that Massinger, thirteen years the elder, had been writing plays for at least thirteen years before he achieved his regular attachment to the King's men, whereas Shirley was ordinary poet at the Phoenix almost from the beginning of his play-writing career. Before Fletcher's death, Massinger had written plays for the Lady Elizabeth's company (*The Honest Man's Fortune*, *The Renegado*, *The Bondman*, *The Parliament of Love*) and for the companies at the Red Bull (*The Virgin Martyr*, *The Maid of Honor*) as well as a number of collaborations, generally with Fletcher, for the King's company.

Indeed, Massinger's contribution to the Beaumont and Fletcher plays are so numerous—he contributed to perhaps as many as twenty plays—that one might suspect that his contractual relationship with the King's men had begun before Fletcher's death. But there are several facts which make such a relationship in the early years doubtful. Since the great majority of the Fletcher plays in question were never published during the lifetimes of either Fletcher or Massinger, and since most of them offer only stylistic and not *external* evidence of Massinger's participation, there is the greatest uncertainty as to how much of Massinger's work in these plays was collaboration, and how much revision which may have been done as one of his normal chores after he became regular dramatist in succession to Fletcher. Indeed, several of these plays showing work of both Fletcher and Massinger have prologues or epilogues in the 1647 folio which explicitly call attention to the fact that they are revisions. In the second place, during the years 1615–1625 Massinger wrote several plays for other companies—*The Old Law* and *A New Way to Pay Old Debts*, as well as the six already mentioned for the Lady Elizabeth's men and the Red Bull companies. The powerful King's company would scarcely have allowed a contracted dramatist to write eight plays or more for rival, if inferior, London troupes.

On the whole, therefore, it seems likely that though in the years 1615 to 1625 Massinger did a good deal of work for the King's company—collaborations not only with Fletcher but with Nathan Field as well—he did not have a contract to work exclusively for them as Fletcher did, but only replaced Fletcher, probably in 1626.

From 1626 to 1639 the evidence that Massinger was the "ordinary poet" for the King's company is fairly clear. In these fourteen years he certainly wrote seventeen or eighteen unaided plays for them at fairly regular intervals; he revised at least three of Fletcher's late, perhaps unfinished, plays, *The Elder Brother*, *Love's Cure*, and *Cleander*, as well as others less certain; and some of his lost and unassignable plays, *The Tyrant*, *The Honor of Women*, *Fast*

and Welcome, The City Honest Man, The Painter, and
The Prisoners, are likely to have been part of his regular
work for King Charles's company in these years.

None of his numerous plays at this time can be assigned
to any other company, with the single exception of *The
Great Duke of Florence,* which was licensed to be performed by Queen Henrietta's men at the Phoenix in July
1627. This manuscript may originally have been prepared
earlier for performance at this same theatre by the predecessors of the Queen's men, for whom Massinger had
written three plays in 1623 and 1624,[5] but in the current
state of our knowledge we must allow it as the single exception to the exclusiveness of Massinger's work for the
King's men.

The evidence of his publication in these years suggests
that Massinger, like Brome and Shirley, had an agreement
not to publish without their consent any of the plays he
wrote for the company. At first glance he seems to have
published too many plays between 1626 and 1639 to allow
any such belief, but a little analysis of the Massinger publications of these years suggests the contrary. Nine of his
plays appeared on the bookstalls in this period. But three
of them, *The Renegado, A New Way to Pay Old Debts,*
and *The Maid of Honor,* had been written for other companies before 1626, and a fourth, *The Great Duke of Florence,* was certainly written for another company, though
the date may be later. A fifth, *The Elder Brother,* is
really a Fletcher play in which Massinger probably collaborated, though only Fletcher's name appears on the
title page of the 1637 edition. This is the only play of
the nine which was printed without a dedication signed by
the author or reviser. I doubt that Massinger had anything
to do with the publishing of this play.

The Unnatural Combat was published by John Waterson in 1639 with a dedication by Massinger in which he

5. *Jacobean and Caroline Stage,* IV, 786–88.

calls it "this old Tragedy" and makes play with old and new fashions. Such evidence as can be collected suggests that it was probably a play of the early 1620s written before Massinger became regular dramatist for the company or had any agreement with them about withholding his plays from the printers.[6]

The remaining three plays, *The Roman Actor*, published 1629, *The Picture*, 1630, and *The Emperor of the East*, 1632, were all published with Massinger's cooperation, for they all carry dedications signed by the author and all have commendatory verses which one may assume that the author collected. Since Massinger certainly wrote at least seventeen or eighteen plays for the company in these years, and very likely several of the undatable and lost ones as well, the publication of only three out of the twenty to twenty-five indicates some restraint on the part of a playwright as interested in publication as Massinger's numerous dedications show that he was. I suspect that these three plays were all published with the consent of the King's men.

The Roman Actor certainly was, for one of the sets of commendatory verses printed in the 1629 quarto was signed by Joseph Taylor, who was a leading sharer in the company and the principal manager of their affairs in 1629 with John Lowin and who had played the lead in the company's production of *The Roman Actor*.[7]

The Emperor of the East, published in 1632, was ill received in the theatre, as two of the three sets of commendatory verses in the quarto explicitly point out. It is therefore not at all surprising that, since the play had been shown to be unpopular in the theatre, Lowin and Taylor should have agreed to its publication soon after performance, as the Stationers' Register entry eight months after Herbert's acting license suggests.

6. Ibid., IV, 821–24.
7. Ibid., II, 590–98.

The Picture, 1630, like *The Emperor of the East*, was printed about a year after Sir Henry Herbert had allowed it to be acted. There are no records of its performance, as there are for many of Massinger's plays, and it was never reprinted, though Waterson, its publisher, assigned it over to Thomas Walkley. I suspect that it too was a failure in the theatre and that the company was willing to see it published.

In sum, then, the records of Massinger's play production strongly suggest that, like Brome and Shirley, he was working under a contract which restrained him from publishing without their consent any of the plays he wrote for the King's men in the years 1626–1639.

Massinger's predecessor as regular dramatist for this company was the extremely popular John Fletcher, as has already been mentioned. Though Fletcher was a prolific dramatist, he was clearly not a publishing dramatist: he is known to have had a hand in about 69 plays, but only nine of them were published in his lifetime. This withholding of 87 percent of his compositions from the printers reveals something of his professionalism as a dramatist: he was writing for the theatre audience, not for readers. A little analysis of the publishing circumstances of those nine plays which did appear in print throws into even stronger relief his attitude as the chief dramatist of King James's company toward publication of the plays he had written for them.

Fletcher's dramatic compositions which the Jacobean public was allowed to read during his lifetime were *The Woman Hater*, *The Knight of the Burning Pestle*, *Cupid's Revenge*, *The Scornful Lady*, *The Faithful Shepherdess*, *Philaster*, *A King and No King*, *The Maid's Tragedy*, and *Thierry and Theodoret*. Only one of the nine offers evidence that Fletcher had anything to do with its publication. Four of them were printed with no author's name on the title page; five were printed with no front matter at all—dedications, addresses to readers, commendatory poems, epistles—though such front matter was used in these years by Jonson, Middleton, Marston, and Webster, and later (for plays published outside their contracts) by Shirley, Brome, and Massinger. The front matter in the other three (excepting *The Faithful Shepherdess*) comes from the publisher, not from the author.

When we look at these plays one at a time, Fletcher's care in withholding from publication without their consent those plays he wrote under his exclusive arrangements with the King's company becomes quite evident.

The Woman Hater was not written for the King's men, but for the Children of Paul's: the anonymous title page of the 1607 quarto records, "*As it hath been lately Acted by the Children of Paules.*"

The Knight of the Burning Pestle, though it may have been the work of Francis Beaumont alone, is also a play for a boy company, and the dedication to Robert Keysar signed by the publisher, Walter Burre, shows one route by which plays came into print without any cooperation from the author. Robert Keysar was the lessor of the Black-friars theatre for the last three years before the King's men took it over, and for three or four years he had been manager of the company of the Children of the Queen's Revels. Burre says that Keysar preserved the play after it had failed in the theatre and "you afterwards sent it to me"; Burre had kept it for two years and then printed it. No author is involved in the transaction.

Cupid's Revenge was also performed by a boy company: the title page of the 1615 quarto notes, "As it hath beene diuers times Acted by the Children of her Maiesties Reuels." The play is printed with Fletcher's name on the title page, but he had nothing to do with the publication. Though the publisher, Thomas Harrison, is not, like Walter Burre, considerate enough to tell us exactly how he got his manuscript, he is kind enough to say in his signed address to the reader:

'Tis the custom used by some writers in this age to dedicate their plays to worthy persons, as well as their other works. . . . But not having any such epistle from the author (in regard I am not acquainted with him) I have made bold myself, without his consent, to dedicate this play to the judicious in general.

The Scornful Lady is a fourth play from the series which Fletcher wrote for boys, "As it was Acted (with great applause) by *the Children of Her Maiesties* Reuels." Though Beaumont and Fletcher are named as authors on the 1616 title page, there is no front matter and no indication of their involvement in the publication. Like several other plays originally written for boys (e.g., *The Silent Woman, The Conspiracy and Tragedy of Charles Duke of Byron, The Faithful Shepherdess*), this one eventually came into the hands of the King's men, and their name is substituted on the title page of the 1625 quarto, but the text is simply the old one reprinted.

The Faithful Shepherdess, published in 1609 or 1610, is the only play of nearly seventy in the Fletcher canon which shows clearly that the author himself was concerned in its publication. He wrote and signed three separate dedications; he wrote and signed an address to the readers; and he collected commendatory verses from his friends Francis Beaumont, Ben Jonson, Nathan Field, and George Chapman. The familiarity of this interesting front matter for *The Faithful Shepherdess* has obscured the fact that such care in presenting a play to readers is unique in the prolific career of John Fletcher. The piece was written for a boy company, and it attained early publication because it was a failure in the theatre, and because Fletcher and his friends, smarting over the failure, were eager to point out its misunderstood character as a pastoral tragicomedy. All the verse writers and Fletcher himself point to the failure of the play on the stage. Evidently the company which owned the piece was not eager to keep it exclusive in their repertory. Unhappily Fletcher had long been dead when his pastoral tragicomedy was presented at court, nearly thirty years later, before King Charles and Queen Henrietta Maria, in costumes which the Queen herself had given to the King's men for the production.

In addition to these five plays never composed for the King's men and therefore not subject to any publication agreement with them, four of the plays which Fletcher *did* write for the royal troupe came into print before he died, *A King and No King*, 1619, *The Maid's Tragedy*, 1619, *Philaster*, 1620, and *Thierry and Theodoret*, 1621. Since he is known to have written alone or collaborated in at least forty-two plays for the company, this small number in itself bears witness to some publication restriction, but an examination of the four texts themselves demonstrates even more. None of the four shows any evidence of the cooperation of the author—no author's dedication, address to the readers, epistle, or commendatory verses. Three of the four do not even have any dramatis personnae, the simplest aid an author, or even a publisher, can provide for a printed play.

The one piece which does have any front matter is *A King and No King*, published in 1619 with a title page asserting that it was "Acted at the Globe, by his Maies*ties Seruants*. Written by *Francis Beaumont* and *Iohn Fletcher*" and "Printed for Thomas Walkley." The only front matter printed with this quarto, which does not have even a list of characters, is an epistle written and signed by the publisher Thomas Walkley. He wrote to Sir Thomas Neville: "I present, or rather return unto your view, that which formerly hath been received from you, hereby effecting what you did desire. . . ." Thus we have explicit testimony that the manuscript of *A King and No King* was not conveyed to the printer by the author or by the acting company, but that Sir Thomas Neville gave Walkley for publication a manuscript which had presumably been made for his private library, since the text shows no sign that it had been set up from a prompt copy.

This analysis of the publication of John Fletcher's plays shows that though his compositions were among the most highly reputed of the productions at Blackfriars, he did not, during the course of his fifteen or eighteen years of exclusive work for the King's company, himself put a single one of them into the hands of the printers. Furthermore, the sharers of the King's company were successful in keeping more than 90 percent of his compositions for them from reaching the hands of the printers by any means—legitimate or illegitimate—during the reign of James I. These facts reflect some nonpublishing arrangement between an ordinary poet and his dramatic company at least as clearly as do the similar ones in the careers of Richard Brome, James Shirley, and Philip Massinger.

John Fletcher's predecessor as regular playwright for the King's company was William Shakespeare. The publishing history of the plays he wrote for the company, though more complex and though studied in infinitely greater detail than the others, is basically the same as the others we have surveyed in its conformity to the patterns of the professional dramatist. In some ways it is even more straightforward: from the formation of the Lord Chamberlain's company in 1594[8] to Shakespeare's death in 1616 there is no evidence that he ever wrote any play for any other company—a longer period of fidelity than that known for any other dramatist, and one which was never interrupted, as Massinger's, Shirley's, and Brome's appear to have been.

Shakespeare's pattern is again like that of the other at-

8. It is possible that the plays written *before* 1594 were also prepared for this company in its earlier form. But the precise antecedents from which the Lord Chamberlain's men were derived are so obscure and confused that it is safer and simpler to begin with 1594. See Chambers, *William Shakespeare*, I, 57–64.

tached professionals in that he did not himself take to the
printers any of the plays he wrote for the Lord Chamberlain–King's company. When his plays were published they
appeared without any indication of the author's sponsorship—no dedications, no epistles, no addresses to the readers, no commendatory verses from friends, not even a list
of characters, and for most of them neither prologue nor
epilogue. Moreover, the multitudes of textual studies of
his plays during the last two hundred years have accumulated so many scores of obvious errors in all the quartos
that one can be sure no author proofread the sheets at the
printing house. Nor can it be hypothesized that the numerous errors may derive from an author who really *was* interested in the publication of his plays, but who was tempera-
mentally careless about the dull chore of proofreading.
This cannot have been the temperament of William Shakespeare, for he did take great pains with his text when he
published his poems. In *Venus and Adonis*, 1593, and *The
Rape of Lucrece*, 1594, he not only provided dedications
but gave his readers excellent texts, far cleaner than those
displayed in any of his play quartos. In whatever manner
Shakespeare's several plays may have come into the hands
of the printers before 1616 (and the possible methods are
various) it is reasonably clear that he himself refrained
from ushering them into print in the fashion of so many
of his contemporaries in these years—Ben Jonson, John
Marston, Samuel Daniel, Barnabe Barnes, John Day,
Lewis Machin, Thomas Middleton, Nathan Field, Thomas
Heywood, John Webster, John Stephens, Wentworth
Smith, Thomas Dekker.

Shakespeare's conformity to the regular professional's
pattern of refraining from publishing the plays he had prepared for his company is shown not only by the character
of the texts of the plays which did get into print during
his lifetime, but equally by the number of those which had
never appeared on the bookstalls by 1616. At the time of

his death slightly more than half his plays remained in manuscript in the archives of the company for which he had prepared them.

THE DRAMATISTS whose publications have so far been discussed had fairly settled careers with well-established companies. But in any activity so precarious as the commercial presentation of plays, it is not usual for organizations to have such long periods of success and prosperity as did the Lord Chamberlain–King's company and Queen Henrietta's men. Much more characteristic of theatrical annals are the obscure histories of such troupes as the Earl of Leicester's men, the Earl of Pembroke's men, the Palsgrave's men, the Lady Elizabeth's men, the Red Bull–King's company, the King's Revels company, and the troupe of Prince Charles [II]. A number of plays are known to have been written for these organizations, but the facts of their histories are so obscure and confused that little can safely be deduced about their relations to the composition and publication of the plays written for them.

But something of the customary pattern of relationship to his regular company, the Earl of Worcester–Queen Anne's men, can be seen in the publications of Thomas Heywood. Most eloquent of his restraint is the fact that in his long life Heywood could have seen in print fewer than twenty plays with his name on the title page. Since Heywood himself said eight years before his death that he "had either an entire hand or at least a main finger" in 220 plays, these figures alone make quite clear his attitude toward the publication of the plays he wrote for his regular company. But twenty-five years before he recorded the number of plays he had written or contributed to, Heywood made an explicit statement about a regular professional playwright's publication of his plays.

In 1608 John Busby and Nathaniel Butter brought out *The Rape of Lucrece* with a title page bearing Heywood's name and the production statement, "Acted by her Maiesties Seruants at the Red Bull." For this edition the author wrote an address to the reader:

It hath been no custom in me of all other men (courteous readers) to commit my plays to the press: the reason, though some may attribute it to my own insufficiency, I had rather subscribe in that to their severe censure, than by seeking to avoid the imputation of weakness, to incur a greater suspicion of honesty: for though some have used a double sale of their labors, first to the stage and after to the press, for my own part I here proclaim myself ever faithful to the first [i.e., Queen Anne's company] and never guilty of the last. Yet since some of my plays [i.e., *If You Know Not Me You Know Nobody*, part 1, 1605, part 2, 1606, *A Woman Killed with Kindness*, 1607, and perhaps others not attributed to Heywood on their title pages] have (unknown to me, and without any of my direction) accidentally come into the printer's hands and therefore so corrupt and mangled (copied only by the ear) that I have been as unable to know them as ashamed to challenge them. This therefore, I was willinger to furnish out in his native habit: first being by consent [i.e., with the permission of the rightful owners, Queen Anne's company] next because the rest have been so wronged in being published in such savage and ragged ornaments. Accept it courteous gentlemen, and prove as favorable readers as we [i.e., Heywood himself and the other members of Queen Anne's company] have found you gracious auditors.

Yours, T. H.

One of these plays printed without any cooperation by the author, or, presumably by Queen Anne's men who owned it, was *If You Know Not Me You Know Nobody, or the Troubles of Queen Elizabeth*. The play had first been published in 1605, and it was reprinted in 1606, 1608, 1610, 1613, 1623, 1632, and 1639. Sometime before 1637 this old, frequently reissued piece was revived at the Phoenix by Queen Henrietta's men, a company which had inherited several plays of the repertory of the long defunct Queen Anne's men. For this revival of his old play Heywood wrote a prologue making explicit application of the charge about unauthorized publication which he had made in his address to the reader in the 1608 quarto of *The Rape of Lucrece*. He published this prologue in 1637 in his collection of miscellaneous verse, translations, and playlets called *Pleasant Dialogues and Dramas*.

> Plays have a fate in their conception lent,
> Some so short liv'd, no sooner showed than spent:
> But born today, tomorrow buried, and
> Though taught to speak, neither to go nor stand.
> This (by what fate I know not) sure no merit,
> That it disclaims, may for the age inherit,
> Writing 'bove one and twenty; but ill nurst.
> And yet received as well performed at first,
> Graced and frequented, for the cradle age,
> Did throng the seats, the boxes, and the stage
> So much that some by Stenography drew
> The plot, put it in print (scarce one word true)
> And in that lameness it hath limped so long,
> The Author now to vindicate that wrong
> Hath took the paines, upright upon its feet
> To teach it walk, so please you sit and see't.

Heywood's own statements in 1608 that he refrained from publishing his plays because such conduct would bring on him "a greater suspicion of honesty" and that such publication by other dramatists constituted "a double sale of their labors, first to the stage and after to the press" show his acceptance of an obligation of restraint. And he further proclaims himself "ever faithful to the first," that is, the acting company for which he wrote, Queen Anne's men. In spite of these explicit declarations, he was concerned with the publication of four other plays, *The Golden Age*, published in 1611, *The Silver Age*, 1613, *The Brazen Age*, 1613, and *The Four Prentices*, 1615, before the final blow to his company, the death of its patron in 1619. The last play was not given to the printer by Heywood, for he says in a dedication that it was fifteen or sixteen years old and

> written many years since, in my infancy of judgment in this kind of poetry, and my first practice; yet understanding (by what means I know not) it was in these more exquisite and refined times to come to the press, in such a forwardness ere it came to my knowledge that it was past prevention, and knowing withall that it comes short of that accurateness both in plot and style that these more censorious days with greater curiosity require, I must thus excuse.

The Golden Age also came to the printer without the knowledge of the author, who says in his address to the reader in the 1611 quarto, "This play coming accidentally to the press, and at length having notice thereof, I was loathe (finding it my own) to see it thrust naked into the world, to abide the fury of all weathers, without either title for acknowledgement, or the formality of an Epistle for ornament."

The other two plays, *The Silver Age* and *The Brazen Age*, were both printed by Nicholas Oakes in 1613. Both were printed with addresses to the reader by Heywood, and neither address indicates that they had come to the press without the knowledge of the playwright. They were probably old plays, and they may have been published with the consent (and perhaps to the profit) of the other sharers of Queen Anne's company, who were beginning to experience those financial difficulties which plagued them for years and led to a series of lawsuits.[9]

Though Heywood was attached to a company more

9. See *Elizabethan Stage*, II, 237–40, and *Jacobean and Caroline Stage*, I, 158–70.

obscure and less successful than the companies of King James and King Charles and that of Queen Henrietta Maria, and though his own canon contains far more lost plays than those of Brome, Shirley, Massinger, Fletcher, and Shakespeare, the evidence which is extant suggests that his observation of restraints on publication of those plays he wrote for his regular company was similar to that of those better-known attached professional playwrights. No one knows how many of his 220 plays had been written for the Worcester–Queen Anne's men, but surely well over half, for he was a leading member of the organization for more than half (and the most active half) of his writing life. After the final disappearance of this struggling troupe, Heywood cannot be shown to have been regular dramatist for any company. He did write several plays for the companies of his former colleague Christopher Beeston at the Phoenix, two or three for the King's men, and a number of Lord Mayor's pageants, and he published seven or eight plays in the 1630s, but there is no evidence of a later contractual attachment.

Lest it be supposed that such attitudes toward publication as these of the attached professional dramatists may well have been characteristic of most playwrights of the period, it may be helpful to give a little attention to the very different publication patterns of a few well-known dramatists who evidently were *not* attached to major acting companies. John Marston is a good example.

For six or seven years at the beginning of the seventeenth century Marston was producing plays fairly regularly; indeed, his output of about two a year was not unlike that of Brome, Shirley, Massinger, Fletcher, and Shakespeare; but he soon gave up play-writing, and for twenty-five years or more appears to have had nothing to do with the stage. But though his output for a time was rather like that of these professionals, his publication pattern was entirely different, as a little attention to dates and quartos will show.

The Marston canon offers fewer problems than the canons of a number of his contemporaries. Eliminating two or three dubious attributions which have been made on stylistic grounds, we find that Marston had a hand in twelve plays, if we include *Jack Drum's Entertainment*, *Histriomastix*, and *Satiromastix*. None has been lost; all twelve were printed during Marston's lifetime, indeed, twenty years or more before his death; all but one or two were published within three years of composition. All but the three doubtful ones were printed with Marston's name or initials on the title page. One-third of them were printed with addresses or dedications signed by Marston; three others have arguments or Latin mottoes or inductions or dramatis personnae which strongly suggest, though they do not prove, the participation of an author. The contrast here with the publishing records of those attached professionals who were Marston's contemporaries—Heywood and Shakespeare—is rather striking.

Similar to Marston in the pattern of his theatrical activities was William Davenant, though he wrote during the reign of Charles instead of at the end of the reign of Elizabeth. Between 1626 and 1639/40, before the closing of the theatres, Davenant wrote eleven plays and five masques. Though he produced plays at a slower rate than the regular professionals, he was like them in staying with one acting company, King Charles's men, who performed nearly everything he wrote. Davenant's publication pattern, however, is different from those of the regular dramatists for this company, Shakespeare, Fletcher, Massinger, and Shirley. None of his plays escaped publication, as did many of those of Fletcher and Massinger, and at least two of Shirley's. About half of them were in print within two or three years of their first performance. Davenant himself was certainly concerned with the publication of at least five of them, for he furnished dedications which he signed, and for three of them he collected commendatory verses. In spite of the fact that his plays were regularly produced by the King's men, Davenant probably had no contract with them; he shows no resolve, as Fletcher and Shirley did, to keep them out of the hands of the printers.

Another Caroline dramatist who produced a good number of plays but did not exercise the attached professional's publication restraint was John Ford, who wrote about sixteen plays (excluding *An Ill Beginning* but including *The London Merchant* and *The Royal Combat*) between 1621 and 1638. Six of them are lost. Of the remaining ten, two of which were collaborations whose manuscripts Ford may not have possessed, three did not achieve print until a decade or two after the author's death. The remaining seven plays were all printed with Ford's cooperation. For all of them he prepared dedications which he signed, and for four of them he collected commendatory verses. Again there is no evidence of publication restraint. Though in the early 1630s Ford wrote five plays for Christopher Beeston's companies at the Phoenix theatre, all five were published with signed dedications within a very few years of performance.

Another writer of plays who showed no hesitation in offering them to the printers shortly after performance was Thomas Nabbes. He wrote seven plays and a masque during the thirties, when Massinger, Shirley, and Brome were functioning as ordinary poets for the principal London companies and restricting their publication of the plays they wrote for their companies. All Nabbes's plays were printed in the years 1637 to 1640; and in 1639, two years before his death, there was even a sort of collected edition, an odd assembly which Sir Walter Greg called a "nonce collection." This consists of copies of the eight dramatic compositions, some with cancel title pages, bound together with a joint title page reading *Plays, Maskes, Epigrams, Ele-*

gies, and Epithalamiums. Collected into One Volume.[10]
Nabbes was not a closet dramatist, for five of his plays have
statements on their title pages informing readers that they
had been performed by Queen Henrietta's company or by
Beeston's Boys. All the plays, including the two apparently
unacted ones, were published with the cooperation of the
playwright, who wrote and signed dedications for seven of
them. The eighth, *Hannibal and Scipio*, was printed two
years after performance with a cast of Queen Henrietta's
men and two sets of verses about the play, one of which,
"To the Ghosts of Hannibal and Scipio," is signed by the
playwright.

Though Nabbes furnished plays for Queen Henrietta's
company fairly regularly during a short period, he seems
to have had no contractual obligation to them as James
Shirley did, and he certainly showed none of Shirley's restraint in taking to the London printers the pieces he had
prepared for the stage at the Phoenix.

By far the most distinguished of the unattached dramatists of the period was Ben Jonson, and his eclectic attitude
toward the London acting companies, as well as his publication patterns, are in sharp contrast with those of Shakespeare, Heywood, Fletcher, Massinger, Shirley, and
Brome.

The most obvious reflection of this eclecticism is the variety of companies which produced his plays: the Lord Admiral's company, the Queen's Revels boys, the Lord Chamberlain's company, the Children of the Chapel, King James's
company, the Lady Elizabeth's company, King Charles's
company, and Queen Henrietta's men. And finally there
are two unfinished plays, *The Sad Shepherd* and *Morti-
mer His Fall*, which were never acted at all. The only
long period when all his plays were acted by the same

10. W. W. Greg, *A Bibliography of the English Printed Drama
to the Restoration*, 4 vols., London, 1939–1959, III, 1098–99.

troupe was 1616 to 1632, when there is no record of any Jonsonian play being given to any company except the King's men. But this record reflects the obvious choice of the most distinguished company by the most distinguished playwright, certainly not an attachment as an ordinary poet, for there are only four certain plays (with the possible addition of contributions to *The Widow* and *The Bloody Brother*) in a period of seventeen years. And for nine years in the middle, 1617 to 1625, there are no plays at all.

Furthermore, Jonson did not think of himself as a servant of the commercial theatres. Fortunately he was so highly articulate, so self-conscious, and so aware of posterity that he left in print an unparalleled number of statements about his conception of himself and of his art.[11] No one who reads through these numerous statements—often arrogant in their independence—can fail to be struck, or even amused, by the violent contrast with the attitude of the attached professional, as expressed by Thomas Heywood:

> ... I had rather subscribe in that to their severe censure, than by seeking to avoid the imputation of weakness to incur a greater suspicion of honesty; for though some have used a double sale of their labors, first to the stage and after to the press, for my own part I here proclaim myself ever faithful to the first and never guilty of the last.

Unfortunately Jonson's unique statements about himself and his work are so much more widely known and discussed than this one, more characteristic of the regular professionals, that many erroneous deductions about the unstated attitudes of other professionals have been derived from them.

Finally, Jonson's publication patterns are quite unlike those of Heywood, Shakespeare, Fletcher, Massinger,

11. See James D. Redwine, Jr., *Ben Jonson's Literary Criticism*, Lincoln, Neb., 1970.

Shirley, and Brome. Most conspicuously abnormal was his collection and publication of his own plays in *The Workes of Beniamin Jonson*, 1616. Never before had plays from the commercial theatres been collected in a single volume, much less published under the aspiring title "Workes." The pretentiousness of the volume, the elaborate engraved title page with its theatrical and symbolic figures, the Latin motto, the numerous sets of commendatory verses, several of them in the language of learning, the formal table of contents, the inclusion of eighteen masques and entertainments prepared for nobility and royalty with plays from the commercial theatres—all this constituted a direct claim to status and permanence unprecedented in the English theatre world and quite foreign to the practices of the attached professional dramatists.

But even before his careful preparation of the folio of 1616 Jonson had himself seen to the publication of most of his plays. Four of the early ones written for Henslowe, mostly collaborations, *Hot Anger Soon Cold*, *Robert II, King of Scots*, *The Page of Plymouth*, and *Richard Crookback*, he chose to suppress and never mentioned in his numerous discussions of his work. But the other plays were all published, usually soon after performance, and with clear evidence of the author's participation in the publication project: *Every Man Out of His Humor*, printed in 1600, with a Latin title-page motto and elaborate characters for the dramatis personnae; *Cynthia's Revels*, 1601, with Latin mottoes; *Every Man in His Humor*, 1601, with Jonson's Latin motto as well as his name on the title page; *Poetaster*, 1602, with a Latin motto and a Latin address to the reader; *Sejanus*, 1605, with a signed dedication and commendatory verses; *Volpone*, 1607, with dedication and commendatory verses; *Catiline*, 1611, with a signed epistle and commendatory verses; and *The Alchemist*, 1612, also with a signed epistle and commendatory verses. The only ones appearing before the folio without clear evidence of Jonson's participation are *The Case is Altered*, 1609, and Jonson's collaboration with George Chapman and John Marston, *Eastward Ho!* 1605. A presumed edition of *Epicoene* of 1612 has been lost.

The publication of Jonson's plays written after the appearance of the 1616 folio is less regular, but the pattern of his production and publication shows no more of the attitude of the regular professionals than does the earlier pattern. From 1616 to 1625 he produced no new play, though he does say that in his fire in 1623 "parcels of a Play" were destroyed. In the twenty-five years between the performance of the last play in the 1616 folio, *Catiline*, and his death in 1637, only six new plays by Jonson reached the London stage, four performed by the King's men in 1616, 1626, 1629, and 1632, *Bartholomew Fair* by the Lady Elizabeth's company in 1614, and *A Tale of a Tub* by Queen Henrietta's men in 1633. Three were prepared for publication by the bedridden Jonson, apparently in a project for a second folio,[12] and were printed in 1631. Two others, *The Magnetic Lady* and *A Tale of a Tub*, did not appear until the second folio, four years after Jonson's death, but again the text appears to have been prepared by the author.[13]

Jonson's independence of the commercial theatres and his deep involvement with the preservation of his plays and his ideas for posterity sets him apart not only from all the attached professional dramatists, but from nearly all the other writers of his time. In his attitude toward his text and toward the significance of the drama he is more Edwardian than Jacobean.

12. See Jonson's correspondence, Herford and Simpson, *Ben Jonson*, I, 211, and discussions of texts of the three plays, VI, 3–8, 145–54, 273–76.

13. Ibid., VI, 501–504 and III, 3–6.

THIS ANALYSIS of the publication patterns of eleven dramatists seems to me to show fairly clearly that there was a distinct difference between the attitudes toward publication displayed by the attached professional dramatists on the one hand, and by those professional writers for the commercial theatres who evidently had no contractual relation with the acting companies for which they wrote on the other. Only in the case of Richard Brome is there extant evidence of a written contract forbidding the dramatist to publish without the company's consent. Yet a study of the timing and sponsorship of the publication of their plays by Shirley, Massinger, Fletcher, Shakespeare, and Heywood seems to me to show that they must have had understandings with the companies to which they were attached that were not unlike Brome's written contract with the players at the Phoenix. It is equally evident that John Marston, William Davenant, John Ford, Thomas Nabbes, and Ben Jonson, who were certainly paid for their plays, observed no such restraint.

Index

Abell, William, 192
Account of our Ancient Theatres
(1790), *see* Malone, Edmond
*Act to Restrain Abuses of
Players, An,* 182
acting companies, dramatists'
relations to, 62-87
actor, 60
actor-dramatists, 64, 66-67,
76, 211-18
actor-sharers, 134
actors' contracts, 70
actors' parts, 156, 160, 196
*Actors' Remonstrance, or
Complaint . . . As it was
presented in the names and
behalf of all our London
Comedians, see* Anonymous
*Acts of the Privy Council of
England, The,* 189
Adams, John Quincy,
*Dramatic Records of Sir
Henry Herbert, The* (ed.),
New Haven (1917), 84, 146,
154, 155, 156, 157, 158,
159, 160, 161, 162, 164,
165, 250, 252, 253, 254,
259; *Shakespearean Play-
house: A History of English
Theatres from the Beginning
to the Restoration* (1917), 6
Address to the Reader, 13,
27, 207, 265, 269, 276,
277, 284, 286
Admiral's company, *see* Lord
Admiral's company
*Adrasta, or the Woman's
Spleen and Love's Conquest,
see* Jones, John
Africa, 250
Al., G., 228
Alaham, see Greville, Fulke,
Lord Brooke
Albumazar, see Tomkis,
Thomas
"Albumazar," see Wright,
William Aldis

293

Chettle, Henry, with Munday, Drayton, and Smith, *Cardinal Wolsey*, 246-47
Children of the Queen's Revels, 32, 35, 39, 169, 200, 211, 276, 277, 288
Christ Church, Oxford, 21, 256
Christmas Comes But Once a Year, see Heywood, Thomas
Chronicle History of the London Stage, 1559-1642 (1890), *see* Fleay, Frederick Gard
Chronicles of the Kings of England, London (1684), *see* Baker, Sir Richard
City Chronologer, 36
City Honest Man, The, see Massinger, Philip
City Match, The, see Mayne, Jasper
City of London, the Corporation of the, 43, 44, 45
City shows, 36
City Wit, The, see Brome, Richard
Clark, Arthur Melville, *Thomas Heywood, Playwright and Miscellanist*, Oxford (1931), 130
Clavell, John, *Recantation for an ill led Life, The*, 18; *Soddered Citizen, The*, 18
clergymen, 4
Clifton, Henry, 47
closet drama, 22
Cockpit at Court, 142
Cockpit in Drury Lane, *see* Phoenix Theatre
Cokayne, Sir Aston, 208-209
collaborating, methods of, 227-34
collaboration, decline of, 221-24

collaborations, 100, 124, 125, 126, 197-234
Collection of Old English, A (1883), *see* Bullen, A. H.
College of God's Gift at Dulwich, 55, 69, 97
college plays, 17-18, 21-22, 49-50, 63, 91-92, 106
Collier, J. P., *Memoirs of Edward Alleyn, Founder of Dulwich College*, London (1841), 97; *History of English Dramatic Poetry to the Time of Shakespeare and Annals of the Stage to the Restoration*, 3 vols. (1831), 5n
Collins, Arthur, *Letters and Memorials of State*, London (1746), 189
Colonel Pride, see Birkenhead, Sir John
comedians, 215-18
Comedies and Tragedies Written by Francis Beaumont and John Fletcher, Gentlemen (1647), *see* Beaumont and Fletcher
commendatory verses, 241, 259, 274, 277, 287, 290
companies, conformity in, 111-12; financing of, 63-74
company hall, 198
company managers, 63-64
compositor, 146
Condell, Elizabeth, 110
Condell, Henry, 5, 110, 151, 159, 164, 262
Conflict of Conscience, see Woodes, Nathaniel
Congreve, William, *Double Dealer, The*, 60
Conquest of Brute, The, see Chettle, Henry

318

(1931), *see* Clark, Arthur
Melville
Three Parnassus Plays, The,
London (1949), *see* Leish-
man, J. B.
Thyestes, see Heywood, John
Tide Tarrieth No Man, see
Walpull, George
Tilney, Edmund, 45, 147,
148-52, 160-61, 174
Time's Trick Upon the Cards,
see Fane, Mildmay
Timon of Athens, see
Shakespeare, William
tire-men, 134
'Tis No Deceipt to Deceive
the Deceiver, see Chettle,
Henry
tobacco-men, 134
Toftrees, Norfolk, 47
Tomkis, Thomas, *Albumazar,*
106
Tottenham Court, see Nabbes,
Thomas
Tourneur, Cyril, 53, 213
Tourneur, Cyril, with Daborne,
Arraignment of London,
The, 231
Townshend, Sir Robert, 31
Toy, The, see Anonymous
Tragedy of Cleopatra, see
Daniel, Samuel
Tragedy of Cleopatra, Queen
of Egypt, The, see May,
Thomas
Tragedie of Miriam the Faire
Queene of Jewry, The, see
Cary, Lady Elizabeth
Tragedy of Philotas by Samuel
Daniel, The, see Michel,
Laurence
Tragedy of St. Albans, The,
see Shirley, James
Tragedy of Sir John van Olden

Barnavelt, The, see Frij-
linck, Wilhelmina P.
Traitor, The, see Shirley,
James
Transactions of the New
Shakespeare Society (1887-
1892), 267
Travels of the Three English
Brothers, The, see Day,
John
Trial of Treasure, see
Wager, W.
Trinity College, Cambridge,
17, 21, 106
Trundle, John, 243
Truth's Supplication to
Candle Light, see Dekker,
Thomas
Tunbridge, Kent, 96
Turnhout, 189
Twelfth Night, see Shake-
speare, William
Two Merry Women of Abing-
ton, see Porter, Henry
Two Shapes, see Caesar's Fall
Tyrant, The, see Massinger,
Philip

Udall, Nicholas, 4, 95
Unfortunate Lovers, The, see
Davenant, William
Unfortunate Mother, The, see
Nabbes, Thomas
unity of place, 81
Unnatural Combat, The, see
Massinger, Philip
Usher, 96, 97

Valiant Scot, The, see W. J.
Variety, The, see Newcastle,
Duke of
Venus and Adonis, see Shake-
speare, William
Vere, Sir Francis, 189

327